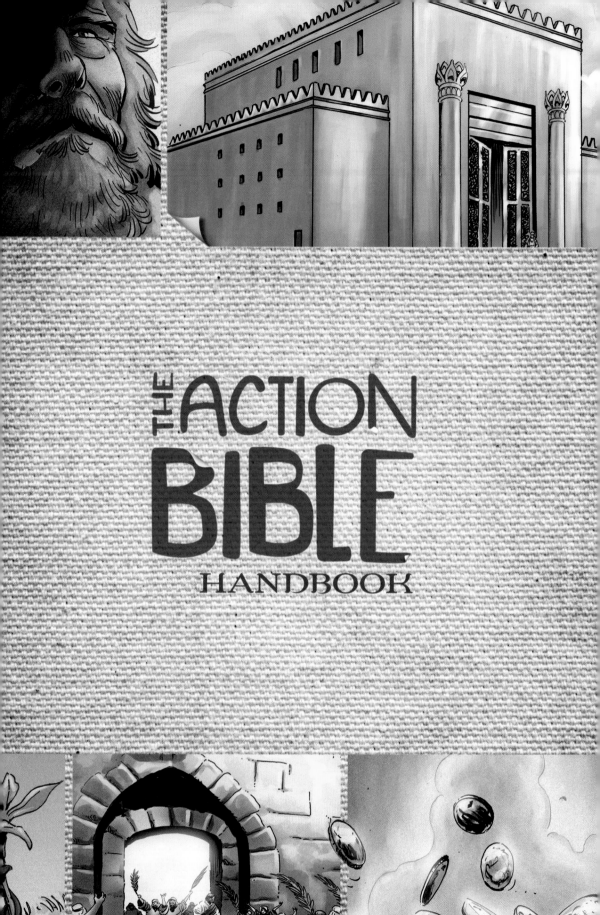

THE ACTION BIBLE
HANDBOOK

THE ACTION BIBLE HANDBOOK

A DICTIONARY OF PEOPLE, PLACES, AND THINGS

ILLUSTRATIONS BY
SERGIO CARIELLO

David C Cook

transforming lives together

THE ACTION BIBLE HANDBOOK
Published by David C Cook
4050 Lee Vance View
Colorado Springs, CO 80918 U.S.A.

David C Cook Distribution Canada
55 Woodslee Avenue, Paris, Ontario, Canada N3L 3E5

David C Cook U.K., Kingsway Communications
Eastbourne, East Sussex BN23 6NT, England

LCCN 2012954694
ISBN 978-1-4347-0483-2
eISBN 978-1-4347-0553-2

Project Manager: Dave Veerman
Project Editor/Writer: Linda Washington
Contributing Writer: Afton Rovik
Project Staff: Joel Bartlett, Bruce Barton, Andy Culbertson, Linda Taylor

The Action Bible Colorists: Patrick Gama, and Wellington Marçal, Priscila Ribeiro,
Fabrício Sampaio Guerra, MaxFlan Araujo, Alex Guim of Impacto Studio

The Team: Don Pape, Jeremy Jones, Nick Lee, Renada Arens, Karen Athen
Cover Design: Amy Konyndyk
Cover Illustrations: Sergio Cariello

Printed in the United States of America
First Edition 2013

2 3 4 5 6 7 8 9 10

HOW TO USE THIS BOOK

The Action Bible Handbook has been created to help you understand God's Word—the Bible. It is filled with definitions and information about the important people, places, and things mentioned in *The Action Bible*. Each definition includes the page number in *The Action Bible* where you can find the defined term. If you're using another Bible (King James Version, the New International Version, the English Standard Version, and so on), we've provided Bible verse references where you can find the person, place, or thing. We've also included cross references to other definitions within this book.

Arranged alphabetically, *The Action Bible Handbook* includes significant persons, places, and terms mentioned in *The Action Bible*, plus many other terms and concepts like *justice* and *forgiveness*. In addition, there is a short summary of every book in the Bible.

May you grow in the knowledge of God and of His Word.

AARON

Israel's first high priest. Aaron was three years older than his brother, Moses. Aaron was Moses's helper during the forty years the Hebrews spent in the wilderness before they entered Canaan. Although Aaron sometimes sinned, he also did some heroic things. Once a large group of Israelites rebelled against Moses and Aaron. God sent a terrible disease as a judgment, and many people died. Aaron took a container with fire and incense from the tabernacle altar and ran among the people so God would forgive them. God stopped the disease.

Aaron and his four sons became the first priests to serve in the tabernacle. Aaron died at age 123, before the people entered the Promised Land.

See The Action Bible *page 125 and Exodus 4:14–Numbers 20:29.*

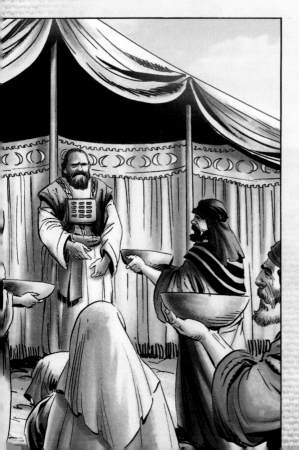

ABEL

The second son of Adam and Eve, and the first person to die. Abel was murdered by his older brother, Cain. Abel was a shepherd and had brought to God an offering—a lamb from his flock. Cain, a farmer, had brought some vegetables he had grown. God was pleased with Abel's offering but not with Cain's. The Bible does not say why, but it may have been because Abel's life pleased God and Cain's did not.

See The Action Bible *page 24 and Genesis 4:1–16; 1 John 3:12.*

ABIGAIL

The wise wife of a foolish sheepherder named Nabal, a mean and stingy man whose name means "fool." When Nabal refused to share food with David and his men, David wanted revenge. Abigail's quick actions as a peacemaker saved her family from disaster. When Abigail told Nabal how close he had come to disaster, Nabal had a stroke that paralyzed him. Ten days later he died. Abigail married David. They had one son, Chileah.

See The Action Bible *page 297 and 1 Samuel 25.*

ABISHAI

David's nephew by his sister Zeruiah and a member of David's fighting forces. He is the brother of Joab. Abishai tried to persuade David to kill Saul while Saul lay sleeping.

See The Action Bible *page 300 and 1 Samuel 24; 26. See also* David; Joab.

ABNER

Saul's cousin and commander of Saul's army. When David defeated the giant Goliath, Abner brought David back to meet Saul. Later, when Saul was trying to kill David, Abner helped Saul look for David and stayed close to Saul to protect him. After Saul's death, Abner helped make Ish-bosheth, son of Saul, the king. This caused two years of war between David's men and those following Ish-bosheth. Abner later tried to convince Saul's followers to be loyal to David, but he was murdered by Joab.

See **The Action Bible** *page 309 and 2 Samuel 2:8–3:39. See also* **David; Joab.**

ABRAM/ABRAHAM

The father of the Israelites, a man who was God's friend. In the beginning, his name was Abram. His family lived in the city of Ur. Then the whole clan moved nearly eight hundred miles northwest to Haran. At Haran, God told Abram to go to Canaan. Abram, his wife, Sarai, and his nephew, Lot, lived in Canaan.

Abram and his nephew, Lot, grew rich; each had many cattle and herdsmen. They eventually separated when their workers kept getting into arguments.

For a long time, Abram and his wife had no children. But God appeared to him and said that someday he would have as many descendants as the stars in heaven. When Sarai still did not have children, Sarai suggested that Abram and a servant woman named Hagar have a child. A son, Ishmael, was born when Abram was eighty-six.

Thirteen years later, God changed Abram's name to Abraham and again promised that he would have a son. This would be a miracle because Abraham and his wife were much too old to have children. But when Abraham was one hundred years old, a son, Isaac, was born!

God tested Abraham's faith by telling him to offer his son as a sacrifice. At the last moment, God stopped him from killing his son as a sacrifice. God only wanted to see how much Abraham trusted Him.

After Sarah's death, Abraham married Keturah and had six more children, even though he was 140 years old!

See **The Action Bible** *pages 44–67 and Genesis 12–25; Romans 4; Galatians 3:6–29. See also* **Sarai/Sarah.**

ABSALOM

The third son of King David, Absalom was known for his long beautiful hair. After he murdered his older brother, Amnon, he ran away from his father's anger and stayed away for three years. Finally he returned, and David forgave him. However, in a few years, Absalom decided to take the kingdom away his father. In a terrible battle between Absalom's men and those of King David, Absalom's hair was caught in the branches of a tree. The mule ran off and left Absalom hanging there. Some of David's men found him and killed him, even though David had forbidden them to hurt Absalom.

See **The Action Bible** *pages 329–346 and 2 Samuel 13–18.*

ACHAN

An Israelite who disobeyed God and caused the Israelites to lose a battle. At the battle of Jericho, God commanded the warriors to avoid taking anything for themselves. Everything made of metal (gold, silver, bronze, iron) was to be given to God; everything else was to be destroyed. But Achan took clothing, gold, and silver and buried it beneath his tent. Because of Achan's disobedience, God let the Israelites be defeated in the battle for the city of Ai. God also showed Joshua how to identify the guilty person. Achan finally confessed. Achan and his family were put to death for Achan's crime.

See **The Action Bible** *pages 201, 203 and Joshua 7:1–26.*

ACTS, BOOK OF

The fifth book in the New Testament. It was written by Luke, a doctor who traveled with Paul on Paul's second and third missionary journeys. The book of Acts was probably written around AD 61 or 62. This book of church history shows how the church grew from a small group of frightened believers who huddled in one room to a courageous, growing church spread across the Roman Empire. The turning point was the coming of the Holy Spirit at Pentecost.

Acts centers mostly on the work of two men—Peter and Paul. Peter is the main person until the end of chapter 12. Beginning in chapter 13, Paul becomes the main character.

Beginning in chapter 13, Paul's missionary journeys are traced as the gospel is told in Asia Minor, Greece, and Rome. The letters of Paul in the New Testament are written to some of the churches he started while on those journeys or to pastors and Christian workers in those churches.

See **The Action Bible** *pages 651–733 and the book of Acts.*

ADAM AND EVE

The first people God created. The name *Adam* means "all people" or "mankind," and *Eve* means "life." God formed Adam from the dust of the ground, but He made Eve from one of

Adam's ribs. She was to be his closest companion. God told Adam and Eve to take care of all He had created.

The Bible does not say how long Adam and Eve lived in the beautiful garden before they ate the fruit of a tree they were forbidden to eat. When Adam and Eve disobeyed God, they had to leave the garden of Eden. After Adam and Eve left the garden of Eden, they had many children, including Abel, Cain, and Seth. Adam was 912 years old when he died.

See The Action Bible *pages 20–28 and Genesis 1:26–5:5. See also* Fall, the; Garden of Eden; Tree of the Knowledge of Good and Evil; Serpent/Snakes.

ADONIJAH

The handsome fourth son of King David. His three older brothers died while they were young men, leaving Adonijah the oldest at the time of David's death. He wanted to become king, even though he knew his younger brother Solomon had been chosen by God to be the next king. When David was old, Adonijah convinced some of David's men to help make him king. But David chose Solomon to be king.

When Adonijah heard the news, he knew his life was now in danger because he had tried to take the throne. He ran to the altar in the tabernacle—a place of refuge where he could be protected from harm. Solomon forgave Adonijah, but later ordered Adonijah to be put to death when Adonijah asked to marry Abishag, David's companion during his last illness. This request was the same as saying that all that had belonged

to David should have belonged to Adonijah.

See The Action Bible *pages 348–351 and 1 Kings 1:1–2:25.*

AEGEAN SEA

The part of the Mediterranean Sea between Greece and Anatolia (Turkey). Paul sailed from Troas across the Aegean to the island of Samothrace.

See The Action Bible *page 708 and Acts 16:11.*

AHAB

The seventh and most evil king Israel ever had. He reigned from about 874 to 853 BC. He was a strong military leader who defeated the army of Syria twice. He married Jezebel, a woman who worshipped idols. To please her, King Ahab built a temple and an altar to Baal. Ahab was king during the famous conflict between the prophet Elijah and the prophets of Baal on Mount Carmel, when God sent fire to consume Elijah's offering. Although Ahab was very rich, he always wanted more. When he tried to take the vineyard of a man named Naboth,

the prophet Elijah predicted Ahab's upcoming death. Ahab lost his life in the next battle with Syria.

See **The Action Bible** *pages 376, 394–399 and 1 Kings 16:29–22:40. See also* **Damascus.**

AHAZIAH

Son of King Jehoram of Judah and Athaliah, whose brother was another Ahaziah, king of Israel. Ahaziah was also the grandson of King Ahab of Israel. Ahaziah became king of Judah at the age of twenty-two and was considered one of Israel's evil kings.

See **The Action Bible** *page 420 and 2 Kings 8:25–9:29.*

AHIJAH

A prophet from Shiloh who met Jeroboam on a road going out of Jerusalem. Ahijah said God would make Jeroboam ruler of the ten northern tribes of Israel. He acted out this prophecy by tearing his clothes into twelve pieces and giving ten of them to Jeroboam. This all came true about 930 BC.

See **The Action Bible** *page 367 and 1 Kings 11:29–40; 14:1–17.*

AHITHOPHEL

One of David's advisers when he first became king. For reasons not stated in the Bible, Ahithophel joined Absalom in rebelling against David. Ahithophel urged Absalom to gather twelve thousand men and attack while David and his army were tired and discouraged. However, Absalom also asked the advice of another man, Hushai. He suggested that Absalom postpone the battle until he could gather a larger army. God caused Absalom to take Hushai's advice instead of Ahithophel's. When Ahithophel saw that his advice was not followed, he killed himself.

See **The Action Bible** *pages 335, 340 and 2 Samuel 15:12, 31; 16:15–23; 17:1–23. See also* **Hushai.**

AI

An old city in central Israel. After Joshua and his army conquered Jericho, Ai was the next city to be attacked. But the army of Israel was beaten by the men of Ai because some Israelites had sinned in the battle of Jericho by keeping some of the treasures of the city. After the sin was found, the Israelites used a clever ambush to defeat Ai. The city was destroyed and burned. It was rebuilt in later years because some men of Ai were among those who returned from captivity in Babylon.

See **The Action Bible** *page 202 and Joshua 7:1–8:29; Ezra 2:28; Nehemiah 7:32.*

ALEXANDER THE GREAT

A great military general, one who conquered almost all of the known world for Greece. In 334 BC, he crossed from Greece into Asia Minor (now Turkey) and conquered the armies of the Medes and Persians. He then went as far south as Egypt, which he took without a battle. There he founded Alexandria, today the second-largest city of Egypt. He traveled across Israel to Babylonia and all the way to India. His army refused to go any farther, and he was forced to stop. He died at age thirty-two of a fever. Because of Alexander the Great, Greek became the common language in most of the known world. This was important in the spread of the gospel after Jesus's death and resurrection. Most scholars think the king of Greece whom the Old Testament prophet Daniel mentions in his book was Alexander the Great.

See The Action Bible *page 516 and Daniel 8:5–8; 11:34. See also the book of Daniel.*

ALMIGHTY

The English version of the word *Shaddai*. God called Himself "God Almighty" (El Shaddai) to Abraham, Jacob, and Moses as a sign of His amazing, unbeatable power.

See The Action Bible *page 437 and Genesis 17:1; Exodus 6:3.*

ALTAR

A structure used in worship that is made of stone, wood, marble, brick, or other materials. The people of Israel and people of other nations used altars for worship. Some altars were very simple; others were fancy. Although Abel offered a sacrifice to God, the first altar mentioned in the Bible was built by Noah. The Jewish tabernacle had two altars. One was the altar of burnt offering, where sacrifices to God were burned. The other was an altar of incense, sometimes called the golden altar. Incense was burned on this altar twice each day to symbolize believers' prayers. The temples built later had altars for sacrifices.

See The Action Bible *pages 25, 163, 165, 351 and Genesis 8:20; 22:9; Exodus 17:15; 27:1; 1 Kings 18:30.*

AMALEKITES

A fierce, warlike tribe of nomads from the family line of Esau. They seemed to wander from what is now the Sinai Desert to Israel. From the time the Israelites came out of Egypt (about 1450 BC) to the time of King Hezekiah (about 700 BC), the Amalekites always seemed to be Israel's enemy.

The Amalekites first attacked the Israelites during the exodus. In that battle, the Israelites kept winning as long as Aaron and Hur held up the arms of Moses. In the book of Judges, the Amalekites swept down upon settlements and took food, animals, and other possessions.

While David and his men left their village of Ziklag, the Amalekites burned it, capturing their wives and children. David later organized a raiding party and rescued the wives and children from the Amalekites. They continued to bother the Israelites until the time of Hezekiah, when they were finally defeated.

See **The Action Bible** *pages 150, 268 and Exodus 17:8–16; Judges 6:3–5; 1 Samuel 30:1–26. See also* Exodus, the.

AMMONITES

Ammon was a son of Lot and the ancestor of the Ammonites. God told Moses not to fight with them when the Israelites left Egypt for Canaan. Many years later, however, the Ammonites became persistent enemies of the Israelites. The Ammonites were fierce and worshipped idols like Molech. Saul once fought and defeated them.

During short periods, they were friendly to David. But the Ammonites mostly remained enemies for nearly a thousand years. When Nehemiah came back from exile to rebuild the walls of Jerusalem about 444 BC, one of those who opposed him was Tobiah the Ammonite. The Ammonites apparently survived until about 100 BC.

See The Action Bible *page 262 and Deuteronomy 2:19; 1 Samuel 11:1–11; 1 Kings 11:1–8. See also* Idol/Idolatry.

AMNON

The oldest son of King David and the half brother of Absalom. Amnon's mother is Ahinoam of Jezreel. An evil deed of Amnon drove Absalom to murder him.

See The Action Bible *page 329 and 2 Samuel 13.*

AMORITES

A large and powerful group of people who once lived in Mesopotamia, later in Babylon, and still later in Israel. They were living in Canaan during the time of Joshua and were defeated by the army of Israel.

See The Action Bible *page 205 and Genesis 15:16; Joshua 10:1–11:14.*

AMOS

A sheepherder and grower of fig trees who became an Old Testament prophet. He lived in Tekoa, a few miles south of Jerusalem in Judah. His preaching and prophesying, however, were mostly in Samaria, the capital city of the northern kingdom of Israel. In his prophecy, he insisted that people should be treated fairly. The rich people should have used their wealth to help the poor. Instead, they used their power to make poor people even poorer.

We don't know whether the people listened and responded to Amos's prophecy. In the end, he was told by the priest of Israel, Amaziah, to go home to his own land (Judah) and do his prophesying there!

See The Action Bible *page 436 and the book of Amos.*

AMRAM AND JOCHEBED

The parents of Moses, Aaron, and Miriam. Amram was from the tribe of Levi.

See The Action Bible *pages 113–117 and Exodus 2:1–10.*

ANANIAS OF DAMASCUS

A Jewish Christian who lived in Damascus. After Saul met the risen Jesus on the road to Damascus, he became blind and was led into Damascus. Three days later, God spoke to Ananias, telling him where to find Saul and saying that he should lay his hands on Saul so that his eyesight would be restored. Ananias was afraid because he had heard that

Saul persecuted Christians. However, he obeyed God, and Saul was healed.

See The Action Bible *page 687 and Acts 9:10–19.*

ANANIAS OF JERUSALEM

Ananias and his wife, Sapphira, sold a piece of their land and pretended they were giving the church all the money they received from it. They kept some of the money. When Ananias presented the money to the apostles, Peter confronted him with his lie, and Ananias fell down dead. Later Sapphira appeared, repeated the same lie—and she too died. The story shows that their sin was in lying to the Holy Spirit rather than in keeping part of the money.

See The Action Bible *page 664 and Acts 5:1–11.*

ANDREW

One of Jesus's twelve disciples. Andrew and his brother, Simon, were fishermen. Andrew also was a disciple of John the Baptist. But one day John pointed to Jesus and said, "Behold, the Lamb of God!" Andrew brought Simon to meet Jesus.

When Jesus wanted to feed five thousand people with five loaves and two fish, Andrew was the one who found the boy with his lunch. After Acts 1:13, Andrew is not mentioned again in the New Testament. However, tradition says he became a martyr for Christ in Achaia (present-day Greece), where he was crucified on an X-shaped cross. That shape is now known as Saint Andrew's cross.

See The Action Bible *page 549 and John 1:35–44; 6:8–13. See also* Peter/Simon.

ANGELS

Supernatural beings—thousands and thousands of them—created by God before He created people. Angels appear many times in the Old and New Testaments. They do not marry; they also never die. But they are not to be worshipped. Angels worship God and serve as His messengers. The Greek word for *angel* (*angelos*) means "messenger." Angels appeared to people many times in the Bible. Here are some of the types of angels mentioned in the Bible:

Angel of the Lord. An angel sent by God to act as His representative. This angel always speaks in the first person, as if God is speaking those very words. An angel of the Lord appeared to several people in the Bible (Hagar, Jacob, Joshua, Samson's parents).

Archangel. A term applied to the angel Michael. It seems to mean the highest rank among the angels. Michael's name means "Who is like God?" Michael's assignment seems to be caring for God's people, the Jews. He also fights against evil.

Messengers. The Bible mentions a messenger angel, Gabriel, several times. Each time, he came with an important message from God. He appeared twice to Daniel to explain visions that Daniel had. He also appeared to Zechariah, the priest, in 6 BC, and to Mary to announce the upcoming births of their sons.

Cherubim. Winged creatures with four faces: man, lion, ox, and eagle. Cherubim and a flaming sword were placed east of the garden of Eden to keep Adam and Eve from returning there. Pictures of cherubim were embroidered on the curtains of the tabernacle; carvings of cherubim were on the walls of the temple. Cherubim made of gold were on top of the ark of the covenant.

Seraphim. Another type of winged angel that appeared in Isaiah's vision of heaven.

See **The Action Bible** *pages 23, 84, 187, 198, 438 and Genesis 3:24; Isaiah 6; Revelation 5:11.*

ANOINT/ANOINTED

Anoint means "to pour oil on a person or a thing." *Anointed* means "sacred or set apart for God's use." Prophets, priests, and kings were anointed with special oil as a sign that God had chosen them for special work. Moses anointed Aaron and Aaron's sons as the first priests of Israel. The tabernacle and its furniture were anointed.

Hosts anointed their guests as a sign of hospitality. People often poured oil on the heads of important visitors to make them feel better. The Holy Spirit's presence is another kind of anointing—an anointing of God's power to do special tasks. Judges like Gideon were anointed by the Spirit. Jesus was anointed by the Spirit of God to do the work God the Father called Him to do.

See The Action Bible *pages 260, 273 and* *Exodus 40:13–16; 1 Samuel 10:1; 16:13;* *Luke 4:18; James 5:14; 1 John 2:20.*

ANTIOCH

The name of sixteen cities founded by Alexander the Great in memory of his father, Antiochus. Two are mentioned in the Bible.

Antioch of Pisidia. This city was on an important trading route in Asia Minor (now Turkey). Paul and Barnabas preached in the synagogue in Antioch on their first journey, and many people were interested in the gospel.

Antioch in Syria. The city where believers were first called Christians. It was fifteen miles from the Mediterranean Sea. It was a business center with many caravan routes going through it. In the time of Paul, it may have had a population of five hundred thousand. Antioch had the first Christian church, made up mostly of Gentiles. When the church at Antioch began to grow, the church at Jerusalem sent Barnabas to help the new Christians. This church sent Paul on his missionary journeys, and between journeys he returned to the Antioch church to tell what had happened. This city still exists today and is now called Antakiyeh.

See The Action Bible *page 693 and* *Acts 11:19–26; 13:14–44.*

APOSTLES/DISCIPLES

The twelve men chosen by Jesus as His special disciples. A disciple is someone who learns from someone else. These twelve were with Jesus during His three years of teaching, traveling, and healing. The list includes Peter, Andrew, James the son of Zebedee, John, Philip, Bartholomew, Thomas, Matthew, James the son of Alphaeus, Simon the Zealot, Thaddeus, and Judas Iscariot, who betrayed Jesus. After Judas killed himself, Matthias replaced him.

After Jesus returned to heaven, the disciples became known as apostles. The word *apostle* means "one chosen and sent" and was later also applied to Paul.

Although the original twelve apostles were the closest followers of Jesus, they did not really understand His mission until after the resurrection. They were frightened and disappointed when He was crucified. They did not expect Him to rise again, but after He did and after the Holy Spirit came, the apostles became leaders and teachers of the first-century church. Most of them later died for their faith in Jesus.

See The Action Bible *pages 550, 566 and* *Matthew 10:1–3, 23; 22:16; Mark 3:18;* *Luke 6:15–16; John 1:43–51; 6:5–6;* *12:20–23; 14:8–14, 22; Acts 1:13. See* *also* Andrew; Judas Iscariot; James; *John; Matthew; Peter/Simon; Thomas.*

AQUILA AND PRISCILLA

A husband (Aquila) and wife (Priscilla) who were leaders in the early church. Like Paul, both were tentmakers. They moved from place to place around the Mediterranean Sea, teaching and preaching the gospel wherever they went. They first met Paul in Corinth, and Paul lived in their home. Later they lived in Ephesus, where they taught a preacher named Apollos about the gospel. They lived for some time in Rome and at Ephesus. Each time, a church met regularly in their home.

See The Action Bible *page 719 and Acts 18:1–3, 24–26; 1 Corinthians 16:19.*

ARABIA

The area roughly the same as what is now Saudi Arabia—a large, dry peninsula between Egypt and the Persian Gulf. It is first mentioned in the Bible when the kings of Arabia brought gold and spices to Solomon. Arabians are mentioned several times in the Old Testament as paying tribute, selling cattle, or being judged by God.

See The Action Bible *pages 173, 363 and 1 Kings 10:15; Galatians 1:17; 4:25.*

ARAM/ARAMEANS

A nomadic group of people living in Mesopotamia (now Syria). They were also known as the Chaldeans. Damascus was one of their major cities. The Arameans defeated the Assyrians, led by King Tiglath-pileser. After becoming king of Israel, David led his troops to defeat the Aramean army. During the time of the prophet Elijah, Ben-Hadad, the king of the Arameans, led his army against the northern kingdom of Israel, but was defeated by King Ahab's army.

See The Action Bible *pages 40, 397 and 2 Samuel 8:5–10; 1 Kings 20.*

ARARAT

The name of a country in biblical times that is now a part of Turkey. It is also the name of a mountain in Turkey. Some modern explorers believe Noah's ark is still buried in the ice on this mountain.

See The Action Bible *page 35 and Genesis 8:4.*

ARK, NOAH'S

The boat God told Noah to build so he could escape the coming flood. Noah was five hundred years old when he built the ark. The boat was like a huge barge made of gopher wood. It was 450 feet long (longer than a football field), 75 feet wide, and 45 feet high. It had three decks or levels—big enough to hold pairs of every type of animal. After the floodwaters receded, the ark came to rest on Mount Ararat in present-day Turkey.

See The Action Bible *pages 30–37 and Genesis 6–9.*

ARK OF THE COVENANT

A wooden chest for storing and transporting the Ten Commandments. It was about four feet long, two and one-half feet wide, and two and one-half feet high. It was covered with gold inside and outside. On top were two golden cherubim (winged creatures that looked both animal and human). Inside the ark were the Ten Commandments written on tablets of stone, a pot of manna, and Aaron's rod that budded.

Because it was considered holy, it had to be carried on poles pushed through four golden rings on the corners. Anyone who touched it died instantly. The ark was placed in the tabernacle. The people of Israel carried the ark for forty years in the wilderness. When the priests carried it across the Jordan River into the Promised Land, the waters rolled back, and all the people passed over on dry land. At the battle of Jericho, the priests carried the ark around the outside of the city before the walls fell down.

The Philistines captured the ark but had diseases for seven months until they sent the ark back. Many years later, David finally brought the ark to Jerusalem. After Solomon built the temple, there was a great ceremony as the ark was placed there. When Jerusalem and the temple were destroyed by the Babylonians in 586 BC, the ark was lost. There was no ark in the second temple or in the temple built by Herod the Great shortly before the time of Jesus.

See **The Action Bible** *pages 163, 196, 200, 251 and Exodus 25:10–22; Joshua 6; 1 Samuel 4–6; 2 Samuel 6; 1 Kings 8:1–21. See also* **Holy/ Holiness; Tabernacle/Tent of Meeting.**

ARMOR

Armor for soldiers was usually made of leather coated with a thin layer of metal for added protection. Strips of the leather were fastened together to form a kind of vest tied at the back

with leather strings. Sometimes soldiers wore a square of bronze over the chest under this armor as a kind of heart guard. Kings often had armor made with more metal. When armor is used in Ephesians 6:11, it refers to all the weapons a soldier used rather than just the leather covering for his body. Paul used armor as a word picture for the spiritual preparedness a Christian needs. This is called the armor of God.

See The Action Bible *pages 279, 289 and Ephesians 6:10–17.*

ARTAXERXES

The king of Persia and the son of Xerxes. Artaxerxes reigned from 465 to 424 BC—the time of Ezra. When the people around Jerusalem complained to Artaxerxes about the rebuilding of the temple, he wrote a letter, ordering the rebuilding to stop. When Ezra returned, the king wrote another letter, allowing the rebuilding to continue.

See The Action Bible *page 512 and Ezra 4; 7–8. See also* Xerxes/Ahasuerus.

ASCENSION

Jesus's return to heaven after His resurrection. The ascension happened on the Mount of Olives. Eleven disciples were with Jesus. When He was taken up into a cloud before their eyes, this was a sign that they would not see Him on earth anymore. After Jesus left, two angels appeared to the disciples and told them that Jesus would someday return. Jesus's return is known as the second coming.

See The Action Bible *page 650 and Acts 1:6–11. See also* Mount of Olives.

ASIA MINOR

Usually refers to a Roman province that included the western section of Asia Minor (now Turkey). But the cities of Asia Minor include those in Anatolia (Troas, Ephesus, Miletus, Smyrna, Pergamum, Sardis, Thyatira, Philadelphia, Alexandria, Lystra, Derbe, Assos, Patara, Colossae, Attalia, Antioch, Iconium, and Tarsus). Paul visited this area on two of his missionary journeys and helped begin churches in several of its cities. The book of Revelation was written to churches in Asia.

See The Action Bible *page 710 and Acts 13–14; 19; Revelation 2–3.*

ASSYRIA

An old and powerful empire northeast of Israel. This nation was an enemy of the Israelites for many years, and finally in 722 BC, it overran the northern kingdom (Israel) and took many of its people into captivity. The most important cities of the Assyrian Empire were Nineveh, Assur, and Calah. The Assyrians worshipped idols and had temples to their gods in many cities. The king of Assyria was also his country's religious leader and commander of its huge army.

Many of the kings of Israel and Judah paid tribute (money, gifts) to the kings of Assyria to keep them from attacking their country. After Sennacherib, a king during the time of Hezekiah, was killed, the Assyrian Empire grew weaker and was conquered by Babylonia. It was never again a great power. The Assyrians who moved into Israel during Israel's exile eventually married Israelites and became the Samaritans mentioned in the New Testament.

See The Action Bible *pages 439–440 and 2 Kings 18:9–19:37; John 4. See also* Exile/Captivity of Israel; Hezekiah.

ATHALIAH

The only woman to reign over Judah. She was the daughter of Ahab. After her son, King Ahaziah, was killed, she ordered all of her grandsons to be killed, so that she could take the throne. She reigned for over six years. One infant son, Joash, escaped with the help of his aunt. When the child was later crowned king, Athaliah heard crowds cheering and went into the temple, arriving just after Joash was crowned. At the order of the priest, she was killed as soon as she left the temple.

See The Action Bible *page 397 and 2 Kings 11; 2 Chronicles 22–23. See also* Jehoiada.

ATHENS

An important city for about three thousand years. It is now the capital of Greece. Its ancient architecture and ruins of old buildings (the Parthenon and several ancient temples) show what a beautiful city it was hundreds of years before the time of Christ. It was the center of Greek art, science, and philosophy and was the most important university city of the ancient world. Athens's time of greatest glory was 459–431 BC when it was a city-state. Later it was defeated in war by the Spartans, then by the Romans, and later by the Goths and the Turks. Paul visited the city on his second missionary journey and spoke to a group of people. In the sermon, he called attention to an altar marked "To an Unknown God" that he had seen in the city. Although some became Christians during his visit, there is no record of Paul beginning a church in Athens.

See **The Action Bible** *page 710 and Acts 17:15–34.*

AUGUSTUS CAESAR

The ruler of the Roman Empire at the time Jesus was born. He was the grandnephew of Julius Caesar, the founder of the Roman Empire. The name Caesar was added to the name of each of the Roman emperors, so it became a title like emperor or king. Augustus Caesar meant the same as Emperor Augustus.

See **The Action Bible** *page 532 and Luke 2:1.*

BABYLON

The capital city of Babylonia, built near the Euphrates River, was probably the largest and richest city in the ancient world. Babylon reached its full glory when Nebuchadnezzar was king (605–562 BC). The people of Judah were captured and taken to live in Babylon during this time.

Babylon was attacked, destroyed, and rebuilt again and again throughout its history. Now Babylon is only a series of mounds near the Euphrates River. In the New Testament, Babylon is used as a word picture for a government that is an enemy of God. When Babylon is used in 1 Peter and Revelation, it probably refers to the city of Rome, the capital of the Roman Empire.

See **The Action Bible** *page 450 and Genesis 11; 2 Kings 24:10–16; Daniel 1–5; Revelation 16:19; 17–18.*

BABYLONIANS

Also known as the Chaldeans and the Amorites, the Babylonians lived in Mesopotamia (Syria today). The Babylonian kingdom got its start under Hammurabi, the king whose code of conduct is sometimes quoted in the Bible. When the Assyrian Empire rose to power, the Babylonians paid tribute money to the Assyrians but later fought for independence. Sennacherib, the king of Assyria, defeated the Babylonians in 703 BC and destroyed Babylon in 689 BC. The Babylonians fought back and destroyed Nineveh. Under King Nebuchadnezzar, the

Babylonians defeated the Egyptians and destroyed Jerusalem.

See The Action Bible *pages 451–483 and 2 Kings 24–25; Daniel 1–5. See also* Babylon; Nebuchadnezzar.

BALAAM

A Midianite prophet in the land of Moab (now called Jordan). When the Israelites camped near Moab, King Balak offered Balaam a reward if he would curse the Israelites. On the way to King Balak's city, an angel of the Lord blocked Balaam's path. This caused his frightened donkey to speak out loud. Balaam was warned to speak nothing but the Lord's words. To King Balak's surprise, Balaam blessed Israel three times. Balaam went home to Peor and helped cause the Israelites to sin. When Israel went to war against Moab and Midian, Balaam was killed. In the New Testament, Balaam is an example of a false teacher who leads Christians away from truth.

See The Action Bible *page 187 and Numbers 22–24; 31:8–16; 2 Peter 2:15.*

BALAK

A Moabite king who sent Balaam, a false prophet, to curse the people of Israel while on their way to Canaan.

See The Action Bible *page 187 and Numbers 22:1–20.*

BAPTISM

In Moses's day, *baptism* was another word for *washing*. But when John the Baptist called the crowds to be baptized, he suggested that they be washed inside and outside. The outside washing showed that the person wanted to be changed on the inside. Baptism meant he was asking God to forgive his sins. So, John baptized people in the Jordan River. Jesus was one of the people John baptized. Jesus had not done anything wrong, but He wanted to show that His work of preaching, teaching, healing, and saving had begun. Today baptism is a way to show that a person has faith in Jesus. The old life has ended and a new life has begun.

See The Action Bible *page 547 and Matthew 3:1–6, 13–17; Romans 6:3–5.*

BARABBAS

A robber who was in prison for murder and rioting when Jesus was arrested. At the Jewish Feast of Passover, the Roman governor Pilate usually set one prisoner free. Barabbas, the criminal, was set free.

See The Action Bible *page 631 and Matthew 27:15–26; Mark 15:6–15.*

BARAK

A military leader of the Israelites. When Deborah was judge of Israel, the people were being oppressed by the Canaanites, who robbed their farms. Deborah told Barak that God wanted him to bring together an army of ten thousand men to fight the Canaanites. Barak said he would do it only if Deborah went along into battle with him. When Barak refused to go unless Deborah went, Deborah proclaimed that victory would belong to a woman.

See The Action Bible *page 213 and Judges 4–5; Hebrews 11:32. See also* Deborah.

BARLEY

Barley was the most common grain grown in Israel. Most of the poor people used it for bread and cereal because it cost less than wheat. Beans, especially dried beans, were a regular part of the diet of poor people in Israel. Dried beans were sometimes ground and mixed with grain to make bread.

See The Action Bible *pages 99, 332 and Ezekiel 4:9.*

BARNABAS

The nickname of a helpful, generous follower of Jesus. His name was Joseph, but the apostles called him Barnabas, which means "son of encouragement."

Barnabas and Paul were good friends. Barnabas spoke up for Paul when the apostles still feared him. He later traveled with Paul as a missionary. Barnabas's young cousin, John Mark, went with them. Later Paul and Barnabas disagreed when planning their second missionary trip. Barnabas wanted to take John Mark along again. Paul didn't, because John Mark left the first trip early. Finally, Paul and Barnabas separated. Barnabas took John Mark and sailed to Cyprus (Barnabas's old home). Paul chose another companion, Silas, and went to Asia Minor (now called Turkey). Some scholars think Barnabas wrote the book of Hebrews, though no one knows for sure.

See The Action Bible *page 664 and Acts 4:36–37; 9:27; 11:22–30; 13:2; 14:28; 15:22–41.*

BARREN

Unable to have children. In Bible times, most men and women were very sad and ashamed when this happened. They thought God was punishing them. Rachel, Hannah, and Elizabeth were unable to have children for a time.

See The Action Bible *pages 248–249 and Genesis 30:1; 1 Samuel 1; Luke 1.*

BASKETS

In the Old Testament, baskets were made from reeds, twigs, or ropes. They were used for carrying fruit, bread, or clay. They were carried by hand, on the head or shoulders, or attached to a pole, depending on their size. As a baby, Moses was placed in a watertight basket and placed on the Nile River. In the New Testament, two kinds of baskets are mentioned. One was like a small backpack. The other was a large, sturdy basket, big enough to hold a person. Paul escaped from Damascus by hiding in a basket, which was lowered down through the city wall.

See The Action Bible *pages 115, 578–579 and Genesis 40:17; Exodus 2:3–4; 29:2–3; Deuteronomy 26:2; Matthew 16:9–10; John 6:13; Acts 9:25.*

BATHSHEBA

A beautiful woman who was married to Uriah the Hittite and lived near King David's palace. Her sin with David caused family problems for David for the rest of his life. Bathsheba's first child with David died, but they had four more sons, one of whom was Solomon.

See **The Action Bible** *page 321 and 2 Samuel 11; 1 Kings 1; 1 Chronicles 3:5.*

BEARS

Bears are mentioned several times in the Old Testament, always as fierce, threatening animals. They were probably Syrian brown bears, which are still found in modern Lebanon. David is said to have fought and killed a bear while guarding his sheep. When teens threatened and made fun of the prophet Elisha, two bears mauled forty-two of them.

See **The Action Bible** *pages 20, 405 and 1 Samuel 17:34–37; 2 Kings 2:23–24.*

BEATITUDES

Short sayings beginning with the word *blessed* that describe actions or thoughts that will give a person joy and peace. In the Old Testament, beatitudes were written by psalmists and prophets. The Old Testament beatitudes often promise blessings of health, peace, prosperity, and family. But most of all they promise that God will be near to a righteous person.

The Beatitudes in the New Testament have one big difference from those in the Old Testament: They stress the joy of belonging to God's kingdom. In the Sermon on the Mount, Jesus says the poor in spirit, those who weep, and those who are persecuted are blessed because they belong to God and enjoy being close to Him.

See **The Action Bible** *page 567 and Psalms 1:1–3; 41:1; 65:4; 84:4–5; 106:3; Proverbs 8:32, 34; Isaiah 32:20; Matthew 5:1–11; Luke 6:20–22.*

BEAUTIFUL GATE

Probably the eastern gate to the temple in Jerusalem. It was beautifully crafted of Corinthian bronze, and it opened into the temple's Court of Women. Peter and John healed a paralyzed man outside the Beautiful Gate.

See The Action Bible page 659 and Acts 3:2–10.

BELSHAZZAR

The last king of Babylon in the family line of King Nebuchadnezzar. Belshazzar did not worship God. At one of his feasts in 539 BC, he praised the idols of gold, silver, bronze, and iron because he drank from cups stolen from the Jerusalem temple. As Belshazzar drank with his thousand guests, a hand appeared on the wall and wrote strange words. Daniel explained what the words meant. That very night, the writing came true. Belshazzar was killed, and his kingdom was taken over by the Medes and Persians.

See The Action Bible pages 481–483 and Daniel 5.

BENJAMIN

(SEE JACOB/ISRAEL)

BEREA

A city in Macedonia. Paul escaped here after a riot broke out in Thessalonica as a result of his preaching. But troublemakers from Thessalonica followed him to Berea.

See The Action Bible page 718 and Acts 17:10–15.

BETHANY

A village two miles southeast of Jerusalem near the Mount of Olives. Simon, a Pharisee with leprosy, Martha, Mary, and Lazarus lived in Bethany. Jesus rose into heaven near Bethany. A town is still there today.

See The Action Bible page 549 and Matthew 26:6–13; Luke 24:50–51; John 11:1–44. See also Lazarus of Bethany; Martha of Bethany; Mary of Bethany; Simon of Bethany.

BETHEL

A town twelve miles north of Jerusalem. When Jacob traveled to his uncle Laban's home in Haran, he camped

for the night near a Canaanite town called Luz and slept on the ground with his head on a rock. Here Jacob had an amazing dream of angels on a stairway. When he awoke, he called the place *Bethel*, which means "house of God," because he had met with God. He later built an altar there.

After the Israelites entered Canaan, the ark of the covenant was kept at Bethel. When the country split into the northern and southern kingdoms, King Jeroboam chose Bethel as a place to set up his golden calves.

See The Action Bible *page 78 and Genesis 28:10–19; Judges 20:26–28; 1 Kings 12:26–30; 2 Kings 23:15–23. See also* Stairway of Jacob.

BETHLEHEM

Best known as Jesus's birthplace and the hometown of King David. The Old Testament prophet Micah predicted the Messiah would be born in Bethlehem. The angels announced Jesus's birth to the shepherds outside the town. All male babies two years old or younger around Bethlehem were sentenced to death by jealous King Herod, who wanted to kill the new king of the Jews. Ruth, Boaz, and Naomi lived in Bethlehem long before Jesus.

See The Action Bible *pages 247, 532 and Ruth 2–4; 1 Samuel 17:12–15; Micah 5:2; Matthew 2:16–18; Luke 2:4–20.*

BIRDS

Of the near four hundred kinds of birds that live in Israel, twenty-six kinds can be found only in Israel and nowhere else. The Bible mentions about fifty kinds of birds. Here are some of them:

Doves. Noah sent a dove to find dry land. Jesus told His disciples to be harmless as doves. The Spirit of God descended on Jesus like a dove. Doves were sold in the temple for sacrifices.

Peacocks. Beautiful pheasants that strutted about Solomon's courts.

Pigeons. Pigeons were common rock doves. They were used by the poor for sacrifices because there were so many around.

Quail. Quail live on the ground and scratch for food. In Bible lands, quail migrate in huge flocks, flying only a few feet off the ground.

Ravens. Ravens were considered unclean because they are scavengers. But ravens also brought Elijah food during a drought.

Rooster. Just before He was arrested, Jesus predicted that Peter would deny Him three times before the rooster crowed—the hours between midnight and 3:00 a.m.

Sparrows. Sparrows are small, seed-eating birds like American sparrows. They busily flit about and chirp constantly. Sparrows were so inexpensive to buy that when four were sold, a fifth sparrow was added free. But Jesus said that God knows about each one.

See The Action Bible *pages 35, 147, 165, 362, 378, 568, 570, 624 and Genesis 8:8–12; 15:9; Exodus 16:13; Numbers 11:31; 1 Kings 17:4; Job 38:41; Psalm 84:3; Matthew 3:16; 10:16, 29–31; 21:12; Luke 2:24. See also* Clean/Unclean.

BIRTHRIGHT

The blessing and double share of wealth a father gave to his oldest son. Esau carelessly sold his birthright to Jacob for a bowl of soup.

See The Action Bible *pages 68–69 and Genesis 25:29–34. See also* Esau.

BLASPHEMY

Speaking lies against God or the name of God. Blasphemy was a crime punishable by death. Jesus and Stephen were falsely accused of blasphemy. God punished King Jeroboam's blasphemy by crippling his hand.

See The Action Bible *page 374 and Leviticus 24:10–16; 1 Kings 13:4–5; Matthew 9:3; Acts 6:11. See also* Sin/Disobedience.

BLESSING

A gift given by God, such as cattle, sheep, wealth, or children. A blessing was also a public statement of favor. Fathers spoke a blessing to their sons. In the New Testament, forgiveness and salvation were blessings—gifts—from God. A person who is blessed is considered favored by God.

See The Action Bible *page 71 and Genesis 27:28–29; Ephesians 1:3.*

BLINDNESS

(SEE DISEASES/CONDITIONS)

BLOOD

Considered to be the basis of life, both in people and in animals. Therefore, God commanded the Israelites to avoid eating meat without draining the blood from it. Blood represented life, and therefore it was needed for forgiveness of sins. The Israelites offered animal sacrifices to God as He commanded. But when Jesus died, He became the final sacrifice for our sins. The phrase "blood of Jesus" refers to His giving His life so that our sins can be forgiven and we can be saved.

See The Action Bible *pages 129, 623 and Exodus 7:14–24; Leviticus 17:10–14; Matthew 26:28; Ephesians 2:13. See also* Plagues on Egypt.

BOAZ

(SEE RUTH, BOOK OF; KINSMAN-REDEEMER)

BODY OF CHRIST

(SEE CHURCH; JESUS)

warfare. First Samuel 31:3 tells that King Saul was wounded by a Philistine archer. Egyptian archers wounded King Josiah so badly that he died.

See **The Action Bible** *page 50 and 1 Chronicles 5:18; 12:2; 2 Chronicles 35:23–24.*

BRICKS

Molded clay used for building projects. The Israelites were forced to make bricks to build the pyramids and cities in Egypt. In making the bricks, they used straw—cut barley or wheat stalks.

See **The Action Bible** *page 127 and Exodus 5.*

BRONZE/COPPER

Copper was used for making tools, furnishings for the temple and tabernacle, and weapons. It was "smelted from ore" as Job discussed with his friends. Many of the outside furnishings for the tabernacle were bronze, which was made from copper and tin. King Nebuchadnezzar of Babylon had a dream in which he saw a statue made of gold, silver, bronze, and iron. This statue was a symbol of the nations that rose to power.

See **The Action Bible** *pages 162, 182–184, 360 and Exodus 25:3; 27:2; Deuteronomy 4:20; 1 Kings 7:45–46; Job 28:2; Daniel 7. See also* **Coins/Money.**

BRONZE SNAKE

When the people of Israel grumbled against God and Moses, God allowed poisonous snakes to bite the people. When people admitted they were wrong, God told Moses to make a

BOOK OF THE LAW

(SEE TORAH)

BOW AND ARROW

Used for hunting animals for food, and also for war. Bows were made of wood; bowstrings were made of oxgut. Arrows were light wood or reeds tipped with metal. When bows and arrows were used as weapons of war, the bows were sometimes as long as five feet. Israelites from the tribes of Reuben, Gad, and Benjamin were famous for their skill with bows and arrows in

snake out of bronze and place it on a pole. Anyone who was bitten had only to look at the snake statue and was healed. While talking with Nicodemus, Jesus mentioned the bronze snake as a symbol for His upcoming death.

See The Action Bible *pages 182–184 and Numbers 21:4–9; John 3:14.*

BROTHERS OF JESUS

(SEE JAMES; JUDE)

BULL

Bulls are male cattle, usually mentioned in the Bible as animals offered as sacrifices to God on special feast days. To be used for sacrifice, a young bull had to be at least eight days old, or in some cases it had to be one to seven years old.

See The Action Bible *pages 383–385 and Leviticus 9:2–4; 22:27. See also* Feasts.

BULRUSH

Bulrush is the papyrus plant, a tall, slender plant that grows in swampy places. The boat for the baby Moses was made from this plant. Bulrushes were also used to make writing material before the days of paper.

See The Action Bible *page 115 and Exodus 2:3.*

BURIAL

Placing a dead body in a grave or tomb. The dead usually were buried in caves, because the ground in many caves consists of rock with only a small layer of soil, so digging is difficult. Sarah, Jacob, Joseph, and others were buried in the cave of Machpelah in Hebron. In Jesus's day, dead bodies were wrapped in clean linen with spices and oils before burial. After His crucifixion, Jesus was buried in the tomb of Joseph of Arimathea.

See The Action Bible *page 641 and* Genesis 23:19; 50:12–14; Joshua 24:32–33; Matthew 27:57–61.

BURNING BUSH

Euonymus alatas is the scientific name for the plant called a burning bush. It gets its common name from its fiery red color and because of the story of God's appearance to Moses in the form of a bush set on fire. God caught Moses's attention because the bush stayed on fire instead of burning to ashes.

See The Action Bible *page 121 and Exodus 3.*

CAESAR

(SEE AUGUSTUS CAESAR)

CAESAREA

A city on the Mediterranean Sea named in honor of Caesar Augustus. It was about sixty-five miles northwest of Jerusalem. During the first century, it was the official capital of Israel. Caesarea was the military headquarters for the Roman army in the area. The first time Peter preached to Gentiles was in Caesarea in the house of Cornelius, a Roman soldier.

See The Action Bible *page 672 and Acts 10; 21:8–9; 23:23–26:32. See also* Cornelius; Philip.

CAESAREA PHILIPPI

An ancient town in northern Israel where Herod the Great built a temple in honor of Augustus Caesar. Herod's son, Philip, enlarged the town and named it Caesarea Philippi so it would not be confused with another Caesarea, the larger city on the coast. While preaching in this area, Jesus asked His disciples who they thought He was. The mountain on which the transfiguration took place was probably in this area.

See The Action Bible *page 584 and Matthew 16:13–28; Mark 8:27–37. See also* Transfiguration, the.

CAIAPHAS

High priest from about AD 18 to 36. Caiaphas was the son-in-law of Annas and seemed to work closely with him. After Jesus raised Lazarus from the dead, Caiaphas and others were eager to kill Jesus. Caiaphas was involved in the trial of Jesus. He is also mentioned in the arrest of Peter and John.

See The Action Bible *page 627 and John 11:45–53; 18:13–28; Acts 4:5–22.*

CAIN

The first son of Adam and Eve—the first child to be born on earth. He was a farmer who brought an offering of vegetables to God. God was not pleased with Cain's offering. The Bible does not explain why. God warned Cain to get control over his temper, but Cain didn't listen. After killing his brother, Abel, Cain was punished by having to leave his parents and become a wanderer, always in fear of being killed. God promised him protection from his enemies. Cain went to a country east of Eden where he married and had a son, Enoch.

See **The Action Bible** *page 24 and Genesis 4:1–17. See also* **Abel***.*

CALEB

One of the twelve men sent by Moses to spy out the land of Canaan. When the people of Israel rebelled against God and refused to enter Canaan, the Lord grew angry and said that none of the adults except Caleb and Joshua would ever enter Canaan. All would die in the wilderness. Forty years later, Caleb and Joshua were the only men of the original group still alive. Caleb asked to settle near Hebron where the "giants" who frightened the other spies lived! Even though Caleb was old, he directed the battle against these people and drove them out.

See **The Action Bible** *page 175 and Numbers 13:1–14:38; Joshua 14:6–15; 15:13–14.*

CALF/CATTLE

Calves are mentioned in the Bible as meat for special occasions. Usually only the wealthy could afford such special foods. In Jesus's parable of the lost son, the father killed the calf that had been set aside in order to celebrate the return of his son.

Calves, like bulls, were also used as sacrifices to God. A perfect, unblemished red cow was used for an important ceremony described in Numbers 19.

The term *cattle* usually refers to larger animals such as oxen, donkeys, horses, and cows rather than sheep and goats. However, cattle can also refer to all domesticated animals. Because cattle were so important to the life of the Israelites, the law of Moses said they should be permitted to rest on the Sabbath just like people.

Cattle were considered part of the spoils of war. A conquering army often took the cattle of the people it had defeated.

See **The Action Bible** *pages 132, 217 and Numbers 19; Luke 15:23. See also* **Idol/Idolatry***.*

CALVARY

The place where Jesus was crucified. The name comes from a Latin word, *calvaria*, meaning "skull." In Aramaic, it is called Golgotha. It may have been called that because it was a place where criminals were executed and skulls were found there, or because the hill itself looked like a skull. The exact location of Calvary is unknown. Two places have been suggested: where the Church of the Holy Sepulchre now stands in Jerusalem; the other is a hill known as Gordon's Calvary. On Gordon's Calvary there are holes in the rocky side of the hill that resemble the eyes and nose of a skull.

See **The Action Bible** *pages 635, 639 and Matthew 27:33; Mark 15:22; Luke 23:33; John 19:17, 41.*

CAMELS

Camels were important in the Middle East because they are very hardy and can live forty to fifty years. They are cud-chewing vegetarians and have a three-part stomach that can store a three-day water supply. The Israelites were not permitted to eat camel meat, but other nations often ate it. Camel hair was used in making cloth. To own camels was a sign of wealth. Job had three thousand camels before his troubles began, and later in life he had six thousand.

See **The Action Bible** *pages 65, 216 and Job 1:3; 42:12; Psalm 50:10.*

CANA

A village in Galilee mentioned several times in the gospel of John. While we don't know its exact location, it was probably west of the lake of Galilee. Jesus performed His first miracle in this town—turning the water at a wedding into wine. It is also the place where Jesus met the nobleman whose son was dying, and Jesus told him his son would live.

See **The Action Bible** *page 552 and John 2:1–11; 4:46–54.*

CANAAN/CANAANITES

One of the old names for Palestine (now Israel); the land God promised to give to the descendants of Abraham. The people who lived there before the Israelites conquered it were called Canaanites.

Canaan was the grandson of Noah and the son of Ham. He was the ancestor of the people who later lived in

the land of Canaan, which was named after him. This group included tribes of the Hittites, Jebusites, Amorites, Hivites, and others. They lived in well-developed cities, each with its own king, army, and taxes. The city-kingdoms often battled each other. The Canaanites worshiped many gods, including Baal. The Israelites had to conquer the Canaanites before they could live in peace in Canaan. But the Israelites never completely conquered them.

See **The Action Bible** *pages 99, 173, 212; and Genesis 15; Exodus 6:4; Judges 4:23 and the books of Exodus; Numbers; Leviticus; Deuteronomy; and Joshua.*

CANDACE

(SEE ETHIOPIAN OFFICER)

CAPERNAUM

A large town on the northwest shore of the Sea of Galilee. Jesus made this town His headquarters during His work in Galilee. He performed many miracles at Capernaum, including the healing of a centurion's servant. Many of His important teachings were spoken there. Because the people did not respond, Jesus predicted the city would be destroyed. His prediction was so completely fulfilled that today no one is sure where the town was.

See **The Action Bible** *page 563 and Matthew 8:5–13; 11:23–24; Luke 7:1–10.*

CAPTIVITY

(SEE EXILE/CAPTIVITY OF ISRAEL)

CARAVAN

A group of people traveling together for protection. In Bible times, travelers in the deserts or foreign lands went in groups to protect each other from robbers, wild animals, or accidents. When families moved, they went in caravans; traders also traveled in caravans. Joseph was sold as a slave to a caravan of Ishmaelites. Mary, Joseph, and Jesus were part of a caravan traveling to Jerusalem for Passover when Jesus was twelve years old.

See **The Action Bible** *pages 64, 92 and Genesis 37:25–28; Luke 2:41–51.*

CAVES

Openings in the earth. In Israel, where the hills are largely limestone or chalk, some are large enough to be used for homes. Lot and his two daughters lived in a cave after Sodom was destroyed. Some of the prophets hid in caves when Jezebel was trying to kill them. Caves were also used for storage and as burial places.

See **The Action Bible** *page 294 and Genesis 19:30; 1 Kings 18:4. See also Burial.*

CEDAR

Trees were often used in Bible times as building material. Cedar was also used to burn the sacrifices. Many cedars were used to build Solomon's temple.

See The Action Bible *page 359 and Leviticus 14:4–6; Numbers 19:6; 1 Kings 5–6.*

CENSUS

Counting of the number of people in an area for taxes or registration for the army. A census was taken soon after the Israelites left Egypt. Another was taken near the end of the forty years in the wilderness. David also made a census when he was king, and the Bible says that David displeased God by doing it.

These census reports counted only men twenty years and older so that they could find out how strong (in number) the army could be. The New Testament says Caesar Augustus once ordered a census. Because each person had to be counted in the place of his birth, Joseph and Mary had to go to Bethlehem. While they were there, Jesus was born.

See The Action Bible *page 532 and Numbers 1:2; 26; 2 Samuel 24; Luke 2:1–7.*

CHALDEANS

(SEE ARAM/ARAMEANS)

CHARIOT

A two-wheeled cart pulled by horses. In ancient times, they were used mainly for war, but also for races and important processions by kings or other high officials. Usually two men rode in a chariot—a driver and a warrior. In some countries, a third man with a shield also rode along.

Joseph rode in Pharaoh's second chariot in Egypt. When the people of Israel left Egypt, Pharaoh's warriors went after them with chariots that became stuck in the mud at the bottom of the Red Sea. Sisera was the commander of the Canaanite army, which had nine hundred chariots. Chariots were not so useful in hilly areas. David and Solomon added chariots to their armies. The strangest chariot mentioned in the Bible was the chariot of fire that came to take Elijah to heaven.

See The Action Bible *pages 105, 144, 400–401 and Genesis 41:43; Exodus 14:21–29; Judges 1:19; 4:3; 2 Kings 2:12.*

CHRIST

The Greek word for "Messiah." Whenever the New Testament refers

to Jesus as Christ, it is saying that He is the Messiah. The disciples realized that Jesus was the Messiah, God's special anointed one, who would fulfill God's purpose. Andrew told his brother Peter that the Messiah had been found.

See The Action Bible *pages 23, 541, 600 and Isaiah 61:1–2; Luke 4:16–21; 1 John 4:14. See also* Jesus; Messiah/Savior.

CHRISTIAN

The term *Christian* was first used in Antioch to point out those who believed in Jesus's teachings.

See The Action Bible *page 693 and Acts 11:26; 26:28; 1 Peter 4:16.*

CHRONICLES, 1 AND 2

Two books in the Old Testament that tell the history of Israel. They cover some of the same events as 2 Samuel and 1 and 2 Kings. But the Chronicles concentrate more on the southern kingdom, Judah, than on the northern kingdom, Israel.

Originally Chronicles was just one book. It was divided into two when the Old Testament was translated into Greek. Though the author's name does not appear in the books, many Bible scholars believe they were written by Ezra, the priest and scribe. After the people of Judah returned to Jerusalem after the exile, Ezra wanted them to know their history and the importance of the reigns of David and Solomon.

The first nine chapters of 1 Chronicles provide genealogies— family histories—of individuals from Adam to King Saul. First Chronicles

1–29 describe the kingdom of David; 2 Chronicles 1–9 tell about Solomon and the temple he built; 2 Chronicles 1–36 provide the history of the southern kingdom, Judah.

See The Action Bible *pages 316–318, 348, 423–430 and 1 and 2 Chronicles. See* Exile/Captivity of Israel.

CHURCH

All Christians throughout time. The church also is called the body of Christ, and Jesus Christ is called the Head. The church grew rapidly soon after the resurrection of Christ and the Holy Spirit's arrival. New Jewish believers in Jerusalem gathered to pray, sing, and encourage each other. Later, in other cities, many Gentiles became Christians and met together to form fellowships or churches, usually meeting in homes. The word *church* also means the believers in a certain city or area. Every local church is part of the body of Christ.

See The Action Bible *pages 693, 704 and 1 Corinthians 16:1–4; Ephesians 1:22–23; 4:15–16; Colossians 1:18–20.*

CITIES OF REFUGE

A place where a person who killed someone by accident could run and avoid being put to death before a trial could take place. The law of Moses named six cities of refuge: Shechem, Hebron, Kedesh, Ramoth, Bezer, and Golan. Three were located on one side of the Jordan and three on the other side.

See The Action Bible *page 208 and Exodus 21:12–14; Numbers 35; Deuteronomy 19:1–13.*

CITY

Ancient cities differ from modern cities. A city always had a high wall around it several feet thick and made of mud, stones, or brick. The wall protected the people from enemy armies and from robbers. Some well-known city walls in the Old Testament include Jericho's walls, which were wide enough to have houses built into them, and the walls of Jerusalem, which were built and rebuilt many times. Nehemiah and some of the people of Israel who returned from exile repaired the walls of Jerusalem. New Testament cities also had walls. Paul escaped from those who tried to kill him by being lowered from the Damascus wall. He later preached in many cities in Asia Minor.

Cities had gates. Some cities had only one gate; large cities might have up to twelve. The gates were closed and barred at night. Some of those walls are still standing today.

Streets in some cities were narrow and winding, without any fixed plan. Ancient cities were usually built to give protection to the farmers who worked in surrounding fields. The people went out to their fields in the daytime and returned at night to sleep. Most cities were built on hills because the people could see approaching enemies better. Cities were often built around a spring or a well because water was scarce in Israel.

See The Action Bible *pages 173, 194 and Deuteronomy 1:28; Nehemiah 1–6; Joshua 6; Acts 9:22–25. See also Athens; Colossae; Damascus; Jericho; Jerusalem.*

CITY OF DAVID

(SEE BETHLEHEM; JERUSALEM)

CLEAN/UNCLEAN

Clean doesn't just mean a person or food that has been washed! It also means something allowable under the law of Israel. *Unclean* refers to thoughts, acts, people, places, and foods that are displeasing to God.

God gave the people of Israel a list of the kinds of clean animals they could eat and the unclean ones they couldn't eat (like pigs). Yet even clean animals could become unclean. An animal that died of natural causes or had been killed by another animal was considered unclean. After Jesus died and rose again, God sent a special vision to Peter to show him that all foods were now clean.

A person could become unclean for several reasons. Anyone who touched a dead person was unclean for seven days and had to go through special washings on the third and seventh days to become clean again. A woman who had a baby was unclean for a week or two weeks. To become clean, she had to offer a young pigeon or a turtledove as a sacrifice. Mary offered two doves after Jesus was born.

See **The Action Bible** *pages 277, 678 and Leviticus 11–12; 15; Luke 2:22–24; Acts 10:9–16.*

CLOTHING

Men and women wore close-fitting tunics with either short or long sleeves. They were usually made of wool and often lined with white cotton so they wouldn't scratch the skin when the undershirt was not worn. Tunics were tied at the waist with a wide sash called a girdle. The girdle was usually a square yard of wool, linen, or silk cloth.

The outer garment was a cloak or mantle. This was used as a coat during the colder seasons of the year and also as a blanket to wrap up in at night. The cloaks were usually made of wool, goat hair, or camel hair.

Men used three kinds of headgear: cotton or wool caps, turbans (long pieces of thick linen material wound around the head with the ends tucked under), or a scarf called a kaffiyeh. This was a square yard of colored cotton, wool, or silk folded into a triangle and draped around the head with the point of the triangle falling down the middle of the back. The man held it in place with a silk or woolen cord coiled around his head.

Women wore headscarves or shawls. These were often pinned

over a cap made of stiff material and decorated with pearls, silver, gold, or other ornaments. Sometimes they were used to form a veil that covered at least part of a woman's face and upper body.

Priests had special clothes. The ephod was a linen garment worn by the high priest. It was embroidered with gold thread. Blue, purple, and scarlet threads also were used to make it. A breastplate was worn over the ephod, which had twelve precious stones—one stone for each tribe of Israel. Other priests wore simpler linen ephods.

Grave clothes were the strips of linen cloth that were wrapped around a body before burial. The hands and feet were tied with more pieces of linen, and another piece was placed over the face. This is the way Lazarus appeared when Jesus raised him from the dead.

See The Action Bible *pages 90–95, 122, 161, 164, 392, 606 and Genesis 37: 3–4; Exodus 22:25–27; 28; 34:29–35; Samuel 2:18; 2 Samuel 6:14; Isaiah 3:18–24; John 11:44; 19:23; 1 Corinthians 11:5–10. See also* Foot Washing; Priests.

COINS/MONEY

Coins of various kinds have existed since the eighth century BC. At the time of King Darius of Persia, a gold coin—a daric—was in circulation. This coin had the image of the king. Phoenician merchants, who traveled all over the known world helped make the use of coins more popular in the fourth and fifth centuries BC. Later, when the Roman Empire conquered much of the known world, other coins were in use. At the time of Jesus, coins were minted in gold, silver, and copper.

Denarius. A silver coin that was the average pay for one day's work. This was the "Roman coin" Jesus asked to see when the Pharisees demanded to know if they should pay taxes to Caesar. Caesar's face was engraved on the coin.

Copper Coins. The smallest denomination of coin used in Jesus's day. This was a Jewish coin called a lepton. The lepton has been in existence, however, since the time of Alexander Jannaeus, king of Judea in 103–76 BC. It is called a "farthing" or a "penny" in some translations of the Bible and was worth about a sixteenth of a denarius. A widow who gave an offering that Jesus admired gave two copper coins. Two sparrows could be bought for one of these coins.

See The Action Bible *pages 92, 235, 601, 615 and Matthew 10:9; Mark 6:8; 12:41–44; Luke 12:6; 20:24. See also* Bronze/Copper; Gold; Silver.

COLOSSAE

An important city for more than a thousand years—from 500 BC to AD 600. It was located in the southwestern part of what is now Turkey. Originally it was on the main road from Ephesus to the east, but the Romans changed the road, and the city became less important. What was left of the city was destroyed by the Turks in the twelfth century AD. No one lives there now, but archaeologists have uncovered some of its ruins. The church at Colossae probably was begun by Epaphras, a friend of Paul, while Paul was living at Ephesus during his third missionary journey. The church met in Philemon's home. Most of the Christians at Colossae were Gentiles.

See **The Action Bible** *page 735 and the books of Colossians and Philemon.*

COLOSSIANS, BOOK OF

A letter written by the apostle Paul to the church in Colossae. Paul was probably in prison in Rome when he wrote this letter about the year AD 61. Epaphras, who had helped begin the church there, had visited Paul and told him of some of the wrong ideas being taught there. Paul wrote this letter to help the Christians understand God's truths. Paul included practical advice in this letter to the Christians about how to live for Christ in the society of their day.

See **The Action Bible** *page 735 and the book of Colossians.*

COMMANDMENT

A rule given by God or a person in authority that must be obeyed. God gave the people of Israel the Ten Commandments to show how He wanted them to live. The first four commandments discuss how people should live in relationship to God. The last six discuss how people should live with each other. God called Moses to the top of Mount Sinai early in the Israelites' journey from Egypt. On two tablets of stone, God wrote these rules as part of the agreement between God and His people.

When asked about the greatest commandment, Jesus named two: to love God and to love one's neighbor.

See **The Action Bible** *page 155 and Exodus 20:2–17; Matthew 22:34–40.*

COMMUNION

(SEE LORD'S SUPPER/ COMMUNION)

CONDEMN/ CONDEMNATION

Condemn means "to judge something or someone wrong and deserving of punishment." People who committed crimes and were caught were condemned to death or thrown in jail. When the prophet Elijah held a contest on Mount Carmel between himself and the prophets of Baal, he knew that King Ahab would condemn him to death if God lost the contest.

The Bible declares that all of us who sinned are condemned and deserving of death. But Jesus died so that we would be declared "not guilty."

See **The Action Bible** *page 383 and 1 Kings 18; Romans 8:1–4.*

CONFESS/CONFESSION

To admit to God that one has done wrong or to declare that one has faith in God. David admitted his sin. The apostle Paul encouraged believers to publicly admit their faith in Jesus.

See The Action Bible *page 326 and 2 Samuel 12; Psalm 51; Romans 10:9–10.*

CONSEQUENCES

The consequences of a decision or wrongdoing. God used prophets like Jeremiah and Isaiah to warn the people of Judah about the consequences of their wrong actions. Because Queen Vashti refused to appear before King Xerxes, she was no longer queen as a consequence of her action.

See The Action Bible *pages 453, 490 and Esther 1; Jeremiah 36; Isaiah 3.*

CORINTH

The capital of Achaia (now southern Greece) and an important seaport in New Testament times. It was known for its luxury but also for having a bad reputation. Most of the seven hundred thousand people who lived in Corinth were Greeks or Romans, but there were also some Jews. More than half the people in Corinth were slaves. Many Corinthians worshipped Aphrodite, the Greek goddess of love.

When Paul visited Corinth on his second missionary journey, he began, as usual, by preaching in the synagogue to Jews. When the Jews refused his message about Christ, another man, Titus Justus, invited Paul to use his house next door to the synagogue. Justus and many others who heard Paul preach became Christians. Paul stayed in Corinth for a while with Aquila and Priscilla. He wrote two letters to the church that began there.

In the years after the New Testament period, Corinth was destroyed and rebuilt several times. In 1858, an earthquake destroyed most of the city, so another city named Corinth was built a few miles away from the old location. The new Corinth also had a destructive earthquake in 1928. But the city was rebuilt.

See **The Action Bible** *page 719 and Acts 18; 1 and 2 Corinthians.* See also **Aquila and Priscilla.**

CORINTHIANS, 1 AND 2

Two letters Paul wrote to the church at Corinth (a city in what is now southern Greece). Paul wrote the letters during his third missionary journey around AD 55 or 56. In the first letter, Paul answered some questions he had received in a letter from the Christians in Corinth. The church at Corinth had many problems. They didn't always get along. Paul reminded the Corinthians that Jesus alone was their Master and that everything they had should be used to honor God.

First Corinthians 5:9 refers to a letter written to Corinth before 1

Corinthians, which was not included in the Bible. The second letter to the Corinthians, however, was written during Paul's third missionary journey, and was a personal message to the church.

See **The Action Bible** *pages 722, 726 and 1 and 2 Corinthians.*

CORNELIUS

A centurion (a commander of one hundred men) in the Roman army stationed at Caesarea. He prayed to God and gave money to the poor. God told Cornelius in a vision to send men to the house of Simon the tanner

in the city of Joppa and to ask for a man named Peter. Cornelius did as he was told. Peter visited Cornelius's home, where he told Cornelius and his family about Jesus and later baptized everyone.

See **The Action Bible** *page 677 and Acts 10–11:18. See also* **Clean/Unclean.**

COVENANT

A special agreement in which both sides (God and a person or two people) decide on an action. God made a covenant with Noah to never again destroy the earth by flood. Jonathan and David made a covenant of friendship. God also made a covenant with David that David's kingdom would last forever. Jesus brought about a "new covenant"—the forgiveness of sins through His death. Those who believe in Jesus are to remember Jesus's death by taking Communion.

See **The Action Bible** *page 623 and Genesis 9:12–17; 1 Samuel 18:3; 2 Samuel 7:9–16; Matthew 26:28; Hebrews 9:15–22. See also* **Lord's Supper/Communion.**

CREATION

God's work in creating the universe. Genesis 1 and 2 tell that God created everything. They do not tell us how God created—just that He spoke everything into being. The Bible describes the days on which certain items were created:

- Day 1—light
- Day 2—sky
- Day 3—seas, land, plants
- Day 4—sun, moon, stars
- Day 5—birds and fish
- Day 6—animals and people

See **The Action Bible** *pages 17–20 and Genesis 1–2; Psalm 19; Job 38–41; Hebrews 11:3.*

CROSS/CRUCIFIXION

Romans used crucifixion, a painful way to die, to execute criminals who were not citizens of Rome. The feet of the condemned person were nailed to an upright plank of wood with the hands spread across another piece of wood—a crossbeam. Together they formed a cross shape. The condemned person usually had to carry the crossbeam to the site of execution. He was then left to hang until he died of fever and infection. Death usually took two to eight days, but Jesus died in a few hours—perhaps because He had been badly beaten before the crucifixion. The cross later became a symbol for Christians. Many people wear crosses to remind them of Jesus's death.

See The Action Bible *pages 632–638 and Matthew 10:38; 27:32–56; Mark 15:21–41; Luke 14:27; 23:26–49; John 19:16–37; 1 Corinthians 1:18. See also* Jesus.

CROWN

The Bible mentions several kinds of crowns. The high priest's crown was a turban. Fastened to it was a gold piece across the forehead bearing the words "Holy to the Lord." The crown meant that the priest had been set apart for a special purpose by God. Kings wore crowns, usually made of gold, as a mark of their royal position.

In the New Testament, *crown* sometimes refers to a head wreath made of myrtle leaves worn by athletes as a sign of victory. *Crown* also stands for the future reward and blessings that Christians will receive from Christ. The apostle Paul compared an athlete's temporary myrtle crown with the future "crown" a believer will receive—one that will not fade away.

Another special crown mentioned in the Bible is the crown of thorns, a circle made of sharp briars that Jesus wore on the cross. To make fun of Jesus, the King of the Jews, the soldiers made Him the crown after Pilate had sentenced Him to death.

See The Action Bible *pages 282–283, 632 and Exodus 28:36–38; Matthew 27:29; Mark 15:17–20; 1 Corinthians 9:25; 1 Peter 5:4.*

CUCUMBERS

The cucumbers the people of Israel remembered fondly from Egypt might have been muskmelons.

See The Action Bible *page 167 and Numbers 11:5.*

CYPRUS

An island in the eastern Mediterranean Sea. It is 148 miles long and about 40 miles across. Paul and Barnabas visited Cyprus on their first missionary journey. On the island, a government official named Sergius Paulus heard the message of Christ and believed. Barnabas and John Mark later came back to Cyprus to preach.

See The Action Bible *page 695 and Acts 13:4–12; 15:36–39.*

CYRENE

(SEE SIMON OF CYRENE)

CYRUS

The founder of the Persian Empire. He was also known as Cyrus the Great. When Cyrus came to power, most of the Jews had been forced out of their own land and sent to Babylonia. Cyrus allowed the Jews to return to their land and to rebuild the temple that had been destroyed. The prophet Isaiah foretold Cyrus's actions long before he was born.

See The Action Bible *page 506 and Ezra 1:1–11; 5:1–6:15; Isaiah 44:28–45:6.*

DAGON

(SEE IDOL/IDOLATRY)

DAMASCUS

The capital of modern Syria. On our maps it is sometimes called Dimashq. It is at least four thousand years old—probably the oldest continually inhabited city in the world. Eliezar, Abraham's servant, came from here. David once captured Damascus, but usually it belonged to Israel's or Judah's enemies.

In Bible times Syria was an area north of Israel. It covered most of the land south of modern Turkey, north of the Sea of Galilee, west of the Arabian Desert, and east of the Mediterranean Sea. The modern nation of Syria covers some of the same territory.

In the New Testament, Saul was going to Damascus when Christ appeared to him in a vision. Saul lost his sight and was taken to Damascus, where it was restored. Disciples in Damascus taught Saul about Jesus, and he began preaching in the synagogue there. Eventually, he had to escape by being let down over the wall in a basket.

See The Action Bible page 686 and Genesis 15:2; 2 Samuel 8:5–6; Acts 9:1–25.

DANIEL

A wise prophet who is best known for being thrown into a den of lions when he refused to stop worshipping God. Daniel also was a high government official. In 605 BC, Daniel was a young man when Babylon defeated his nation, Judah. Daniel and many others were taken from Judah to Babylon. Daniel's gift for interpreting dreams was put to the test twice

when Nebuchadnezzar had troubling dreams. After Nebuchadnezzar's reign, Daniel was called upon to interpret a mysterious message for Belshazzar, the next king.

When the Medes and Persians conquered the Babylonians, Daniel became an adviser to Darius. But envious coworkers plotted to get rid of Daniel. They persuaded Darius to make a law that Daniel broke. As a result, he was thrown into a den of lions, but God protected him.

See The Action Bible *pages 470–488 and the book of Daniel. See also* Clean/Unclean.

DANIEL, BOOK OF

Records the life and prophetic ministry of Daniel. Chapters 1–6 describe his rise from captive to king's counselor and the dreams he interpreted. The second half of the book, chapters 7–12, describes the visions Daniel had.

See The Action Bible *pages 470–488, 517 and the book of Daniel.*

DARIUS

The name of several rulers of the Medo-Persian Empire. Darius is mentioned in the story of Daniel. He was the king who made Daniel one of his officials. Another King Darius appears later in the book of Ezra. During his reign, some people tried to stop the rebuilding of the temple in Jerusalem. Darius looked through old records and found a decree from Cyrus, king of Persia, saying that the Jews were free to rebuild the temple. Darius ordered that the rebuilding could continue.

See The Action Bible *page 484 and Ezra 6:1–15; Daniel 6.*

DAVID

King during Israel's time of greatest glory. He was a skilled leader and musician who wrote about seventy-three psalms in the book of Psalms. David was born in 1040 BC, the youngest of eight sons in a family of shepherds. He served first as a musician in Saul's court and later as his armor-bearer. David grew popular after he killed Goliath, a Philistine giant. Fearing that David would take over his throne, Saul tried to kill David. David was on the run from Saul and his men for many years.

After the deaths of Saul and his sons, David became king only of Judah (the southern portion of Canaan). After seven years, the northern tribes also accepted him as their king. David then captured Jerusalem and made it the capital of Israel.

Though David was a great king, his family life was sad. He had many wives, among them Bathsheba, whom he took from another man. Some of his own children killed each other, and two sons led rebellions against him.

Near the end of his life, David ordered that the people be counted. This was against the will of God, and God sent a plague that killed seventy thousand people. It was miraculously stopped at a place just north of Jerusalem. David purchased that land and built an altar to God there. Later Solomon built the temple there. Jesus was born in David's family line.

See **The Action Bible** *pages 270–352 and 1 Samuel 16–1 Kings 2. See also* **Armor; Jonathan; Saul, King of Israel.**

DAVID'S MIGHTY MEN

An elite fighting force of men who traveled with David. Some of these men were relatives of David. Among this group were two groups of superior fighters: the Three and the Thirty.

See **The Action Bible** *pages 290–292 and 1 Samuel 22–23; 2 Samuel 17:8, 10; 23:8–39. See also* **Abishai.**

DEAD SEA

A lake located in southern Israel toward the end of the Jordan Valley. The Dead Sea has four times as much salt as the ocean. It is called dead because nothing lives in it. Even someone who cannot swim can float on the Dead Sea because it is so salty. Its surface is 1,300 feet below sea level, and in some places the water is more than 1,000 feet deep. It is sometimes called the Salt Sea in the Bible. The Dead Sea is forty-seven miles long and about seven miles across—the largest body of water in Israel. Sodom and Gomorrah were somewhere near the Dead Sea. This lake was mentioned in one of Ezekiel's visions. John the Baptist preached west of this area.

See **The Action Bible** *page 173 and Ezekiel 47:8. See also* **Jordan River.**

DEBORAH

A prophet and the only woman among the judges of Israel. When Deborah told Barak to go to war against the Canaanites, he refused unless she also went. Deborah then predicted that the victory would go to a woman. Although Barak and the soldiers defeated the enemy on Mount Tabor, they didn't kill Sisera, the commander of the army. Jael, the wife of Heber, killed Sisera. After the victory, Deborah and Barak composed and sang a song of praise to God.

See **The Action Bible** *page 212 and Judges 4–5. See also* **Judge.**

DELILAH

A Philistine woman who pretended to be in love with Samson. She wanted to find out the secret of his great strength. Three times he lied to her when she asked where his superstrength came from. Finally he admitted that he was strong because of his vow to God that he would never cut his hair. While he slept, she called in his enemies to cut his hair. His strength was gone, and he was captured.

See **The Action Bible** *page 235 and Judges 16:4–22. See also* **Samson**.

DELIVERANCE

The act of saving or rescuing someone. Moses and the people of Israel sang praise to God for delivering them from slavery in Egypt and from the Egyptian army, which wanted to drag them back to Egypt.

See **The Action Bible** *page 144 and Exodus 15. See also* **Salvation**.

DESERT

(SEE WILDERNESS)

DEUTERONOMY, BOOK OF

The fifth book in the Old Testament reviews many of the laws God gave to the people through Moses. The name *Deuteronomy* comes from a Greek word meaning "second law." As the people of Israel gathered at the edge of the Jordan River, Moses reminded them of God's agreement with them. He repeated many of the stories of their years in the wilderness. The closing chapters tell how Joshua would now lead the people to conquer Canaan after the death of Moses.

See **The Action Bible** *page 189 and the book of Deuteronomy.*

DEVIL/SATAN

The former angel who is an enemy of God and Christians. He has many names and forms in the Bible: Beelzebub, Abaddon, the great dragon, the Devil, the serpent, and the deceiver. Jesus was tempted by Satan in the wilderness following His baptism. Judas betrayed Jesus after Satan entered into him.

The Bible does not say directly where Satan came from, but he was already in the garden of Eden when Adam and Eve were created. Although the serpent is not called Satan, he used that creature to tempt Eve. He does not normally have a physical body.

Satan is the ruler of a kingdom made up of demons. Demons are evil spirits. They are often mentioned in the Bible. The New Testament teaches that Jesus has power over demons and protects His followers from them. At the end of the world, all demons will be destroyed with Satan, their master.

See **The Action Bible** *pages 22, 40, 548 and Genesis 3:1–15; Matthew 4:1–11; 12:24; 25:41; Luke 22:3; John 13:27; Romans 16:20; 2 Corinthians 11:14; Revelation 9:11; 12:9; 20:2–3, 7–10.*

DISCIPLINE

To correct the behavior of someone. Parents are encouraged to discipline or correct their children when they do wrong. God does the same for His children. Jeremiah warned the people of Judah that God tried to discipline them over and over. Because they ignored Him, He would allow them to be punished.

See **The Action Bible** *page 451 and Proverbs 3:11; 15:5; Jeremiah 26; Hebrews 12:4–11.*

DISEASES/ CONDITIONS

Many people in the Bible suffered from illness or other conditions. Those mentioned in *The Action Bible* include the following:

Blindness. Inability to see. Some blindness was caused by eye infections while some people were born blind. Moses gave special instructions to provide for the blind and the deaf. Jesus healed several blind people. Sometimes blindness is used as a word picture of a person who refuses to see what God wants him to do. Jesus spoke of the Pharisees as "blind guides." Peoples like the Philistines and Amalekites often blinded the captives they took in war. The Philistines blinded Samson when Samson was captured.

Boils. Swellings of the skin caused by different diseases. Job's boils may have been smallpox. The boils of the cattle (one of the plagues on Egypt) may have been anthrax. Hezekiah's boil might have been a carbuncle—a painful swelling. The prophet Isaiah prescribed a fig poultice for his boil.

Leprosy. A skin disease known as Hansen's disease today. In Bible times, a number of skin diseases were called leprosy. The Old Testament book of Leviticus provides instructions for people dealing with skin diseases. Leprosy could be crippling. Some lepers lost fingers and toes. Since a form of leprosy was contagious, lepers were ordered to stay away from other people for a certain amount of time until signs of healing could be seen. They also were ordered to shout, "Unclean! Unclean!" to warn other people they were about to pass on the road.

Paralysis. An inability to move the muscles in a part of the body. The paralysis may have been due to polio, birth injuries, or other illnesses.

Plagues. Any serious epidemic among a group of people. God sometimes allowed a plague among people who rebelled as a consequence for their disobedience. The plague in 1 Samuel 5–6 might have been bubonic plague. Bubonic plague causes high fever, swelling, and swift death. It is usually spread by rats.

Sores. Infections on the skin, often developing around wounds or bruises that become infected. Lazarus had sores.

Withered Hand. A form of paralysis that affected the hand only. It may have been caused by polio. Withered hand is mentioned in Matthew 12:9–14.

Worms. Worms caused the death of Herod Agrippa. They were probably roundworms. These worms form a tight ball and block the intestine, causing death.

See The Action Bible pages 41, 46, 54, 132, 172, 374, 415, 560, 564–565, 685 and Exodus 9:9; Leviticus 13; Numbers 14:37; Judges 16:20–21; 2 Kings 20:7; Job 2:7; Matthew 12:9–14; 15:14; 20:30–34; Mark 3:1–6; 8:22–25; Luke 6:6–11; 16:20–21; John 9:1–7; Acts 12:21–23.

DOGS

Dogs are mentioned many times in the Bible, and in most instances they are considered undesirable. They were scavengers and disease carriers. Although they were used to guard sheep, they were not considered pets

or companions. Only in the story of Jesus's encounter with a Canaanite woman is there any suggestion of a dog as a pet.

The prophet Elijah predicted that wild dogs would eat the remains of Queen Jezebel. That prophecy came true.

See The Action Bible *pages 396, 399 and 1 Kings 21:23; 2 Kings 9:30–37; Matthew 15:26–27.*

DONKEYS/MULES

Donkeys in the Bible are the same as our modern donkey. They were used for heavy farmwork and were also ridden with a saddle. Mules are a cross between male donkeys and

female horses. While horses were used for war, rulers and great men usually rode donkeys when they were on a peaceful journey. When Jesus rode into Jerusalem on a donkey, this action fulfilled a prophecy made by the Old Testament prophet Zechariah.

See The Action Bible *pages 40, 187–188, 611 and Numbers 22:21–34; Zechariah 9:9; John 12:12–19.*

DOORPOST

The board or stone across the top of a door or window. The doorpost supports the wall above it. On the first Passover, every Israelite family brushed the blood of a lamb on the front doorposts and lintel of its house.

See **The Action Bible** *page 136 and Exodus 12:22–23. See also* Feasts.

DOUBT

Inability to believe; uncertainty. Many people in the Bible doubted at times. The people of Israel doubted God and grumbled against Moses while in the wilderness. Thomas doubted Jesus's resurrection until Jesus appeared to him.

See **The Action Bible** *pages 147, 646 and Exodus 16; John 20:24–29.*

DREAMS AND VISIONS

Dreams were used by God to communicate with people. Many times He gave people the ability to explain those dreams. A baker and a butler working for the pharaoh of Egypt had dreams that Joseph explained. Later Pharaoh had a dream of seven fat cows and seven thin ones. Joseph knew that the dream meant a famine would happen. God spoke to Joseph, the husband of Mary, twice through dreams: once before the birth of Jesus, and again before he fled with Mary and Jesus to Egypt.

A vision is something like a dream, except that it is given by God and reveals truth in pictures. Most prophets were awake and alert when they received visions from God. Isaiah and Ezekiel saw a vision of God on the throne. Daniel was with others when he saw the vision God gave him. His companions did not see it, but they felt great fear and ran away. A newly blinded Paul saw Ananias in a vision coming to restore Paul's sight. The Lord spoke in a vision to Ananias, telling him to go to the house where Paul stayed and to heal Paul.

See **The Action Bible** *pages 97, 171, 437 and Genesis 40:1–20; 41:14–36; Isaiah 6; Ezekiel 1; Daniel 10:4–8; Matthew 1:20–24; 2:13–14; Acts 9:1–19. See also* Daniel; Joseph, son of Jacob.

EBED-MELECH

The Ethiopian servant working in the palace of King Zedekiah who rescued Jeremiah from a cistern.

See The Action Bible *page 465 and Jeremiah 38:1–13; 39:15–18.*

EBENEZER

A word that means "stone of help." The Israelites camped at this location during a battle with the Philistines. After a later battle that Israel won against the Philistines, the prophet-judge Samuel took a stone and named it Ebenezer. This stone was a memorial stone to show that God helped them win the battle.

See The Action Bible *page 257 and 1 Samuel 4:1; 7:12.*

ECCLESIASTES, BOOK OF

An Old Testament book of wisdom. Some scholars believe the author was Solomon, writing in his old age. Ecclesiastes 1:1 and 1:12 say the writer was the son of David and king over Israel. The word *ecclesiastes* means "preacher." The writer called himself "the Preacher" and said he had tested out many things and found these activities meaningless. He tried pleasure and found it to be vanity, or emptiness. He saw that wisdom was better than foolishness. The Preacher also gave some wise advice. He said people should enjoy their work, go to God's house, keep their promises to God, and be trustworthy.

See The Action Bible *page 358 and the book of Ecclesiastes.*

EDICT

The written law of a king. After his seal was put on it, the law was read in public. Disobeying a king's edict was a crime punishable by death. Pharaoh made an edict that all Hebrew boy babies were to be killed. In the time of Esther, the king made an edict that all Jews were to be killed. Many of these laws could not be changed, even by the king.

See The Action Bible *page 484 and Exodus 1:22; Esther 8:8–9; Daniel 6.*
See also Xerxes/Ahasuerus; Darius.

EGLON

(SEE EHUD)

EGYPT

In the Old Testament, Egypt covered about the same territory as it does today. It is about the size of Texas and Colorado combined. The only thing that keeps the land from being all desert is that the Nile River floods every year.

The Pyramids and Sphinx tell us that the Egyptians were an ancient, highly civilized people. The Israelites called Egypt "Mizraim." They asked Egypt for help during times of famine. The seven years of famine during the time of Joseph were probably caused by the Nile not flooding to its usual level. Interesting details of ancient Egyptian life are told in the stories of Joseph's life and the slavery of the Hebrews up to the exodus. Egypt was at war with Israel several times in the Old Testament period.

See The Action Bible *pages 94–138 and Genesis 12:10; 37; 39–50; Exodus 1–15; 2 Chronicles 12:1–9; 35:20–27.*
See also Pharaohs of Egypt.

EHUD

During the period when Israel was led by judges, Ehud served as a judge. The Moabites, led by King Eglon, conquered and oppressed the people, demanding money from them. Ehud, who was left-handed, strapped a short sword to his thigh and killed the unsuspecting King Eglon.

See The Action Bible *page 210 and Judges 3:12–30.*

ELEPHANTS

While elephants are not mentioned in the Bible, ivory is, however. So, elephants must have been somewhere in the area. Records other than the Bible show that elephants were common in Syria.

See The Action Bible *page 362 and 1 Kings 10:22; 22:39. See also* Damascus.

ELI

A judge and high priest of Israel for forty years. He lived at Shiloh, near the tabernacle. Eli thought Hannah was drunk in the tabernacle because she cried loudly as she prayed for a son. Eli had two grown sons, Phinehas and Hophni, who had bad reputations. But

Eli did not correct them. A prophet warned Eli that his two sons would die on the same day and that Eli's family would no longer serve as God's priests. When Eli was ninety-eight years old, the Philistines captured the ark of the covenant, and Eli's sons were killed. When the sad news was brought to Eli, he fell over backward and died of a broken neck.

See **The Action Bible** *page 248 and 1 Samuel 1:1–4:18.*

ELIEZAR

(SEE REBEKAH)

ELIJAH

An Old Testament prophet famous for his fiery words and for courageously opposing Queen Jezebel. Elijah lived during the reigns of King Ahab, his son Ahaziah, and his grandson Jehoram. Elijah would appear without warning with a message from God to Israel's rulers—and then he would disappear again. Kings listened to his words because they recognized that he was a prophet of God.

Elijah's story begins in 1 Kings 17, where he told King Ahab there would be no rain. The Lord cared for Elijah during the drought and later sent him to stay with a widow in Zarephath.

Meanwhile, King Ahab and his wicked wife, Queen Jezebel, kept on worshipping Baal and encouraging the people to do so. Elijah challenged the prophets of Baal on Mount Carmel to determine who was God—the God of Israel or Baal. God won. Elijah then prayed for rain to end the three-year drought, and God sent rain.

Elijah's triumph caused Queen Jezebel to mark him for death. A depressed Elijah ran for his life to Mount Horeb. Later Elijah returned to Israel and anointed Elisha to be a prophet after him. When King Ahab and Queen Jezebel murdered a man named Naboth so they could steal his vineyard, Elijah told Ahab and his family that God would punish them.

Elijah never died. Instead, God took him to heaven in a whirlwind with fiery horses and a chariot. Many centuries later, the prophet Malachi said God would send another Elijah. Jesus said that John the Baptist fulfilled Malachi's prediction. Elijah and Moses met with Jesus on the Mount of Transfiguration.

See **The Action Bible** *pages 376–402 and 1 Kings 17–2 Kings 2:12; Malachi 4:5–6; Matthew 11:14; 17:1–3.*

ELIPHAZ, BILDAD, AND ZOPHAR

The friends who tried and failed to comfort Job. These men were probably older than Job and considered themselves wiser. Because they spoke of God in a dishonoring way, God told Job to pray for them.

See **The Action Bible** *page 42 and the book of Job.*

ELISHA

An Old Testament prophet who did many miracles through God's power. He was a counselor and adviser to several kings (Jehoram, Jehu, Jehoahaz, and Jehoash), always delivering the message God had given him. He took Elijah's place when Elijah went to be with God. Some of the miracles Elisha did included the following: made a dry path through the Jordan River by striking the water with Elijah's cloak; turned the bad waters of a spring good; saved a widow from losing her sons to slavery by making her oil supply keep going until she had enough to pay her debts; brought the dead son of a Shunammite woman back to life; saved prophets from dying after eating poisonous food; healed Naaman from leprosy; made a borrowed iron axhead float; and led the newly blinded Syrian army into Samaria. Elisha also prophesied some miraculous military victories, such as the defeat of the army that threatened Samaria. He ordered Jehu to be anointed the next king of Israel, in place of Ahab's descendants.

When Elisha was old and sick, King Jehoash came to visit him. The dying prophet used the little strength he had left to do one final prophetic act. He told Jehoash to shoot an arrow through a window. The king did so, and Elisha assured him it was the Lord's arrow that would conquer the Syrians. The prophecy came true, but Elisha did not live to see it.

See The Action Bible *pages 392, 400–423 and 2 Kings 2–13.*

ELIZABETH

The mother of John the Baptist and the wife of a priest named Zechariah. Like Zechariah, she was from the family line of Aaron. Elizabeth could not have children at first. When Zechariah and Elizabeth were too old to have children, an angel told Zechariah that Elizabeth would have a son. When Elizabeth was six months pregnant, her cousin Mary came to visit her. Elizabeth greeted Mary with Spirit-filled words, and Mary rejoiced by singing a song of praise to God. Elizabeth's son was John the Baptist, who prepared the people of Israel for the coming of the Lord.

See The Action Bible *page 527 and Luke 1:5–57.*

ELYMAS

A Jewish magician and a false prophet. His real name was Bar-Jesus, which means "son of Jesus (or Joshua)." He was called Elymas because that name was connected with magic. Paul and Barnabas met Elymas when they came to the town of Paphos. A Roman officer Sergius Paulus wanted to hear Paul's message about Jesus, but Elymas tried to prevent that. Paul proclaimed that Elymas would be blinded for a time. Paul's words came true.

See The Action Bible *page 695 and Acts 13:4–12. See also* Paphos.

EMMAUS

A village about seven miles from Jerusalem. Two of Jesus's disciples walked to Emmaus with Christ after His resurrection. They finally recognized Him when He broke bread at dinner.

See The Action Bible *page 644 and Luke 24:13–35.*

ENCOURAGEMENT

Words or actions that instill hope within someone. Encouragement is one of the

gifts of the Spirit. Joseph, a missionary who traveled with Paul, was called Barnabas, a name that means "son of encouragement." Barnabas tried to encourage Paul when Paul expressed disappointment about Mark's leaving.

*See **The Action Bible** pages 468, 696 and Acts 4:36; Romans 12:8. See also **Barnabas.***

EPAPHRODITUS

A messenger between the church at Philippi and the apostle Paul. The church at Philippi sent Epaphroditus with gifts for Paul, who was in prison in Rome. Epaphroditus became sick and almost died while he was with Paul. Paul sent him back to the church with the letter to the Philippians that is now a part of our New Testament.

*See **The Action Bible** page 734 and Philippians 2:25–30; 4:18.*

EPHESIANS, BOOK OF

Paul wrote this letter when he was a prisoner in Rome around AD 59–61. It probably went to many small churches in the province of Asia (now part of Turkey). Paul's friend Tychicus delivered the letters we call Colossians and Philemon at the same time. Paul uses many pictures to show how the church is related to Jesus. All Christians are like a body, and Jesus is the Head. Christians together are like a building, and Jesus is the important cornerstone.

*See **The Action Bible** pages 734–735 and the book of Ephesians.*

EPHESUS

The capital city of the Roman province called Asia (now a part of Turkey). It was an important, old, beautiful city during the time of the New Testament. In Ephesus, an enormous white temple dedicated to the goddess Diana (whose Greek name was Artemis) was one of the seven wonders of the ancient world. In the center of the temple was a sacred stone, perhaps a meteorite, that had fallen from the sky. People said it looked like the goddess. Many merchants in Ephesus made their living by selling silver statues of Diana.

Paul stayed in Ephesus for nearly three years on his second missionary journey and helped many people become Christians. The merchants were afraid people would stop buying the idols they made, and so they started a riot. Despite this, a strong church was established at Ephesus.

See The Action Bible *pages 723–725 and Acts 18:19, 24–19:40.*

EPHRAIM

Manasseh and Ephraim were the sons of Joseph by his wife, Asenath, the daughter of an Egyptian priest. Ephraim was the younger son. When Ephraim's grandfather, Jacob, was old, he adopted both boys as his own sons. Jacob blessed them, but gave Ephraim the firstborn's rights, even though Joseph disapproved. Their descendants formed one tribe of Israel.

See The Action Bible *pages 110, 213 and Genesis 41:50–52; 48:8–20. See also Manasseh.*

EPISTLES

Letters written by individuals. Examples of epistles in the Old Testament include David's letter to Joab in 2 Samuel 11:14–15; Queen Jezebel's letter in 1 Kings 21:8–10; Sennacherib's letter to Hezekiah in 2 Kings 19:10–14; and the letters in Ezra 4. However, the word *epistle* usually refers to twenty-one books in the New Testament. These letters were written by Peter, Paul, James, John, Jude, and the author of Hebrews. Paul wrote thirteen letters. Here are the the best known epistles of the Bible: Colossians, 1 and 2 Corinthians,

Ephesians, Galatians, Hebrews, and James.

See The Action Bible *pages 716–726, 734–741. See also* James, brother of Jesus; John, the apostle; Jude; Paul/ Saul of Tarsus; Peter/Simon.

ESAU

The firstborn son of Isaac and Rebekah and the twin brother of Jacob. Before their birth, God told Rebekah that the elder would serve the younger. This was the opposite of the custom of that time—usually the older person had more authority.

Esau loved hunting, but he seemed to care nothing for God. Once when he was hungry, he sold his birthright to Jacob for a bowl of bean soup. When the time came for Isaac to bless his sons, Jacob tricked his father into giving him the blessing that belonged to Esau. As a result, Esau planned to murder Jacob, but Jacob escaped.

Years later, when Esau was living at Mount Seir, he heard that Jacob was returning. Jacob sent a large gift of cattle and sheep to Esau because he was afraid. Esau took four hundred men with him when he went to meet Jacob. But when he saw him, Esau ran to his brother and forgave him.

See The Action Bible *pages 68–88 and Genesis 25:21–25; 25:27–34; 26:34–35; 27:1–45; 33:1–9. See also* Birthright; Jacob/Israel.

ESTHER

A Jewish orphan who became the queen of Persia. Her name originally was Hadassah, but it was changed to Esther, a Persian name. Her story is told in the Old Testament book of Esther. After Vashti was rejected as the queen, a contest was held to find a new queen for Xerxes, the king of Persia. Esther was chosen from a large group of beautiful women.

Esther had been brought up by her cousin Mordecai, who told her not to tell anyone that she was Jewish. Mordecai kept in touch with Esther after she became queen. One day Mordecai heard of a plot against the king's life. He told Esther, and she

told the king, so she saved his life. A worse plot came later, when Haman convinced Xerxes to sign a decree that all the Jews were to be killed. The king signed, not knowing that Esther was Jewish. Esther risked her life to go before the king and explain Haman's plan. He could not change the law he had made, but he gave permission for the Jews to protect themselves. Jewish people today still celebrate the Feast of Purim to remember how God saved the people because of the actions of this brave queen.

See The Action Bible *pages 489–505 and throughout the book of Esther. See also* Xerxes/Ahasuerus; Feasts; Haman.

ETERNAL LIFE

Life forever. Eternity is all that is past and all that is yet to come. Our part in God's eternity begins when we accept Jesus as Savior and seek to do the things that please Him. Even though we will die on earth, we will live again after death.

See The Action Bible *pages 555, 623 and John 3:36; 10:28.*

ETHIOPIA/CUSH

A country whose history stretches back to before Moses's time. It was south of Egypt along the Red Sea. In Old Testament times it included much of today's Sudan as well as modern Ethiopia. The people of Israel called Ethiopia "Cush" and its people "Cushites." Cush was the grandson of Noah, and his descendants formed Ethiopia. Moses married an Ethiopian woman. In the days of King Hezekiah, the Ethiopian king,

Tirhakah, attempted to conquer Judah but failed. In New Testament times, Ethiopia was ruled by Queen Candace.

See The Action Bible *pages 209, 671 and Genesis 10:6–10; Numbers 12:1; 2 Kings 19:9; Acts 8:27.*

ETHIOPIAN OFFICER

A treasurer for Candace, the queen of Ethiopia. He was a Gentile who had become interested in the Jewish religion. After he traveled to Jerusalem to worship, he was sitting in his chariot, reading aloud in Isaiah 53. Philip the evangelist, who was sent by the Holy Spirit, asked if he understood what he was reading. Philip explained that Isaiah 53 was a prophecy about Jesus the Messiah. The officer believed in Jesus and was baptized.

See The Action Bible *page 671 and Isaiah 53:7–8; Acts 8:26–40. See also* Philip.

EUTYCHUS

The young man who fell asleep during one of Paul's sermons at Troas. Not much is known about this young man other than the fact that he fell to his death out of a window. Paul raised him from the dead by the power of the Holy Spirit.

See The Action Bible *page 727 and Acts 20:7–12.*

EVE

(SEE ADAM AND EVE)

EVIL

Anything that is against the will of God. These include bad thoughts, hatred, fighting, loving something more than we love God, complaining, excluding people from our groups, and many other actions. Evil hurts our relationships with other people and with God. Evil damages everything God created.

Evil began in the world when Adam and Eve disobeyed God. God later sent a flood, because most of the actions of the people were evil. Satan and demons are described as evil. Sometimes in the Bible, evil is called "the works of the flesh."

God did not create evil, but He allows it to exist. He created people with the ability to choose for themselves whether to do evil or good. One day God will create a new heaven and a new earth, and evil will not exist.

See **The Action Bible** *pages 36, 573 and Genesis 3; 6:5–13; Romans 1:18–32; Galatians 5:19–21; Revelation 21:1–5.*

EXILE/CAPTIVITY OF ISRAEL

The seventy-year period when many of the people of Judah were forced to live in Babylon. Because of the wrongdoing of the people of Israel and Judah, God promised that He would allow their enemies to conquer them and force them to leave their land. The northern kingdom (Israel) was defeated by Assyria in 722 BC. More than twenty-seven thousand upper-class Israelites (the wealthy and the leaders) were forced to move to Assyria, and many Assyrians were sent to live in Israel. This was a common wartime custom to keep a conquered country from rebelling. The southern kingdom (Judah) was defeated by Babylon. Much of Jerusalem was destroyed by the army of King Nebuchadnezzar in 586 BC. The wall around the city was broken and the temple destroyed.

While away from their land, the people of Israel and Judah were not prisoners. They were free to build homes, start businesses, or work at their trade. But they could not return to their own land. While in Babylon, the Jews gathered in small groups to pray and study the law of Moses. Many scholars believe these small groups were the beginning of Jewish synagogues. After Nebuchadnezzar died, his country was conquered by the Persians in 539 BC. Cyrus, the king of the Persians, allowed the people of Judah to return to their land.

See **The Action Bible** *pages 451–508 and 2 Kings 24–25; Ezra 1–2; Jeremiah 34–39. See also* Zedekiah.

EXODUS, THE

The time when the people of Israel left slavery in Egypt to go to the Promised Land of Canaan. The Israelites left from Rameses in Egypt and went to Succoth. Succoth was about thirty-two miles southwest of Rameses. They avoided the land of the Philistines along the coast of the Mediterranean Sea, which would have been the closest route to Canaan.

After they crossed the Red Sea, the people of Israel went into the wilderness of Shur and came to a place called Marah. This was an oasis in the Sinai Desert about halfway down the coast. They camped at Mount Sinai, in the southern part of the peninsula, for about a year. They wandered between Mount Sinai and Kadesh Barnea for forty years.

See **The Action Bible** *page 139 and Exodus 12–15.*

EXODUS, BOOK OF

The second book of the Bible, Exodus is the story of God's deliverance of the people of Israel from slavery in Egypt and their journey to the Promised Land of Canaan. The first twelve chapters of Exodus tell how Moses's people—the Hebrews—lived as slaves for four centuries. God chose Moses to lead His people out of Egypt. God sent ten plagues on Pharaoh and the Egyptians before they were willing to let the Hebrews leave Egypt. Chapters 13–19 tell how God worked miracles and provided food and water for the grumbling Israelites as they traveled across the wilderness. Chapters

19–40 tell how God gave the Ten Commandments and other instructions to Moses on Mount Sinai. These instructions include those for building the tabernacle and for the priests who would help the people worship God.

See **The Action Bible** *page 112 and the book of Exodus.*

EZEKIEL

A Jewish prophet from the family line of priests. Ezekiel was forced to move from Jerusalem to Babylon in 597 BC. The army of King Nebuchadnezzar captured the city and took many of the furnishings of the temple. Nebuchadnezzar forced thousands of priests, scribes, and skilled workers to

move to Babylon, about nine hundred miles away.

Ezekiel built a house for himself and his wife in Babylon. He taught the people to be faithful to God's laws even though they had no temple in which to worship. He encouraged them to gather to pray and study the Scriptures. Many scholars believe this was how Jewish synagogues became the place of worship instead of the temple.

When Ezekiel had been living in Babylon five years, God called him to be a prophet, and he saw an amazing vision of God on a throne. It was the first of many visions that Ezekiel received.

Ezekiel was often told to help people remember his prophecies by acting out the message. Before Jerusalem was finally destroyed in 586 BC, he made a brick model of Jerusalem with armed soldiers around it.

After the final destruction of Jerusalem, Ezekiel encouraged his people by prophesying that Jerusalem and the temple would be restored. These prophecies began to be fulfilled about fifty years later, in 538 BC, during the time of Ezra and Nehemiah. Ezekiel died in Babylon without ever returning to his own land or seeing Jerusalem restored.

See **The Action Bible** *page 456 and the book of Ezekiel.*

EZEKIEL, BOOK OF

Written while Ezekiel lived in exile in Babylon (after 597 BC). The book of Ezekiel contains many visions and word pictures of God and the temple. Ezekiel foretells the destruction of Jerusalem (chapters 4–5); describes Ezekiel's vision of the sinful worship practices in the temple (chapters 8–11); and proclaims God's judgment on false prophets and His people (chapters 1–24), as well as other nations (chapters 25–32).

See The Action Bible *pages 456–460 and the book of Ezekiel. See also* Ezekiel.

EZRA

A priest, scribe, and scholar who helped his people start worshipping God again. Ezra had been in exile in Babylon. There, scribes like Ezra who knew how to read and write Hebrew made copies of the Old Testament by hand for use in worship.

Ezra was an adviser to the king about the Jews and their religion. He asked the king for permission to return to Judah so he could teach God's Law there. The king approved and also gave him authority to appoint judges to enforce the Jewish laws.

Ezra returned with about five thousand others. He found that many of the people who lived in Judah were not keeping God's commands. He wept in sorrow. Ezra began offering sacrifices to the Lord at the temple. He gathered the people of the land, read the law of Moses to them, and encouraged them to obey God and keep the required feasts.

See The Action Bible *page 512 and the books of Ezra and Nehemiah. See also* Exile/Captivity of Israel; Nehemiah.

FAITH

Trust or belief. In the Bible, many times faith means belief in God and in His Son, Jesus. When you see the phrase *the faith*, it means the whole message of the good news of Jesus: that He died for the sins of all and came back to life.

In the Old Testament, Abraham obeyed God because he had faith. In the New Testament, Jesus's disciples showed their faith—their belief that Jesus was the promised Savior—by leaving their jobs and following Him. Hebrews 11 lists many other people who had faith: Abel, Enoch, Noah, Joseph, Moses, and others. Hebrews 11:6 says that without faith it is impossible to please God.

The letters Paul wrote in the New Testament explain what faith is and why we need it. The book of James in

the New Testament explains that faith is seen in what we do. When we trust God, we show our faith by obeying Him.

See The Action Bible *pages 62, 739 and Galatians 2:20.*

FAITHFULNESS

Loyalty and dependability. This quality is part of God's character and is a fruit of the Spirit. God sent the rainbow after the flood as a sign that He would be faithful to keep His promise. David and Jonathan were friends who promised to be faithful to each other.

See The Action Bible *pages 36, 287, 468 and Genesis 9:12–17; Exodus 34:6; 1 Samuel 19; Galatians 5:22. See also Fruit of the Spirit.*

FALL, THE

Adam and Eve's first sin in the garden of Eden. God told Adam and Eve that they could eat from any tree in the garden except from the Tree of the Knowledge of Good and Evil. But the serpent (Satan) tempted Eve, and she ate fruit from that tree. She gave some fruit to Adam, and he also ate. Their disobedience caused the fall. They "fell" out of their good relationship with God. Because of their sin, every human being born since then has been born with a desire to do wrong things.

See The Action Bible *page 21 and Genesis 3. See also Adam and Eve; Tree of the Knowledge of Good and Evil; Serpent/Snakes.*

FASTING

Going without food or water for a period of time. Many people fasted when they were sad about someone's death. Others fasted to gain God's answer to prayer or to concentrate and depend more on God. Jesus fasted for forty days when He was in the wilderness after His baptism. Some Pharisees fasted every Monday and Thursday.

See The Action Bible *pages 327, 547 and Exodus 34:28; Matthew 4:2; Acts 13:2–3.*

FATHER

The Bible uses *Father* in a special way to describe God. In the New Testament, God is the Father of Jesus. All who believe in Jesus become children of God. We follow Jesus's example and pray to God as our Father.

See The Action Bible *page 599 and Malachi 2:10; Matthew 6:9; John 1:12.*

FEASTS

The Bible mentions two kinds of feasts: those held by kings or other people in celebration of events like weddings; and worship feasts required by Jewish law to celebrate God's goodness. The worship feasts included the following:

The Feast of Passover. The most important feast. It was held during the middle of April to remember how God rescued the people of Israel from slavery in Egypt. The name *Passover* comes from the way death "passed over" those homes with lambs' blood on the doorposts. Passover begins at sundown on the fourteenth day of the Jewish month Nisan and lasts for twenty-four hours. During Bible times, special meals were prepared. The story of Israel's deliverance was told, songs of thanksgiving were sung, and prayers of praise were spoken to God. In New Testament times, the Feast of the Unleavened Bread, which lasts seven days, was celebrated with Passover, making it an eight-day feast.

The Feast of Weeks or *Pentecost.* Also called the Feast of the Harvest because it was a one-day celebration at the end of the wheat harvest. The feast was held fifty days after Passover. The Jewish people sang and danced and made sacrifices to thank God for watching over their crops. Later they also used this occasion to thank God for giving them His Law. The Feast of Weeks or Pentecost received a new meaning for Christians when the Holy Spirit came to the church on that day. Many churches today celebrate Pentecost to thank God for sending His Holy Spirit.

The Feast of Tabernacles or *Booths.* An important eight-day celebration in autumn. It began five days after the Day of Atonement. Because this feast was held at the end of the final harvest of olives and fruits, and because it was near the beginning of the Jewish year, the people celebrated it like Thanksgiving and New Year's Day combined. They thanked God for giving them good crops, and they asked Him to watch over them in the year ahead. The people camped out in little shelters called booths to remember how their ancestors had lived while they wandered in the desert for forty years. Jesus secretly traveled to Jerusalem one year to go to the Feast of Booths.

The Feast of Dedication or *Lights.* Lasts for eight days in December. It is also called Hanukkah (or Chanukah), which is the Hebrew word for "dedication." This celebration is to remember how Judas Maccabeus cleansed and rededicated the temple in Jerusalem in 165 BC. During the Feast of Dedication the Israelites sang, danced, and marched to the synagogues, carrying lit torches. At the synagogues children were told about the brave deeds of Judas Maccabeus.

The Feast of the New Moon. A one-day festival held in October on the first new moon of the Hebrew month Tishri to celebrate the first day of the Hebrew New Year. On this day silver trumpets were blown all during the day. All work was stopped, special sacrifices were offered to God, and families gathered for a special meal. A public reading of God's Law took place.

The Feast of Purim. This two-day festival in March celebrates the victory of Queen Esther and Mordecai over Haman, who wanted the people of Israel to be killed. It begins with people gathering in the synagogue to hear a reading of the book of Esther. Whenever Haman's name is mentioned, the people boo and hiss! They also thank God for rescuing His people.

See The Action Bible *pages 80, 136, 197, 505 and Exodus 12; 23:16; 34:22; Leviticus 23; Numbers 28–29; Esther 9:2–32; Amos 8:5; John 7; 10:22; Acts 2; 1 Corinthians 5:7. See also* Plagues on Egypt.

FESTUS

A governor of Judea. After hearing Paul's defense, Festus wanted to send Paul back to Jerusalem for trial. Paul preferred to go to Rome to stand trial before the emperor, so Festus allowed him to go. Festus died in Judea in AD 62.

See The Action Bible *page 731 and Acts 25.*

FISH

Fish were an important food for the Jewish people. Hooks, nets, and spears were used to catch fish. Fish are mentioned in many parts of the Bible. One of the plagues against Egypt was the killing of all fish in the Nile River. Jonah was swallowed by a great fish. And at least seven of Jesus's disciples were fishermen. After He was resurrected, Jesus appeared to His disciples while they were fishing.

The fish is also used as a symbol. When it was illegal to worship Jesus, Christians in the Roman Empire used secret codes to announce meeting places. One of those secret codes was the Greek word for *fish*: ICHTHUS. The letters of that word in Greek were also the first letters of the words "*Jesus, Messiah, God, Son, Savior.*"

See The Action Bible *pages 434, 647 and Exodus 7:20–21; Jonah 1–2; Matthew 4:18–22; Luke 5:1–11; John 21:1–13.*

FLEECE

The wool of a sheep. The phrase "to put out a fleece" means to ask God for a sign. When told that he was to lead the people of Israel against the Midianites, Gideon asked God for a sign involving a fleece.

See The Action Bible *page 219 and Judges 6:36–40.*

FLOOD, THE

When God allowed water to destroy much of the earth's population. God saw how evil people had become and was sorry He had made them. Only Noah and his family and the animals with them on the ark were saved from the flood. God sent rain that lasted forty days and nights. This may have been the first time rain ever fell on earth. Water also rushed up from springs below ground. Soon everything was under water and remained that way for more than a year.

See The Action Bible *pages 30–37 and Genesis 6:9–9:17; Matthew 24:37–39; Hebrews 11:7; 1 Peter 3:20; 2 Peter 2:5; 3:3–7.*

FOOD

In Bible times food did not have much variety. Only rich people ate meat regularly. Poor people served meat when they had important guests, or at special celebrations, or when they made a sacrifice to God. Then a certain portion was given as a sacrifice, another portion to the priest, and the rest was eaten by the family. Because there was no refrigeration, meat had to be eaten within a few hours after the animal was killed, or else it would spoil.

Cows and goats were raised for their milk rather than meat. Sheep were raised for their wool or for

sacrifices. Milk was made into cheese and yogurt. Abraham served curds and a cooked calf to the angels who visited him.

The most common food in the Bible was bread. It was the main part of every meal. This is why Jesus taught His disciples to pray for "our daily bread." Poor people usually ate bread made from barley. Wealthy people ate bread made from wheat. Jesus used barley bread—a child's lunch—to feed over five thousand people.

The vegetables eaten included onions, cucumbers, leeks, garlic, beans, and lentils. Beans and lentils were used in stews and sometimes mixed with flour to make bread. Esau traded his birthright for a pot of vegetables.

People usually ate two meals a day. Workers often took some flatbread and cheese or dried fruit with them to work. A light meal was eaten sometime between ten o'clock and noon just before a midday rest from the hot sun. Ruth ate roasted grain after gleaning in Boaz's fields. A large meal was eaten in the evening. This was a time for fellowship and having guests. Banquets and feasts were always held in the evening. At ordinary meals women ate with the men, but only men were invited to banquets.

In Abraham's time people usually sat on the ground for meals. But in New Testament times diners stretched out on the floor or on couches on three sides of a large, low, square table, leaving the fourth side free for serving. Knives, forks, or spoons were not used.

People dipped bread into the pot or used their fingers.

See The Action Bible *pages 52, 69, 381, 610 and Genesis 18:8; 25:27–34; Ruth 2:14; Matthew 6:11; 15:36; Luke 14:12–13; John 6:5–13. See also* Feasts.

FOOT WASHING

A special way to greet guests after they traveled. After a long journey, their feet would be tired and dirty from the dusty roads. Servants would use a bowl of cool water and fresh towels to bathe the feet of the travelers. Jesus shocked His disciples by washing their feet at the Last Supper. He taught them to serve one another. Some churches today have foot-washing services to remember Jesus's example.

See The Action Bible *page 621 and Genesis 18:4; 1 Samuel 25:41; John 13:1–17; 1 Timothy 5:10. See also* Last Supper.

FORGIVENESS

The erasing of the sin and guilt of a person through the action of another. All people have done wrong things. These wrong things made us enemies of God. We should be punished, but Jesus died to take the punishment for our wrong actions. Because of that, God offers forgiveness—a free pardon from the guilt of sin. This means God acts as if the wrong things we did never happened. All we have to do is ask for it. What a gift!

God wants His people to forgive others. When Peter asked Jesus how many times a person is expected to forgive someone for the same wrongdoing, Jesus's answer surprised him: "Seventy-seven times" (Matt. 18:22 ESV). What Jesus really meant was that forgiveness has no limits. We are to always forgive, just as God forgives us. If we don't forgive, God can't forgive us.

See **The Action Bible** *pages 161, 588, 636 and Matthew 6:12; 18:21–35; Luke 23:34; Colossians 1:13–14.*

FOXES

Foxes are mentioned nine times in the Bible. They were probably similar to the red fox in America.

When Samson wanted to take revenge against the Philistines, the enemies of Israel, he caught three hundred foxes, tied torches to their tails, and set the Philistines' grain fields on fire. Jesus called Herod Antipas a "fox" because of Herod's crafty nature.

See **The Action Bible** *page 229 and Judges 15:3–5; Matthew 8:20; Luke 13:32. See also* **Herod.**

FRANKINCENSE

A sweet-smelling perfume made from the sap that comes from a terebinth tree in northern India and Arabia. These trees grow in warm, dry places. When a cut is made in its bark, a resin comes out that is used in incense. It was used in the tabernacle and the temple. The wise men brought a gift of frankincense to Jesus when He was a child. The Israelites used frankincense in worship ceremonies.

See **The Action Bible** *page 537 and Exodus 30:34; Isaiah 60:6; Matthew 2:11.*

FRIENDSHIP

Many people in the Bible were friends. David and Jonathan were best friends. The book of Ruth tells of the beautiful friendship between Ruth and her mother-in-law, Naomi. Jesus had many friends, including Mary, Martha, and Lazarus. God called Abraham His friend. Jesus offers His friendship to those who trust Him as Savior. We prove that we're His friends if we obey His commands. The book of Proverbs has good advice about friendship: how to be a friend and how to recognize a good friend.

See **The Action Bible** *pages 282, 597 and Ruth 1; 1 Samuel 18:1–4; Proverbs 17:17; 18:24; Ecclesiastes 4:9–10; Luke 10:38–42; John 11:11; 15:14; James 2:23.*

FROGS

The most known reference to these amphibians is the plague of frogs that came as a result of the pharaoh's stubbornness.

See **The Action Bible** *pages 130–131 and Exodus 8:1–14.*

FRUIT OF THE SPIRIT

Actions and characteristics that show the influence of the Holy Spirit. These nine characteristics—love, joy, peace, patience, kindness, goodness, faithfulness, gentleness, and self-control—are the results of the Holy Spirit helping a person grow in Christ.

See The Action Bible *page 713 and Galatians 5:22–23.*

FURNACE

Used for baking pottery and bricks; for melting silver, gold, copper, brass, and bronze; and for smelting iron and other ores. They were of many sizes and were usually made of stone and brick. Daniel's three friends—Shadrach, Meshach, and Abednego—were thrown into a furnace for their refusal to worship a statue set up by King Nebuchadnezzar. Jesus compared the agony of hell with a "fiery furnace."

See The Action Bible *page 479 and Proverbs 17:3; Daniel 3:13–30; Matthew 13:42.*

GABRIEL

(SEE ANGELS)

GAD

The prophet who helped David during most of his life. Usually court prophets prophesied only good things to their king. But Gad delivered God's message to David whether it was good news or bad. Gad once gave David advice on how to escape when Saul was trying to kill him. When David angered God by counting his fighting men, Gad brought God's message of punishment to David. Gad was also a musician and a writer who helped David arrange musical services for the temple. He wrote a history of David's reign in Israel.

See The Action Bible *page 293 and 1 Samuel 22:5; 1 Chronicles 21:9–17; 29:29; 2 Chronicles 29:25.*

GALATIA

A large province in central Asia Minor (now Turkey). Cities like Lystra and Derbe were located in a region—Lycaonia—that was part of this province. Paul visited Galatia on his missionary journeys and wrote a letter (Galatians) to the churches in that province.

See The Action Bible *page 702 and Acts 14; the book of Galatians.*

GALATIANS, BOOK OF

A letter the apostle Paul wrote to the churches in the province of Galatia in Asia Minor (now the western part of Turkey). Some of these churches were at Antioch of Pisidia, Iconium, Lystra, and Derbe. Paul established these churches during his first missionary journey. The Christians there were confused by some of the teachings they had heard. Paul wrote this letter to try to help them understand God's truths.

See The Action Bible page 702 and Acts 14; the book of Galatians.

GALILEE

The northern province of Israel in Jesus's day. Jesus grew up in Nazareth, a city of Galilee, and preached His first sermon in the synagogue there. Almost all of His disciples were from Galilee. The southern part of Galilee, where Jesus grew up, had more cities and people than the northern part. Southern Galilee had a mild climate that was good for farming. Olive trees grew in the northern part.

See The Action Bible page 551 and Luke 5.

GALLIO

A Roman official known for his fairness. Some Jews in Corinth brought the apostle Paul before Gallio, saying that Paul persuaded people to worship in ways that were against the Jewish laws. But Gallio refused to listen to their charges. Paul was freed.

See The Action Bible page 720 and Acts 18:12–17.

GAMALIEL

A well-known Pharisee and teacher living in Jerusalem. The apostle Paul was one of his students before Paul became a Christian. When the church was just beginning in Jerusalem, the Pharisees and priests ordered the apostles not to preach about Christ. When the apostles said they must obey God rather than men, the Pharisees and priests wanted to kill them. The highly respected Gamaliel advised

against that action. The council took his advice.

See The Action Bible *page 667*
and Acts 5:27–40; 22:3.

GARDEN OF EDEN

The beautiful place God created for the first man and woman, Adam and Eve. In it grew many fruit trees and two special trees: the Tree of Life and the Tree of the Knowledge of Good and Evil. Adam and Eve lived in the garden until they sinned against God by eating the fruit of the Tree of the Knowledge of Good and Evil, which God had told them not to eat.

People have always wondered where the garden of Eden was located. The only clue is Genesis 2:10–14, which says a river in the garden divided into four rivers: Pishon, Gihon, Tigris, and Euphrates. The Tigris and Euphrates Rivers are in western Asia. The location of the Pishon and Gihon Rivers remains unknown, however. The Bible says the Pishon flowed through a place called Havilah, where gold was found. This may have been India. The Gihon perhaps flowed through Ethiopia.

See The Action Bible *page
21 and Genesis 2–3.*

GAZA

A Philistine city on the coast of the Mediterranean Sea. It still exists but is now called Chazzah. It is the most important city on the Gaza Strip in the southwest corner of Israel. Gaza is best known as the city where Samson died. He pulled down the pillars of the temple of Dagon and killed the crowd inside—including himself. The city was not fully defeated by the Israelites until the time of Hezekiah, about 713 BC. Gaza is mentioned in the New Testament only once. Philip the evangelist told an Ethiopian about Jesus on the road that ran from Jerusalem to Gaza.

See The Action Bible *pages 232,
671–672 and Judges 16:21–30;
2 Kings 18:8; Acts 8:26.*

GENESIS, BOOK OF

The first book of the Bible and a book about beginnings. It tells how God created the world and people. It tells about the beginning of sin, the beginning of God's judgment on sin, and His mercy to sinners. It also tells about the beginning of the nation of Israel, from which the Redeemer of the world—Jesus—would be born many years later. Stories of the patriarchs—the fathers of the people of Israel (Abraham, Isaac, and Jacob)—can be found in Genesis.

See The Action Bible *page 21
and the book of Genesis.*

GENTILES

All people who are not Jewish by nationality or religion. In Bible times, Jews and Gentiles did not have much to do with each other. Gentiles often persecuted the Jews for their religion, and the Jews hated the Gentiles and looked down on them. Jesus rarely taught Gentiles, but He healed them when they came to Him. He healed the servant of a Gentile soldier. After Jesus's death and resurrection, the church began to include both Jews and Gentiles who believed in Christ.

The apostle Paul was sent by the risen Jesus to preach the gospel message to Gentiles.

See The Action Bible *page 679 and Luke 7:2–10; John 12:20–36; Ephesians 2:11–22.*

GETHSEMANE/GARDEN OF GETHSEMANE

The walled garden where Jesus prayed just before He was arrested and then crucified. It was located on the Mount of Olives, just outside Jerusalem.

See The Action Bible *page 625 and Matthew 26:36–56; Mark 14:32–50; Luke 22:39–54.*

GIANTS

In the Bible, giants refer to actual human beings (not make-believe creatures) who are tall and powerful. Tribes of these very large people lived in Canaan before the Israelites conquered it. Goliath, who fought David, was one of these. He was more than nine feet tall. His armor weighed 125 pounds! Very large people are often called Rephaim or Nephilim in the Old Testament. There is no reference to these people in the New Testament. Og, the king of Bashan, slept in a bed thirteen and a half feet by six feet. He was the last of the Rephaim.

See The Action Bible *pages 174, 217 and Deuteronomy 3:11; 1 Samuel 17.*

GIBEON

A city in Canaan about fifteen miles west of Jerusalem. When the Gibeonites heard that the Israelites had defeated Jericho and other cities, they tricked Joshua into making a treaty with them by pretending they came from far away. When Joshua discovered that they lived in the area, he said they would have to become servants of the Israelites, but he would keep his word and see that they were not destroyed. Later, others attacked the Gibeonites because they had made peace with Joshua. The Gibeonites called for help, and Joshua came with his army. God sent giant hailstones on the enemies and miraculously lengthened the day to give the Israelites time to defeat them. Saul once tried to kill the Gibeonites despite the treaty, but God punished Saul's family as a result.

See The Action Bible *page 204 and Joshua 9:3–27; 10:1–14; 2 Samuel 21:1–14.*

GIDEON

One of Israel's judges during the period of the judges. The Midianites made life miserable for the people of Israel, stealing their cattle and destroying all their crops. God's angel appeared to Gideon and told him that the Lord would help him defeat the Midianites. But fearful Gideon demanded a sign from God. God used a fleece to help Gideon know that he was the one chosen to lead the army against the Midianites.

To prove that God was the one who would help the Israelites be victorious, God cut Gideon's army down from twenty-two thousand to three hundred. Gideon gave each of the the hundred men a trumpet and a jar with a torch inside. One hundred men went to each of three sides of the Midianites' army camp. They all broke their pitchers and blew trumpets at the same time. The Midianites were so frightened and confused they began killing each other. Gideon's men won a great victory. Later, the Israelites wanted to make Gideon king, but he refused. He said God should rule over them. The Israelites had peace for forty years.

See The Action Bible *page 217 and Judges 6:1–8:33. See also* Fleece.

GILGAL

The place where Joshua and the people of Israel first made camp after crossing the Jordan River.

See The Action Bible *page 197 and Joshua 4.*

GLEANING

Going into the fields after the main harvesting to find whatever grain is left. In Old Testament law, farmers were told they should let the poor come into their fields and glean the remaining grain. Ruth gleaned grain in the field of Boaz to find food for her mother-in-law, Naomi, and for herself.

See The Action Bible *page 243 and Leviticus 19:9–10; 23:22; Deuteronomy 24:19–22; Ruth 2.*

GNATS

The plague Egypt suffered directly after the plague of frogs was a plague of gnats. This two-winged fly most likely was a mosquito. Jesus quoted a popular proverb about a gnat when He scolded the Pharisees.

See The Action Bible *page 131 and Exodus 8:16–19; Matthew 23:34.*

GOATS

Goats were important sources for milk and meat. They were also used in sacrifices. Their hair was made into clothing and their skins into containers for water and wine. Young goats are called kids and were used for food on special occasions and sometimes as sacrifices. In Exodus 23:19 the Jews were told, "You shall not boil a young goat in its mother's milk" (ESV). This command is why many Jews still do not eat meat and milk at the same meal.

See The Action Bible *page 165 and Exodus 8:1–14.*

GOD

The Creator; King; God of all creation. The Bible never tries to prove God exists; it assumes that everyone knows He does. The Bible shows us what God is like by letting us see what He does and how He responds to people and the things they do. But the most important way we know who God is and what He is like is to see Jesus Christ. Jesus Christ was God in a human body.

The Bible tells us many things about God: He loves us. He is everywhere. He knows everything. He has always existed and always will. He neither began (like a baby is born) nor will He ever die. He is holy. Unlike people, He has never done anything wrong, and could never do so. Only He is perfect. God is Spirit. He does not have a physical body as people have, although Jesus had a physical body because He became a man on earth.

The Bible does not tell us everything about God. No one could ever understand all there is to know about God. But we can understand enough to know that God wants us to believe Him, trust Him, love Him, and obey Him. We can start by learning about Jesus, who came to earth to be our Savior and to reveal God to us.

See throughout The Action Bible *and throughout other versions of the Bible. See also* Holy Spirit/Spirit of the Lord; Jesus.

GOLD

Gold was valuable in early times just as it is now. In Bible times gold was used for jewelry, as money, and to decorate fine furniture, pottery, spoons, and other household things. But its main use was in decorating palaces and temples and the things used inside them. Gold was a gift fit for a king. When the wise men visited the child Jesus, they brought gold, frankincense, and myrrh. The heavenly city in the apostle John's vision of heaven had walls made of gold.

See The Action Bible *pages 156–157 and Genesis 2:11–12; 24:53; 44:2; Exodus 25:3, 10–17; Matthew 2:11; Revelation 21:21. See also* Coins/Money.

GOLGOTHA

(SEE CALVARY)

GOMER

(SEE HOSEA)

GOOD SHEPHERD

(SEE SHEEP/LAMB)

GOSPEL, THE

"Good news." The good news is that God has provided a way for any person to become His child: through faith in Jesus. Jesus died so that we could be forgiven by God and someday live forever with God. Christians are to spread the message of the gospel throughout the world.

See The Action Bible *page 649 and* Matthew 28:19–20. *See also* Gospels.

GOSPELS

The first four books of the New Testament: Matthew, Mark, Luke, and John. Each one tells about the life, death, and resurrection of Jesus Christ. Information about the life of Jesus was spread by word of mouth, but the growing community of believers needed a more permanent record of Jesus's words and actions. Matthew, Mark, and Luke are called the "synoptic" Gospels. *Synoptic* means "seen together." These three accounts tell many of the same things, sometimes in ways that are very much alike.

See **The Action Bible** *pages 523–650 and the gospels of Matthew, Mark, Luke, and John.*

GRACE

Being treated better than deserved. Instead of punishing people for the wrongs they do, God allowed His Son to die as payment. We can do nothing to earn grace. This is a gift God offers.

See **The Action Bible** *page 705 and Ephesians 2:8–10.*

GRAIN

(SEE BARLEY; WHEAT)

GRAPES

(SEE VINEYARD)

GRASSHOPPER

Grasshoppers were among the foods allowable for the Israelites. When twelve spies reported on the land of Canaan, ten of the spies claimed that the people of Israel were like "grasshoppers" compared to the huge people of Canaan.

See **The Action Bible** *page 175 and Numbers 13:33; Ecclesiastes 12:5.*

GREAT SEA

(SEE MEDITERRANEAN SEA)

HABAKKUK

A little-known prophet working in Judah around the time of the prophet Jeremiah. Habakkuk wrote his Old Testament book sometime between 605 and 586 BC. In his book, Habakkuk asked questions and then quietly listened to God's answers. He asked why the people of Judah had become so wicked. He told them to be sorry for their wrongdoings and be willing to change. If they refused, God

would allow their enemies to the north, the Chaldeans, to destroy Judah. But even after bad times come to God's people, Habakkuk said, they must remember God's faithfulness and trust Him. The last chapter of Habakkuk is a lovely poem expressing Habakkuk's faith in God's power and control of the world.

See The Action Bible *page 450 and the book of Habakkuk.*

HAGAR

Sarah's Egyptian maid and the mother of Abraham's son Ishmael. Sarah became jealous of Hagar and her son, even though Sarah came up with the idea for Hagar and Abraham to have the child. Sarah treated Hagar badly. Abraham did not stop Sarah from being mean to Hagar, and eventually Hagar took her son and ran away. But through an angel, God promised Hagar that the descendants of her son Ishmael would become a large nation. They later became the Ishmaelites. Joseph's brothers sold Joseph to Ishmaelite traders.

See The Action Bible *page 50 and Genesis 16; 21:1–21; 37:28.*

HAGGAI

A prophet who wrote an Old Testament book about 520 BC. The Jews had returned from captivity in Babylon and had started to rebuild the temple at Jerusalem. But they stopped work because the lack of rain had ruined their crops, and poverty discouraged them. Haggai encouraged the Jews to go back to the rebuilding.

See The Action Bible *page 509 and the book of Haggai.*

HAMAN

Prime minister of Persia during the reign of Xerxes. He greatly wanted to be admired. When Mordecai, a relative of Queen Esther, refused to bow down to Haman, Haman came up with a plan to have all of the Jews killed. But Queen Esther showed the king what Haman was up to, and Haman himself was hanged on the gallows he had built for Mordecai.

See The Action Bible *page 496 and Esther 3–7. See also* Xerxes/Ahasuerus; Esther; Feasts; Mordecai.

HANNAH

A godly woman who dedicated her firstborn son, Samuel, to serve God. When Hannah had no children, she prayed for a long time that she would have a child. One feast day in the tabernacle she promised God that if He gave her a son she would bring him to serve in God's house. Later, when Hannah and her husband, Elkanah, had a baby boy, Hannah dedicated

him to God's service. She was so happy she sang a beautiful song of praise. After Samuel moved into the tabernacle to serve the priest Eli there, God gave Hannah three more sons and two daughters.

See **The Action Bible** *page 248 and 1 Samuel 1–2.*

HARAN

A city in northern Mesopotamia. Abraham buried his father, Terah, here after their family left the city of Ur. In this city Abraham's brother, Nahor, decided to stay while Abraham set off for Canaan. Later Abraham sent his servant to find a wife for his son Isaac among his relatives there. Still later, Isaac's son Jacob fled to Haran and met his wives there.

See **The Action Bible** *page 45 and Genesis 11:31; 12:4; 24:4; 29:4–5.*

HARP

(SEE MUSIC/MUSICAL INSTRUMENTS)

HATE

A word used in two different ways in the Bible. God hates evil, idolatry, unfairness, and religious pretending. Believers also should hate these things. Even though God hates these sins, He still loves the persons who do them, and Christians should too. Christ said we are to love our enemies. John says that anyone who hates his brother is a murderer and is sinning.

Hate in the Bible is sometimes a word picture of turning away from something or someone. When God said He "hated" Esau, it meant that Esau and his descendants were not chosen by God as His special people. Jesus used *hate* as an exaggerated word to show us that we should not love someone more than we love God.

See **The Action Bible** *page 86 and Deuteronomy 12:31; Proverbs 6:16–19; Malachi 1:2–3; Matthew 5:44; Luke 14:26; 1 John 3:15.*

HAZAEL

King of Aram (the city-state of Damascus). He first served as an official of Ben-Hadad, the Syrian king. God told the prophet Elijah that Hazael would be king and would be part of His plan of judgment on the nation of Israel. Hazael murdered Ben-Hadad and became king, then went to war against Israel.

See **The Action Bible** *page 391 and 1 Kings 19:15–17; 2 Kings 8:7–15; 9:14–15.*

HEALING

Curing someone of a disease or condition. Sometimes God healed people directly or worked through a prophet like Elisha to heal people. Healing was an important part of Jesus's ministry. He often healed the sick. When He sent His disciples out to tell about salvation, He gave them a special gift—the ability to heal the sick as He did. After Jesus returned to heaven, the leaders of the early church received the gift of healing.

See **The Action Bible** *pages 172, 409, 553 and 2 Kings 5; Luke 4:33–39; 9:1; Acts 3:1–16. See also* Diseases/Conditions.

HEAVEN

Either the part of the world that arches over the earth or the place where God lives. Ancient peoples saw the universe as being in two parts: the earth and the heavens. They saw the heavens as a kind of dome over the earth. From the heavens came the rain and the sunlight needed for life. The beauty of the heavens reminded the people of God.

Heaven is also the place where God lives and where His children will live with Him after the resurrection. Right now, Jesus is in heaven, praying for His followers and helping to run the universe. We don't know where heaven is or what it looks like, but the word pictures in the book of Revelation tell us it is a happy place where everyone enjoys God.

See **The Action Bible** *page 479 and Genesis 28:17; Psalm 8; Matthew 5:12; Hebrews 9:24; and the book of Revelation.*

HEBREWS, BOOK OF

We do not know who wrote this letter. Some scholars believe that Paul, Barnabas, Priscilla, or Aquila could have written it. The book itself does not say, and no other New Testament books tell us for certain. The author's purpose was to show readers that Jesus was greater than angels, Moses, and any high priests. All Christians are on their way to a heavenly city to which Jesus has already gone. They will find eternal rest and joy at the end. So we shouldn't be weary or lose hope.

See **The Action Bible** *page 740 and the book of Hebrews.*

HEBREWS/JEWS

(SEE ISRAEL; JUDAH)

HEBRON

A city of refuge as well as a hill outside of Hebron. This area was known for having good soil. At one point Abraham lived in Hebron. Later, during the time of the dividing of Canaan, this area was given to Caleb, one of the twelve spies sent to look over Canaan. David lived in Hebron while king of Judah.

See The Action Bible *page 207 and Joshua 14:9–13; 2 Samuel 2:3. See also* David.

HELL

The eternal place of those who reject Jesus. It is a place of punishment for those who have chosen to turn away from God. It is the place of the Devil and his angels. The Bible has many word pictures to show how terrible it is to be forever separated from God.

See The Action Bible *page 742 and Matthew 5:22, 29–30; 18:9; Mark 9:47–48; 2 Peter 2:4.*

HELMET

Helmets for soldiers, during most of the Old Testament period, were made of leather; those for kings were of bronze. In New Testament times, soldiers' helmets were made of bronze.

See The Action Bible *page 149 and Ephesians 6:17.*

HEROD

Herod was the family name for several rulers. Although all the Herods were under the authority of the Roman emperor, they could rule their own country as long as they did not rebel against the Romans. Here are the Herods:

Herod the Great. King over Israel and some surrounding areas about 73 to 4 BC. Herod the Great was known

for his building projects, including the temple in Jerusalem. Jesus was born during Herod's reign. Herod ordered the killing of all baby boys in Bethlehem when he heard a new king had been born.

Herod Archelaus. The son of Herod the Great who became ruler of Judea and Samaria after his father died. God warned Joseph in a dream of the danger from this king. So he took his family and settled in Nazareth when they returned from Egypt. Archelaus's rule was short. He was banished to what is now France in AD 6.

Herod Antipas. Another son of Herod the Great who became ruler of Galilee after the death of his father. Jesus called him "that fox." Herod Antipas was the ruler who had John the Baptist killed.

Herod Agrippa I. Grandson of Herod the Great. He ruled most of Israel from AD 40 to 44. He is the ruler who had the apostle James killed and Peter imprisoned. He died suddenly in AD 44 at age fifty-four after he permitted his followers to say he was a god. God struck him with intestinal worms.

Herod Agrippa II. Known in the Bible as King Agrippa. He was the son of Herod Agrippa I. He ruled Galilee and some areas east of the Sea of Galilee from AD 53 to 70. He is the ruler who heard Paul defend himself against Jewish charges.

Herod Philip. Another son of Herod the Great and the builder of Caesarea Philippi.

See The Action Bible *pages 519, 536, 681, 731 and Matthew 2; 14:1–12;*

Mark 6:14–29; Luke 3:1, 19–20; Acts 12:1–23; 25: 23–26: 32.

HEROD'S PALACE

A beautiful palace Herod the Great built during his reign as king of Judea. This was one of the places where Jesus was put on trial. It was destroyed in AD 70.

See The Action Bible *page 524 and Luke 23:6–12.*

HERODIAS

The granddaughter of Herod the Great. Herodias was the wife of her uncle Philip but left him to marry his brother. Because John the Baptist confronted her about her illegal marriage, Herodias told her daughter Salome to ask for the head of John the Baptist after Salome danced for Herod Antipas.

See The Action Bible *page 576 and Matthew 14:1–12. See also* Herod.

HEZEKIAH

The thirteenth king of Judah. He came to the throne when he was twenty-five and ruled for twenty-nine years. Hezekiah was a good ruler who tried to restore proper worship of God. Later in his life, pride was his downfall.

When Hezekiah came to power, many of the people in Judah had stopped worshipping God. There were also political problems, with Egypt and Assyria wanting to conquer Judah. Hezekiah reopened the temple, destroyed altars to idols, and led a Passover celebration. But he had a hard time. The Assyrians captured many of the cities of Judah and threatened to take Jerusalem. Hezekiah offered to pay them not to attack Jerusalem. The Assyrians, under King Sennacherib, decided to attack anyway. But God saved the people in an amazing way.

Later, Hezekiah became sick. He prayed, and God gave him another fifteen years of life. But as Hezekiah got older, he became proud. When ambassadors came from Babylon to see him, he showed off his great wealth. Isaiah the prophet scolded him for his foolish pride and predicted that this nation would later carry away these treasures. And that is exactly what happened, but not during Hezekiah's life.

See The Action Bible *page 439–445 and 2 Kings 18–20; 2 Chronicles 29–32. See also* Assyria.

HILKIAH

A high priest during the time of King Josiah who discovered the long lost book of the Law in the temple. Hilkiah helped get the temple cleaned up and proper worship of God restored. His grandson Seraiah was later executed when the Babylonians destroyed Jerusalem.

See The Action Bible *page 447 and 2 Kings 22–23.*

HOLY/HOLINESS

Set apart or separate. It is a word that describes God. God is pure and loving, and completely unable to sin. God's holiness means He is completely separate from sin. Like oil and water, God and sin don't mix.

Because Jesus also is God, He has the same character as God. This means He is without sin too. That's why He was the perfect sacrifice to die for the wrongs everyone else did. His sacrifice gives those who believe in Him the power to be holy. This means we are set apart as God's people. We are to act differently than those who don't believe in God.

Items used in the tabernacle and temple were considered holy. Some could be handled only by priests. The ark of the covenant had to be carried with poles. Anyone who touched it died instantly.

See The Action Bible *page 437 and Exodus 15:11; Leviticus 20:7; Psalm 30:4; Isaiah 6:3; Mark 1:24; Luke 1:35; Romans 12:1; Hebrews 12:14. See also* Ark of the Covenant; God.

HOLY OF HOLIES/ HOLY PLACE/MOST HOLY PLACE

(SEE TABERNACLE/ TENT OF MEETING)

HOLY SPIRIT/SPIRIT OF THE LORD

God's presence in the world. Jesus called the Holy Spirit the Helper or Comforter. The Holy Spirit would convince people about the truth of Jesus and of their sin.

Many word pictures in the Bible help us understand the Holy Spirit. Wind and breath are the most common. Wind shows the power of the Holy Spirit; breath in the Bible stands for life itself. Other word pictures include a dove, oil, and fire. The dove is a picture of the peace of God; the oil (for a lamp) shows the Holy Spirit as light that shines in darkness. The fire pictures judgment.

In Old Testament times the Holy Spirit gave certain individuals power for certain work. This happened to David and many of the judges of Israel.

After Jesus had gone back to heaven, the Holy Spirit came in a new, permanent way on the day of Pentecost. Instead of providing power for a time, He came to live within those who trusted Jesus as their Savior. He provides power to tell others about Jesus. He also gives many different gifts to believers to help them serve God and help others.

See **The Action Bible** *pages 224, 547 and Genesis 1:2–3; Job 32:8; 33:4; Ezekiel 37:9–10; Matthew 3:16; Mark 1:10; Luke 1:15, 47, 67; John 1:32; 14:15–17; 15:26–27; 16:7–15; 20:22; Acts 2; Romans 12:6–8; 1 Corinthians 12–14; Galatians 5:22–23; 1 John 2:20, 27. See also* **Fruit of the Spirit.**

HOPE

The expectation of a good result. Because the Bible often connects hope with God, hope and trust often have the same meaning in some passages. The person who hopes waits for God to act in some way: to keep a promise He made or to bring about a rescue.

Job proclaimed his hope—his trust—in God, even though terrible things happened to him. After delivering bad news to the people of God, Old Testament prophets often spoke words of hope to encourage the people. For example, though Jeremiah predicted the fall of Jerusalem, he included a message of hope: God's mercy was new every day. For Christians, Jesus provides the ultimate hope: eternal life with God.

See The Action Bible *pages 445, 468 and Job 13:15; Proverbs 13:12; Lamentations 3:21–25; 1 Corinthians 13:13.*

HORSES

Horses have been tamed for thousands of years. In Bible times, horses were used mostly for war. They pulled chariots and were sometimes ridden by kings and important people. In the story of Esther, Mordecai was honored by being allowed to ride the king's horse around the capital city.

In the time of Moses, the Israelites were told not to collect a large number of horses. However, Solomon had about twelve thousand horses.

See The Action Bible *pages 118–119, 365, 503 and Deuteronomy 17:16; 1 Kings 4:26; Esther 6:6–11.*

HOSEA

An Old Testament prophet who called his people back to God. God told Hosea to use marriage as a picture of God's relationship to His people Israel. God was the bridegroom; Israel was the bride. God told Hosea to marry a woman who would be unfaithful to him. Her name was Gomer. They had three children. But Gomer fell in love with other men and left Hosea, just as Israel found other gods to worship. But Hosea, like God, brought Gomer back to his house and loved her even after what she had done.

See The Action Bible *page 436 and the book of Hosea.*

HOSPITALITY

The act of welcoming someone and providing for that person's needs. As they traveled far from home, many people in the Bible depended on the hospitality of others. Abraham showed hospitality to angels sent from God. When Jesus sent His disciples out to preach about the kingdom of God, He told them to depend on the hospitality of others. Later, the apostle Paul and his fellow missionaries often stayed in the homes of others while preaching the good news of Jesus.

See The Action Bible *pages 51, 711 and Genesis 18; Matthew 10:11–14; Romans 12:13; 3 John 8.*

HOUSE

While the homes of many people in Israel were tents, many others lived in houses. These houses had flat roofs. There was no need for a slanting roof in a land with so little rain. Walls were usually made from stone or brick. From the street, one would first enter a small open-air courtyard that often served as the kitchen. Beyond the courtyard, doors opened into a living room. Small bedrooms were beyond the living room. The owner and his family often shared the house with farm animals.

The floor of the house was clay or stone, depending on what the owner could afford. When a group of men tried to bring their paralyzed friend to the crowded house where Jesus taught, they tore up the roof to lower the man into the house. Doors were made of wood, cloth, skins, or woven rushes. The windows were small and high. Since there were no chimneys, smoke from the indoor stoves—used for cooking and heating—escaped through windows or doors.

The flat roofs were important to people of Bible times. They could be used for extra sleeping space, for drying flax, and for other activities. Stone steps often led from the courtyard to the roof.

Houses of richer people sometimes had an upper room built on the roof. Stairs to the upper room were usually outdoors. After Jesus's death, the disciples met in the upper room of the home of John Mark's mother. This is also the site of the Last Supper.

See The Action Bible *pages 529, 537, 560 and Mark 5:2–4; 14:15; Acts 1:13; 12:12. See also* **Upper Room.**

HUMILITY

The attitude opposite of pride and arrogance. Moses was a humble man. The best example of humility in the Bible is Jesus's life. Jesus showed humility when He came to earth to live as a man and die for wrongs He didn't commit. When He preached the Sermon on the Mount, He said that those who were humble were blessed.

See The Action Bible *pages 123, 134 and Numbers 12:3; Matthew 5:5; 11:28–30; Philippians 2:6–11.*

HUSHAI

A spy for King David when David's son Absalom led a rebellion against his father. Hushai pretended to have changed from David's side to Absalom's. When Absalom asked him about attacking King David, Hushai gave advice that delayed the attack.

Then David had time to escape across the Jordan River.

See The Action Bible *page 339 and 2 Samuel 16:15–19; 17:5–15. See also* **Ahithophel.**

I AM WHO I AM

God addressed Himself by this name to Moses. This is God's way of saying, "This is what I am like—a God who can be trusted." When Jesus later used this name for Himself, a crowd tried to stone Him for blasphemy.

See The Action Bible *page 123 and Exodus 3:14; Psalm 50:21; John 8:48–59.*

ICONIUM

A city in what is now Turkey. It still exists but is now called Konya. In New Testament times Paul visited there on his first and second missionary journeys. On his first visit, Paul and Barnabas preached to Jews and Gentiles. Many believed, and a church was formed. However, the two men were forced to leave when some unbelieving Jews threatened to stone them. Some of them followed Paul to Lystra, where they stoned him and dragged him out of the city. But Paul and Barnabas went back to Iconium after a while, continued to preach, and encouraged the church. Paul and Timothy visited Iconium later.

See The Action Bible *page 701 and Acts 14:1–7, 19–23; 16:1–5.*

IDOL/IDOLATRY

Worshipping false gods. Idolatry includes not only the worship of objects made by people, but also

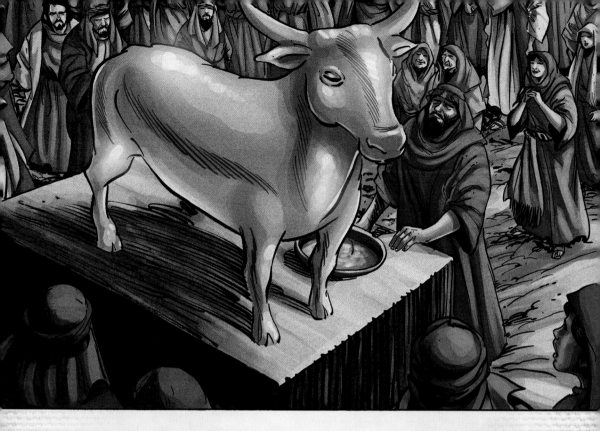

the worship of the sun, moon, trees, or stars. Idols were statues or other images made of wood, stone, metal, or some other material. These were meant to represent a god.

In the Old Testament, the nations around Israel worshipped many idols. That's why one of the Ten Commandments speaks against the worship of idols. The Israelites often disobeyed, and God sent many prophets to warn them against this.

In the New Testament, Christians were told not to eat meat that had been offered to idols. Idolatry doesn't just mean worshipping statues. Idolatry also means making anyone or anything a higher priority than God.

Some of the idols worshipped in Bible times include the following:

Baal and Asherah. Baal was the chief god of the people of Canaan. Asherah was his mother. Those who worshipped Baal believed that he ruled their land, crops, and animals. He was pictured as a warrior holding a thunderbolt spear in one hand and a shield in the other. Poles were set up and dedicated to Asherah. During the time of the prophet Elijah and during other periods as well, many Israelites worshipped the god Baal, thanks to kings like Ahab.

Dagon. The chief god of the Philistines. Scholars are not sure whether Dagon was a fish-god or a god of agriculture, but the people built many temples to honor this god. When Samson was blinded by the Philistines, they brought him to a temple of Dagon to make fun of him. Another time when the Philistines fought the Israelites, they captured the ark of God in a battle and took it to a temple of Dagon. The next day they found the image of Dagon facedown in front of the ark.

Golden Calf. An image Aaron made while Moses was on the mountain receiving the Ten Commandments from God. The people had become impatient because Moses had been gone so long. The statue was probably similar to the Egyptian bull-calf statues that the people had known. Much later, King Jeroboam made two golden calves because he did not want his people to go to the temple in Jerusalem to worship.

Greek and Roman Gods. When Paul traveled throughout Macedonia and Asia Minor on his missionary journeys, he saw many temples and statues dedicated to the Greek and Roman gods (Zeus, the chief god; Artemis/Diana, the goddess of the hunt; Hermes, the messenger of the gods; and many others). Silversmiths in Ephesus grew wealthy making statues of Artemis/Diana. In Lystra, Paul and Barnabas were believed to be Hermes and Zeus, respectively, after they healed a crippled man by the power of the Holy Spirit.

Molech. A god worshipped by the Ammonites before Israel arrived in Canaan. The Phoenicians worshipped this god. Often children were sacrificed to Molech. God warned His people to have nothing to do with this horrible practice. But Solomon later allowed his wives to persuade him to worship Molech. God warned Solomon that most of the kingdom would be torn away from his family.

Others. During the time of Daniel, King Nebuchadnezzar of Babylon ordered a ninety-foot statue built. This statue was to be worshipped whenever a certain tune was played.

See The Action Bible *pages 29, 156–160, 216, 253–254, 475, 477, 700, 721–725 and Exodus 20:4–5; 32; Leviticus 18:21; 20:1–5; Judges 16:23–30; 1 Samuel 5; 1 Kings 12:25–33; 18; 1 Chronicles 10:10; Jeremiah 19:5; Daniel 3; Hosea 8:5–6; Acts 17:16–21; 1 Corinthians 8:4–13. See also* Ahab; Elijah; Jezebel.

INJUSTICE

An unfair action. God wanted judges to be fair and provide justice equally to all. But sometimes judges weren't fair. They treated those who had money better than they treated the poor. Nathan told David a story about an injustice. This was God's way of warning David that his wrongdoing had been seen.

See The Action Bible *pages 324–325 and 2 Samuel 12; 2 Chronicles 19:7. See also* Justice.

INN

A resting place (something like a camp) for individuals or caravans as they traveled. Such inns would be near a well and might have some protection with rocks and trees. An inn could also be a large courtyard with a gate that could be locked. Around the sides were rooms or stalls for animals and travelers. A well would be in the courtyard. Travelers carried food for themselves and their animals. Sometimes an inn was a guest room in a private home.

Innkeepers of ancient times had bad reputations, especially those who had large inns with a courtyard and a gate. This is one of the reasons Christians were urged to welcome traveling Christians into their homes.

See **The Action Bible** *page 532 and Luke 2:7.*

INSCRIPTION ON THE CROSS

The words written on the sign fastened to Jesus's cross, which explained the charge against Him. The sign read, "Jesus of Nazareth, the King of the Jews." Jesus was charged with plotting to overthrow the government.

See **The Action Bible** *page 633 and Matthew 27:37; Mark 15:26; Luke 23:38; John 19:19–21.*

IRON

Iron was used to make axes and other tools. When the Israelites first came into Israel, they had very little iron. This kept them poor because they did not have good farming tools or swords and spears for their armies. Later, when they defeated the Philistines and took over the land, they were able to learn how to melt and shape iron. The army of the Canaanites had nine hundred chariots made from iron.

See **The Action Bible** *pages 213–215 and Judges 4:3.*

ISAAC

The only son of Abraham and Sarah, born by a miracle of God when

Abraham was one hundred years old and Sarah was ninety. God promised that the nation of Israel would be born through the family line of Isaac.

When Isaac was a young boy, God told Abraham to sacrifice Isaac to Him on a mountain in the land of Moriah. With great sorrow, Abraham went to Moriah and got ready to sacrifice Isaac. When everything was set, God appeared to Abraham and prevented him from killing Isaac.

At age forty, Isaac married Rebekah, a relative from Mesopotamia and had twin sons, Esau and Jacob. When Isaac was about a hundred years old and his eyesight was poor, he was tricked into giving the birthright blessing to Jacob instead of Esau. Isaac died at age one hundred eighty.

See The Action Bible *pages 56–77, 88 and Genesis 17:17–19; 18:9–15; 21:1–8; 22:1–14; 24; 27; 35:27–29.*

ISAIAH

An Old Testament prophet who is quoted more times in the New Testament than all other prophets combined. Many of the Old Testament prophecies about Jesus Christ are in the book of Isaiah. We do not know much about the prophet Isaiah except that he prophesied from 740 to 680 BC during the reign of four kings of Judah—Uzziah, Jotham, Ahaz, and Hezekiah. He was married to a female prophet whose name we don't know. They had two sons. Isaiah warned the people that God was more interested in right living than in animal sacrifices.

See The Action Bible *pages 437–445 and the book of Isaiah; Luke 4:16–21.*

ISAIAH, BOOK OF

Written by Isaiah around 740–681 BC. The book of Isaiah is the first of the major books of prophecy in the Old Testament. Besides Isaiah's remarkable prophetic poems, the book of Isaiah also has sections about the history of Judah and surrounding nations. Chapters 36–37 tell how King Sennacherib of Assyria threatened to overrun Jerusalem. When Hezekiah received Sennacherib's threatening

letter, he took it to the temple, spread it before the Lord, and prayed for deliverance. God answered and destroyed the Assyrian army.

Isaiah was a prophet of great imagination and skill as a writer. He used colorful word pictures to describe the sins of his people. He showed God as the great, holy Creator of the universe—one who has great power and knowledge but also loves His people deeply. Isaiah warned the people that God was more interested in right living than in animal sacrifices. Probably the most well-known chapter is Isaiah 53, where the picture of a suffering Savior describes the life and ministry of Jesus with stunning accuracy. Isaiah also prophesied the upcoming birth of the Savior, which took place seven hundred years later. The importance of the book of Isaiah is shown in the fact that Jesus began His public ministry in Nazareth by reading from Isaiah 61.

See The Action Bible *pages 437–445 and the book of Isaiah; Luke 4:16–21. See also* Isaiah.

ISH-BOSHETH

The fourth son of Saul. He was king over Israel for two years after Saul and Saul's three older sons died in battle. He was proclaimed king by Abner, the captain of Saul's army. But the tribe of Judah had made David king. Ish-bosheth fought against David for two years until Abner turned his loyalty to David. Later, Ish-bosheth was murdered by his own captains.

See The Action Bible *pages 309, 315 and 2 Samuel 2:8–4:12.*

ISHMAEL

The son of Abraham and Hagar, the Egyptian maid of Sarah, Abraham's wife. Ishmael was fourteen years old when Abraham and Sarah had a son, Isaac. Sarah did not want Isaac to be brought up in the same house with Ishmael, and when Ishmael was sixteen, she urged Abraham to send Ishmael and Hagar away. Abraham did not want to do this, for he loved Ishmael. An angel appeared to Abraham, however, and told him to let them go, for God would make the children of Ishmael into a great nation.

When Ishmael and his mother went into the wilderness, he almost died of thirst. Then an angel of God appeared to his mother and assured her that God would care for them. When his father, Abraham, died, Ishmael went back to Canaan and helped Isaac with the funeral. Ishmael died when he was 137 years old. The people in his family line were the Ishmaelites and were known for their skill with bows and arrows. Some Ishmaelites bought Joseph from his brothers and took him to Egypt.

See The Action Bible *pages 50, 56 and Genesis 16:1–7; 17:20; 21:9–21; 25:7–18; 37:25–28.*

ISRAEL

The land called Canaan, which includes what is now known as Israel. This area is about 70 miles wide and 150 miles long—between the Mediterranean Sea and the Jordan River. It is about the size of the state of Vermont. The history of the people

known as the Israelites (the Hebrews) started with the time of Abraham, about 2000 BC. Abraham, his son Isaac, and Isaac's son Jacob are the ancestors or founders of the Israelites.

Israel became known as the northern kingdom between 930 and 722 BC, after separating from the tribes of Judah and Benjamin after the death of Solomon. This kingdom, which included ten of the original twelve tribes, was also called Ephraim—the name of one of the strongest tribes. The northern and southern kingdoms had separate kings and sometimes fought each other. Its capital was Samaria.

Although all of Israel is hilly, the northern part has the most rugged hills. The central part has the best farmland. There are fertile valleys between the hills, and the climate is good for farming. Much of southern Israel has so little rainfall that it is barely usable for grazing sheep and camels. There is some land around wells that can be farmed.

See **The Action Bible** *page 368 and throughout the Bible. See also* **Judah**.

JABESH GILEAD

A city east of the Jordan River. King Saul rescued the people of this area from the Ammonites. After the Philistines hung up the dead bodies of Saul and his sons, the men of Jabesh Gilead risked their lives to take down the bodies and buried them honorably.

See **The Action Bible** *page 308 and* **Judges 21:8–12; 1 Samuel 31:11–13.**

JACOB/ISRAEL

The younger of twin sons born to Isaac and Rebekah. Jacob's name was later changed to Israel, and from that name came the word *Israelites*. Jacob is most known for stealing the birthright of his brother, Esau. Because of this trickery, Jacob had to go live with his uncle, Laban. After he had stayed with Laban for twenty years, Jacob took his family back to Beersheba, where he was later forgiven by Esau. Jacob settled in Shechem, in Canaan.

Jacob had twelve sons, the families of which later formed the twelve tribes of the nation of Israel. The twelve sons are (in birth order) Reuben, Simeon, Levi, Judah, Dan, Naphtali, Gad, Asher, Issachar, Zebulun, Joseph, and Benjamin.

Jesus came from the tribe of Judah. When Jesus visited the territory of Zebulun, He fulfilled a prophecy recorded in Isaiah 9:1–2. King Saul and the apostle Paul were both from the tribe of Benjamin. Deborah, a judge of Israel, was from the tribe of Issachar. Moses and Aaron came from the tribe of Levi.

See The Action Bible *pages 68–110 and Genesis 25:23–34; 27–50; Matthew 1; 4:12–16. See also Ephraim; Israel; Joseph, son of Jacob; Laban; Leah; Manasseh; Rachel.*

JAIRUS

The ruler of a synagogue whose twelve-year-old daughter was raised from death by Jesus. Jairus went to Jesus, seeking help for her. But before Jesus arrived at Jairus's home, messengers told him his daughter had died. Jesus insisted on going anyway, and when He arrived, the people were weeping and mourning. Jesus sent everyone out of the house except Jairus and his wife and Peter, James, and John. Jesus took the girl's hand and commanded her to rise.

See The Action Bible *page 573 and Mark 5:21–24, 35–43.*

JAMES, BROTHER OF JESUS

The half brother of Jesus and writer of the book of James in the New Testament. James and his other brothers were not followers of Christ during His life. But after Jesus rose from the dead, they became believers and were in the upper room, waiting for the coming of the Holy Spirit.

Jesus appeared to James in a miraculous way after the resurrection. James became a leader in the church in Jerusalem. He was in charge when Paul and Barnabas came to Jerusalem to discuss the serious problems arising when Gentiles became believers in Christ. James was stoned to death by the Jewish high priest in AD 62, according to the Jewish historian Josephus.

See The Action Bible *page 729 and John 7:5; Acts 15:1–21; 21:17–19; 1 Corinthians 15:7; the book of James.*

JAMES, THE APOSTLE

One of Jesus's twelve disciples. His brother was the apostle John. James was a fisherman in Galilee when Jesus invited him to become one of His disciples. He was one of the three most well-known disciples along with

Peter and John. These three were with Jesus at several important moments—such as Jesus's time on the Mount of Transfiguration where Jesus's appearance was changed; when Jesus prayed in Gethsemane before His crucifixion; and when Jesus raised the daughter of Jairus from death. James was killed by Herod Agrippa I in AD 44.

See The Action Bible *page 566 and Matthew 26:36–46; Acts 12:1–3.*
See also Transfiguration, the.

JAMES, BOOK OF

James, the brother of Jesus, wrote this letter possibly as early as AD 48 to tell believers to do more than talk about their faith—they must do what is pleasing to God. James is very plain about the things that do not please God. Christians should be careful about what they say. Christians are not to honor people because they are rich. Everyone is to be treated alike. James urges Christians to pray for each other, to resist temptation, to be humble before God, to seek wisdom from God, and to realize that every good thing we have is a gift from God.

See The Action Bible *page 740 and the book of James. See also* James, brother of Jesus.

JASON

A Christian at Thessalonica who invited Paul and Silas to stay at his house while they were preaching. Some of the Jews who were jealous of Paul's success in winning converts gathered a crowd and attacked Jason's house. Paul and Silas were not there at the time, so the mob took Jason and some of his friends to the city judge and accused him of protecting criminals. This made it sound as though Paul and Silas were trying to overthrow the government. The judge made Jason promise that Paul and Silas would leave the city and not come back again.

See The Action Bible *page 717 and Acts 17:1–10.*

JAVELIN/SPEAR

Javelin, spear, and lance were roughly the same—long, slender pieces of wood with heads of stone or metal. They were used in war either to thrust or to throw at the enemy. King Saul threw a spear in an attempt to murder David and Jonathan.

See The Action Bible *pages 149, 283 and 1 Samuel 19:9–10.*

JEHOIADA

A high priest and uncle of Joash, a king of Judah. When Joash was a baby, Jehoiada and his wife, Jehosheba, rescued him from being killed by his grandmother, Athaliah. Jehoiada and Jehosheba hid Joash in the temple. When Joash was seven years old,

Jehoiada told the palace guards that the true heir to the throne was alive. Jehoiada planned with them to have the boy crowned king when Queen Athaliah was away. The plan worked. Jehoiada later became an important adviser to Joash. He directed the destruction of many of the altars to the false god Baal. Jehoiada and Joash also arranged to have the temple repaired. Because of his importance and his good work, Jehoiada was buried among the kings when he died at age 130.

See The Action Bible *page 425 and 2 Kings 11:1–12:16; 2 Chronicles 22:10–24:16. See also* Athaliah.

JEHOIAKIM

The eighteenth king of Judah, who ruled from 609 to 598 BC. He became king when his brother was taken captive by Pharaoh Neco, the ruler of Egypt. Neco made Jehoiakim king of Judah and told him what to do. Jehoiakim had to tax the people very heavily and give the money to Neco. Jehoiakim treated the prophet Jeremiah very cruelly because Jeremiah prophesied that Babylon would conquer Judah. This prophecy came true. The Babylonians captured most of Israel, and Jehoiakim had to take orders from King Nebuchadnezzar. Later, Jehoiakim tried to rebel against Nebuchadnezzar but was taken captive and killed.

See The Action Bible *page 451 and 2 Kings 23:34–24:6; 2 Chronicles 36:3–8. See also* Babylonians; Nebuchadnezzar.

JEHOSHAPHAT

King of Judah and an ally of Ahab, king of Israel. Like his father, Asa, Jehoshaphat was one of the good kings of Judah. When threatened by a huge army from Ammon and Moab, Jehoshaphat prayed. God caused Judah's enemies to destroy each other.

See The Action Bible *page 397 and 1 Kings 22; 2 Chronicles 17–20.*

JEHOSHEBA

(SEE JEHOIADA)

JEHOVAH

The Jews had a special name for God that was so sacred they would not even say it out loud. When reading the Old Testament, they would substitute another name (Lord) for their special name for God.

Originally, all Hebrew words were written without vowels. A name such as *Peter* would be written PTR. The special name for God, Yahweh, was written YHWH. Because the Jews never said the name, they eventually forgot how to pronounce it. Hundreds of years later, the vowels for *Adonai*, the Hebrew word for "Lord," were used with the letters YHWH, and from these two Hebrew words (the consonants of one and the vowels of the other) came the word *Jehovah,* which is used in some translations of the Bible. Most translations now use the word LORD in capital letters for this special name for God.

See The Action Bible *page 451 and Psalms 24:10; 59:5; Isaiah 1:24; Jeremiah 36 and other places in the Bible where "Lord" is used.*

JEHU

The eleventh king of Israel. While serving in the army, Jehu was chosen by God to take the place of King Joram, the son of Ahab. The prophet Elisha told a younger prophet to go to the army post where Jehu was stationed and anoint him king of Israel. The prophet told Jehu that he must strike down the rulers who were relatives of Ahab. Jehu did as he was told. Joram was killed and so was Jezebel, wife of Ahab. Jehu was king for twenty-eight years.

See The Action Bible *page 418 and 2 Kings 9:1–13; 10:1–29.*

JEREMIAH

One of the greatest Old Testament prophets and also the most unpopular. He was a prophet during the reigns of five kings of Judah—Josiah, Jehoahaz, Jehoiakim, Jehoiachin, and Zedekiah—about forty years.

God called him to be a prophet when he was a young man. The messages God gave Jeremiah made the people of Judah angry. He told them that God would judge them for their evil acts, and that a great power from the north would soon come and conquer them. So Jeremiah spent much of his time as a prisoner or hiding from angry kings.

But God still spoke to him, so Jeremiah put his words in writing instead, with the help of his friend Baruch. Baruch came from a noble

family in Jerusalem. He could have been a powerful friend of the king. Instead he chose to be the friend and assistant of Jeremiah. He wrote down Jeremiah's words and read them to the people.

Because Jeremiah told the king to submit to the rule of the Babylonians, he was considered a traitor and was placed in a dungeon half full of mud. But nothing could stop God's words from coming true. The Babylonians conquered the city of Jerusalem. Jeremiah was left in Jerusalem with the others. The few who were left later decided to go to Egypt and try to make new lives for themselves there. They forced Jeremiah to go with them. In Egypt Jeremiah continued his prophecies, urging the people to turn away from idolatry and worship God again. Jeremiah died in Egypt.

See **The Action Bible** *pages 446–469 and the book of Jeremiah. See also* **Exile/Captivity of Israel.**

JEREMIAH, BOOK OF

The longest prophetic book in the Old Testament. Even though the book of Isaiah has more chapters, they are shorter than the chapters in the book of Jeremiah. It was written by the prophet Jeremiah about many events in his life and in the history of Judah (the southern kingdom) between 625 and 580 BC. The book also gives many of the prophecies of Jeremiah. However, the events were not written in the order in which they occurred. The book seems to be arranged roughly this way: prophecies and sermons about Judah (chapters 1–25); events in the life of Jeremiah

(chapters 26–45); prophecies about other countries (chapters 46–51); and the fall of Jerusalem and events that followed (chapter 52).

Although Jeremiah's prophecies were usually about the bad things that would happen to Judah and other countries, he also wrote about a new agreement God would make with His people. This new agreement is mentioned in several places in the New Testament.

See **The Action Bible** *pages 446, 451–467 and the book of Jeremiah; Hebrews 8:7–13; 10:15-18. See also* **Jeremiah.**

JERICHO

The oldest known city in the world—dating five thousand years before the time of Abraham. It is located about one mile southeast of where the city was in Old Testament times. Jericho is famous because its walls fell down after Joshua and his army marched around it for seven days. At God's command, Joshua and his men destroyed everything in the city. The city was not rebuilt for more than five hundred years. It became an important city but was later destroyed.

The Jericho of the New Testament is near the modern town of Jericho. It was a great city, built by Herod as his winter capital because it has a tropical climate. Jesus often taught and healed there. Zacchaeus, who climbed a tree to see Jesus, lived in Jericho. Jesus's famous story about the Good Samaritan is placed on the lonely, winding road between Jerusalem and Jericho—a distance of about twenty miles.

See The Action Bible *pages 200,
608* and Joshua 6; Mark 10:46–52;
Luke 10:29–37; 19:1–10.

See The Action Bible *pages 366–375*
and 1 Kings 11:28–39; 12:20, 26–31;
12:32–13:10. See also Ahijah.

JEROBOAM

The first king of the northern kingdom of Israel, who ruled from about 931–910 BC. He began as a counselor under King Solomon. He helped stir up anger against Solomon over the high taxes the people had to pay.

The prophet Ahijah announced that Jeroboam would become the leader of ten tribes of Israel. Ahijah warned Jeroboam to obey God's laws. After King Solomon's death, the prophecy came true, and Jeroboam became king. He forgot about obeying all of God's laws.

A prophet told Jeroboam that God would judge his actions. When Jeroboam ordered the prophet arrested, Jeroboam's hand shriveled up! Jeroboam pleaded with the prophet to ask God to heal him. The prophet did, and Jeroboam was healed. But Jeroboam did not return to worshipping God.

JERUSALEM

The most famous city on earth. Its name means "city of peace." Jerusalem was the capital of Israel under David and Solomon. It was captured by David from the Jebusites. David later made this part his royal home when he became king. In this city, Solomon erected his beautiful temple to God. After Israel was divided into northern and southern kingdoms in 930 BC, Jerusalem continued to be the capital of Judah, the southern kingdom.

The city was destroyed by King Nebuchadnezzar in 586 BC when the southern kingdom was defeated and many of its people taken into exile in Babylon.

Around 538 BC, some Jews were able to return to Jerusalem and start to rebuild the temple. Nehemiah led the rebuilding of the walls of the city, beginning about 445 BC. During the next five hundred years, Jerusalem

was ruled by a number of countries including Greece, Persia, Egypt, Syria, and, finally, Rome. It was during the Roman rule that Jesus visited Jerusalem several times and once wept about how it wouldn't listen to His message. He was finally crucified there. After He rose from the dead, He appeared to His disciples in Jerusalem and went back to heaven from a hill near the city.

The first Christian church was formed in Jerusalem after the Holy Spirit came upon the disciples during the Feast of Pentecost. The city was completely destroyed by the Romans in AD 70. After it was rebuilt beginning in AD 136, it came under the control of many rulers. The city became part of the modern nation of Israel in 1967. Today it is considered a sacred city by Jews, Christians, and Muslims. The Muslim Dome of the Rock (where Abraham is said to have offered his son as a sacrifice to God) now stands on part of the area where the temple once stood.

See **The Action Bible** *page 316 and 2 Samuel 5:5–7; Matthew 21:1–11; 23:37–39.*

JESUS

The most important person in the Bible. The name *Jesus* is the same as the Old Testament name *Joshua*, meaning "the Lord is my salvation." The word *Christ* comes from the word *anointed* in Greek. Jesus is called Christ and Messiah because He was anointed or chosen by God for His special work as Savior of the world.

Though He was born on earth, many passages in the Bible say He existed before that, because He is both God and man. His mother was Mary, who was engaged to marry Joseph, a carpenter.

When Jesus was about thirty years old, He began to preach and teach. His teachings were different from those of other Jewish teachers and priests. He told interesting stories and used plain words. He became very popular, especially when the people learned that He could perform miracles. He healed people who had terrible diseases, fed thousands of people with just five loaves of bread and two fish, and made a terrible storm go away.

Because of these wonderful works, many people wanted to make Jesus king. But that was not the kind of king Jesus came to be. His kingdom was one in which God ruled the hearts of people. The religious leaders of His time, the Pharisees and scribes, became angry with Jesus and jealous of His popularity. So they began to figure out ways to have Jesus put to death by the Romans.

Finally one of Jesus's disciples betrayed Jesus, which led to His arrest, trials, and crucifixion. On the day we now call Good Friday, Jesus was put to death as a criminal along with two thieves. Even on the cross, He thought about others. He asked John to take care of His mother. He told one of the thieves that the thief would be in heaven with Him. He prayed for the soldiers and for the people who wanted Him to die. After six hours of suffering, He died.

On the third day, Jesus rose from the dead and appeared again to women who were His followers, and to the disciples. For forty days, Jesus appeared occasionally to His followers, talked with them, and taught them. Then He returned to heaven before the startled eyes of His disciples. Angels soon appeared, telling the disciples that Jesus would return the same way He left.

See **The Action Bible** *pages 528–650 and throughout the books of the New Testament. See also* **Apostles/Disciples; Ascension; Bethlehem; Joseph, husband of Mary; Judas Iscariot; Mary, mother of Jesus.**

JETHRO

Moses's father-in-law. Moses lived with him in Midian and shepherded his sheep for forty years before Moses returned to Egypt to lead the Israelites out of slavery. While Moses was in the wilderness with the people of Israel, Jethro came to visit him. He saw how overworked Moses was as he tried to advise the people. He suggested that

Moses appoint judges to help him in less important matters. Moses took his advice.

See **The Action Bible** *page 153 and Exodus 18.*

JEZEBEL

The scheming wife of Ahab, king of the northern kingdom. Jezebel came from Phoenicia, a country near the mountains of Lebanon. She wanted the people of Israel to worship gods like Baal. Because of this, she had many of the prophets of God put to death.

When the prophet Elijah had her prophets of Baal killed, Jezebel ordered Elijah to be killed. He escaped and later told Ahab that God's judgment would fall on Jezebel and Ahab. Ahab died in battle, and Jezebel died when she was thrown from a window in her palace.

See **The Action Bible** *page 376 and 1 Kings 16:32; 19; 21; 22:34–40; 2 Kings 9:30–37.*

JEZREEL

A city about sixty miles north of Jerusalem. King Ahab had a palace here. Near the palace, a man named Naboth had a vineyard that King Ahab wanted for his vegetable garden.

See **The Action Bible** *page 419 and 1 Kings 21:1–16; 2 Kings 9:30–37. See also* Naboth.

JOAB

Commander of David's army and David's nephew. He was a skilled fighter, but he was also a cruel man. He killed Abner, the commander of an opposing army, who was trying to make peace with David. When Absalom, David's son, led a rebellion against David, David ordered that Absalom not be harmed. Joab killed him anyway. David then made Amasa (probably Joab's cousin) commander of his army instead of Joab. Joab pretended to be Amasa's friend—and then one day suddenly stabbed him to death. When David was dying, Joab supported Adonijah as the next king instead of Solomon. After Solomon was made king, he ordered Joab to be killed.

See **The Action Bible** *page 310 and 2 Samuel 3:20–30; 18:9–15; 20:4–10; 1 Kings 2:28–34.*

JOASH

The ninth king of Judah, who ruled for forty years (835–796 BC). When he was a baby, everyone else in the royal family, including his father, was murdered. Joash was saved by his aunt

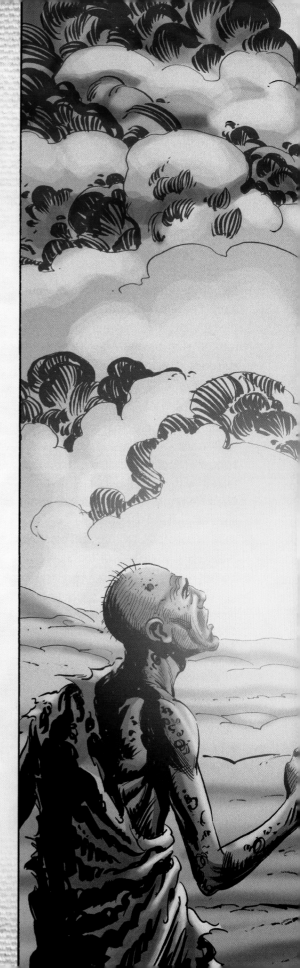

and uncle, who hid him for seven years. At first he took advice from his godly uncle and ruled well. Later he began to worship idols. When Zechariah, the son of the priest, told him he was doing wrong, he had Zechariah killed. Joash was wounded in a battle with the Syrians, but he was killed in his own bed by his servants because he had ordered Zechariah killed.

See **The Action Bible** *pages 423–430 and 2 Chronicles 24:1–24. See also* **Jehoiada.**

JOB

A wise, rich, and good man who suffered terrible losses. No one knows when Job's story took place. We know that his ten children died on the same day. He lost all his wealth and became ill with a painful skin disease. Three friends who visited tried to explain why these dreadful things had happened. Job became very discouraged and angry with God for letting such bad things happen, but he still believed in God and trusted Him. Job realized that his trust in God did not depend on the things that happened to him. Later, God restored Job's health, made him twice as rich as he had been before, and gave him ten more children.

See **The Action Bible** *page 40 and the book of Job.*

JOEL

An Old Testament prophet who wrote a short book. No one knows exactly who he was or when he wrote the book. We do know that he wrote about a terrible plague of locusts that had invaded the land, stripping the crops and ruining orchards. Joel told the people that the locusts had come as a punishment because they had not been faithful to God. The most famous part of Joel's prophecy is a section the apostle Peter quoted on the day of Pentecost: Joel 2:28–32.

See **The Action Bible** *page 436 and the book of Joel; Acts 2:17–21.*

JOHN, 1, 2, AND 3

All three letters were written between AD 85 and 100 by John, one of Jesus's twelve disciples. First John was probably sent to the churches in Asia (now Turkey), where John lived toward the end of his long life. In this

letter, John warned his readers about the false teachers in the area who preached untrue things about Jesus. John wrote to explain the truth. In 2 John, John again warned the church about false teachings. Believers were to avoid inviting false teachers into their homes. Third John was written to Gaius, a leader in one of the churches. John praised Gaius for inviting some of the traveling Christian teachers to stay in his home. He also said that Diotrephes, another man in the church, was not pleasing God by the way he treated John and other Christians.

See The Action Bible page 741 and the books of 1, 2, and 3 John; Hebrews 8:7–13; 10:15–18. See also John, the apostle.

JOHN, GOSPEL OF

Written by John, one of Jesus's disciples, when John was an old man. It was probably the last of the four gospels to be written. The apostle John tells many things about the life of Christ that the other three do not. Most of John's gospel is about Jesus's teachings, travels, and miracles in Judea. These are some of the miracles that are described only in the gospel of John: turning water into wine at a wedding (2:1–11); healing a lame man at the pool of Bethesda (5:1–15); healing the man who had been blind from birth (9:1–41); and raising Lazarus from the dead (11:1–44). John's gospel also tells many teachings of Jesus that are not in the other gospels, including Jesus's identifying Himself as the Bread of Life (6:25–59) and the Good Shepherd (10:1–18).

See The Action Bible pages 523, 586, 592, 741 and the gospel of John. See also John, the apostle.

JOHN, THE APOSTLE

Known as "the disciple whom Jesus loved." He was involved in the writing of five New Testament books—the gospel of John, 1 John, 2 John, 3 John, and Revelation. John was a fisherman when Jesus chose him to become a disciple. Jesus nicknamed him "Son of Thunder." This probably meant that when John was young, he did things on the spur of the moment and had a hot temper. He is the only one of Jesus's disciples known to have lived to an old age. When he was older, he was known for his gentleness and loving spirit.

He was one of the three disciples—Peter, James, and John—who were closest to Jesus and saw Him do some miracles that no one else saw, such as raising the daughter of Jairus from the dead. Jesus took these three with Him into a garden to pray just before His trial and crucifixion. John was the only disciple who the Bible says watched the crucifixion. Jesus saw him and asked him to take care of His mother.

After Jesus returned to heaven, John became one of the leaders of the Christians in Jerusalem. He was exiled much later on the island of Patmos because of his faith. There God gave John visions. He wrote them in what we know as Revelation—the last book of the Bible. John was probably later released from Patmos and died in the city of Ephesus when he was an old

man. We don't know exactly when he wrote the parts of the New Testament that carry his name.

See **The Action Bible** *page 549 and Mark 3:17; the gospel of John; John, 1, 2, 3; the book of Revelation.*

JOHN, THE BAPTIST

A prophet who was a relative of Jesus. His parents, Zechariah and Elizabeth, were quite old when he was born. When he was a young man, John preached in the wilderness near the Jordan River just north of the Dead Sea. There he lived simply, eating locusts and wild honey, and wearing rough garments of camel hair. He told his listeners that they must be willing to change, treat people fairly, and share what they had with others. Many thought John was the coming Messiah. John's job was to prepare people for the coming Savior.

John baptized those who wanted to turn to God and change their ways. One day as John was baptizing, Jesus asked to be baptized. At first John refused, but Jesus insisted. Some of John's followers, like Andrew, became

disciples of Jesus after John told them that Jesus was the promised Savior.

Later, John the Baptist was imprisoned by Herod Antipas, the ruler of Galilee. John had said that Herod was wrong to have married the wife of his half brother. While in prison, John sent some of his friends to ask Jesus if He really was the promised Messiah. Jesus told them to assure John that He was. John was killed after Herod's stepdaughter asked for his head as a reward for her dancing at one of Herod's banquets.

See The Action Bible *pages 545, 576 and Matthew 11:2–15; 14:1–12; Mark 6:14–29; Luke 1:5–25, 57–80.*

JONAH

An Old Testament prophet who had to be swallowed by a huge fish before he was willing to obey God. When God called him to preach in a Gentile city, Nineveh, in about 745 BC, Jonah did not want to go. He was afraid the people would repent and God would spare the wicked city. After all, the Assyrians, whose capital city was Nineveh, had been very cruel to the people of Israel. Jonah wanted God to destroy this city. God allowed Jonah to be swallowed by a fish until Jonah obeyed God.

See The Action Bible *page 431 and the book of Jonah.*

JONAH, BOOK OF

Most known for the story of Jonah and the great fish, the book of Jonah shows that God was concerned for all the people of the world—not just the Israelites, who were His chosen people.

See The Action Bible *pages 431–435 and the book of Jonah. See also* Jonah.

JONATHAN

The oldest son of King Saul. He was David's best friend and was a skilled and courageous soldier. When Saul saw that David was popular among the people, he hated him so much he plotted to kill him. Jonathan tried to show his father that he had no reason to kill David. But Saul refused to listen to Jonathan and even tried to kill him! Jonathan warned David of Saul's plan to kill him, and this helped David escape.

Jonathan knew that David would become the next king of Israel even though, as Saul's oldest son, he should have been the next king. The love of David and Jonathan for each other was so deep that jealousy never hurt their friendship. At the end, Jonathan and King Saul were both killed in the same battle with the Philistines. Later King David wrote a song in Jonathan's honor.

See The Action Bible *pages 263, 285 and 1 Samuel 14:1–45; 18:1–3; 20:17–42; 31:1–6; 2 Samuel 1:19–27.*

JOPPA

An ancient seaport very near where Israel's largest city—Tel Aviv—now stands. Joppa is now called Jaffa and is a suburb of Tel Aviv. The old Joppa was a walled city that existed before the time of Moses. Here, Jonah caught a ship for Tarshish when he was trying to run away from God's command. Joppa is mentioned in the New Testament as the city where Peter raised Tabitha to life. It was also where Peter saw a vision that made him realize the gospel was for Gentiles as well as Jews.

See The Action Bible *pages 431, 672–677 and Jonah 1:3; Acts 9:36–43; 10. See also* Tabitha.

JORAM

Son of Ahab and king of Israel while Ahaziah (Joram's nephew) was king of Judah. The prophet Elisha prophesied that Jehu would become king of Israel because God wanted to carry out the judgment proclaimed by the prophet Elijah. Joram was killed by Jehu.

See The Action Bible *pages 407, 420 and 1 Kings 21:21–24; 2 Kings 5:5; 8:25–9:24.*

JORDAN RIVER

The most important river in Israel's history. It begins in the mountains north of the Sea of Galilee, runs into the Sea of Galilee, then out and down to the Dead Sea, where it ends. Because it is so winding, it actually travels about two hundred miles to cover its sixty-five-mile route. It is not a river that can be used for shipping; it has too many rapids and is only three to ten feet deep. The nation of Israel had to cross the Jordan to enter Canaan. God miraculously made it possible for them to cross over on dry land. John the Baptist preached in the wilderness along the Jordan River, and Jesus was baptized there by him.

See The Action Bible *pages 173, 197 and Joshua 3–4; Matthew 3:1–5. See also* Dead Sea.

JOSEPH, HUSBAND OF MARY

A carpenter who lived in Nazareth. When Mary was pregnant, an angel told Joseph that the Holy Spirit was the father of the child to be born and that Joseph should go ahead and marry her instead of ending their engagement. He was with Mary when Jesus was born in a stable in Bethlehem. After God spoke in a dream, Joseph moved his family to Egypt until King Herod died. Then they all returned to Nazareth, where Joseph taught Jesus the carpenter trade. Joseph is last mentioned in the Bible in the story of the family trip to Jerusalem when Jesus was twelve. Most scholars believe Joseph died before Jesus began His ministry.

See **The Action Bible** *pages 529–544 and Matthew 1:18–25; 2:13–23; Luke 2:41–52.*

JOSEPH OF ARIMATHEA

A rich Jewish man who was a member of the ruling council when Christ was crucified. He secretly believed in Jesus but was afraid to tell others. After Christ died on the cross, Joseph asked Pilate for permission to remove the body. He helped place Jesus's body in a new tomb he owned.

See **The Action Bible** *page 640 and Matthew 27:57; Mark 15:43; Luke 23:50–53; John 19:38–41.*

JOSEPH, SON OF JACOB

Joseph's father, Jacob, was ninety years old when Joseph was born, and Jacob favored Joseph over all his other sons. The older brothers were jealous and sold Joseph as a slave to a caravan of strangers going to Egypt. They made their father think that Joseph had been killed by a wild animal.

Meanwhile, Joseph was sold to Potiphar, an officer of the pharaoh. Joseph proved so trustworthy and skillful that he was given much responsibility. Later he was thrown into prison because Potiphar's wife lied about him. In prison, Joseph became known as a man who could tell what dreams meant. After he interpreted the dreams of the pharaoh, he became the chief ruler of the land—second to the pharaoh.

Several years later, Joseph's brothers came to Egypt to buy grain. They met Joseph but did not recognize him. Joseph put them through several tests to see if they were still cruel and thoughtless. Their actions showed that they had changed. Joseph then told them who he was and invited them to bring their father and their families to live in Egypt.

See The Action Bible *pages 89–111 and Genesis 37; 39–50.*

JOSHUA

Moses's assistant and military commander through Israel's forty years in the wilderness after the escape from Egypt. When Moses died just before Israel entered Canaan, Joshua became the new leader. He was at least seventy years old at that time. He led the army into battle against Jericho and many other cities. He also assigned specific areas to the tribes and encouraged them to drive out the remaining Canaanites in their areas. Joshua then dissolved his top command post and retired to an area near Mount Ephraim. He died at age 110.

See The Action Bible *pages 150, 173, 189–208 and Numbers 13–14; 27:15–23; Deuteronomy 34; the book of Joshua.*

JOSHUA, BOOK OF

The book of Joshua tells the stories of the battles Israel fought in Canaan and how the land was divided up among the various tribes. The book begins with Joshua taking over after Moses's death and ends with the death of Joshua. The first twelve chapters tell about the conquest of Canaan. Chapters 13–22 describe the division of Canaan. Chapters 22–24 tell how Joshua called all the leaders of Israel together and reminded them of all that God had done for them.

See The Action Bible *pages 189–208 and the book of Joshua. See also* Joshua.

JOSIAH

The sixteenth king of Judah and one of the godly kings in the Old Testament. He became king when he was eight years old, after his father had been killed by slaves in the palace. The people were worshipping idols. Worship of the Lord had almost been forgotten. When Josiah was sixteen, he ordered his men to break down the altars to foreign gods. When Josiah was twenty-six, the high priest discovered the book of the law that had not been seen or read for years. After getting the advice of the prophet Huldah, Josiah gathered all the leaders and many of the people of Judah to listen while the book of the law was read.

Josiah decided to do all that the book commanded. He ordered the Passover feast to be held. The Passover had not been celebrated for hundreds of years. Josiah was killed in a battle with Egypt in 609 BC when he was thirty-nine years old.

See The Action Bible *page 446 and 2 Kings 22:1–33:30; 2 Chronicles 34–35. See also* Hilkiah.

JUDAH

The tribe descended from Judah, the son of Jacob. When Joshua led the Israelites into Canaan, the tribe of Judah was assigned the land between the Dead Sea and the Mediterranean Sea. It was one of the largest territories, nearly forty-five miles wide and fifty miles long. The tribe of Simeon was assigned a large area south of Judah, but a lot of it was almost desert land. Over a period of hundreds of years, the tribe of Simeon became a part of Judah. King David came from the tribe of Judah, and so did Mary and Joseph.

Judah was the southern kingdom when the Israelites divided into two separate kingdoms after the death of King Solomon (around 930 BC). It was composed of Judah and Simeon, plus a small part of Benjamin, and also the kingdom of Edom. The southern kingdom was less than half the size of the northern kingdom, and much of its land was desert. It had a population of only about three hundred thousand.

At first Judah tried to force the northern kingdom to reunite with it but could not. This kingdom lasted until the capital city, Jerusalem, fell to the Babylonians in 586 BC. About forty years later, Babylonia was conquered by Persia. The Persian king, Cyrus, allowed the Jews to return to their own land. At least forty-three thousand went back to live and to rebuild the city of Jerusalem.

See The Action Bible *page 290 and 1 Kings 12–2 Kings 25. See also* Israel.

JUDAS ISCARIOT

The disciple who betrayed Jesus. He served as treasurer for the disciples. Although they trusted Judas, Jesus knew all along that Judas would betray Him.

When a woman came and put expensive ointment on Jesus's feet, Judas complained that the money it cost could have been used to feed many poor people. However, he did not really care about the poor—he just wanted the money.

We do not know why Judas finally decided to lead the enemies of Jesus to Him. The Bible says the chief priests paid him thirty pieces of silver. After Jesus was arrested, Judas felt so guilty for what he had done that he took the money and tried to give it back to the priests, but they refused it. He finally threw it on the floor of the temple. Then he went and hanged himself.

See The Action Bible *pages 566, 626, 634 and Matthew 26:47–50; 27:3–5; John 6:64; 12:3–8; 13:29.*

JUDE

The half brother of Christ and the writer of the book of Jude—one of the shorter books of the New Testament. His father was Joseph the carpenter. Like his brother James, Jude did not believe in Jesus at first, but later did.

See The Action Bible *page 741 and Matthew 13:55; the book of Jude.*

JUDE, BOOK OF

One of the shortest books in the New Testament. This letter was written by Jude, one of the half brothers of Jesus who did not believe in Jesus until after the resurrection. In this short letter, Jude warns his readers against false teachers. Jude writes that Christians must stay close to Jesus and obey Him.

See The Action Bible *page 741 and the book of Jude. See also* Jude.

JUDEA

The Old Testament name for the part of Palestine to which many Jews returned after they had been exiled in Babylonia. Since most of these people were from the tribe of Judah, the land was called Judea. In the New Testament, Judea refers to the southern part of Israel. It extended from the southern part of the Dead Sea north about sixty miles. It included Bethlehem, Jerusalem, and Jericho.

See The Action Bible *page 555 and Matthew 2:1; Acts 1:8.*

JUDGE

A government official who had different duties at different periods of history. In the time of Moses, judges settled arguments among the people. During the four hundred years before the Israelites asked for a king, God spoke through judges who led His people. They ruled during peacetimes and led in wars. Deborah, Gideon, and Samuel were well-known judges. After kings began to rule Israel, judges again became those who settled disputes and took care of official business. Six thousand Levites were appointed to be officers and judges.

See The Action Bible *pages 209–241 and Exodus 18:13–23; the book of Judges; 1 Samuel 7:15–16; 1 Chronicles 23:2–4.*

JUDGES, BOOK OF

This book of history tells what happened to the Israelites during the 350 years before Saul became king. There were several small nations or groups of people still in Canaan who often made war against the Israelites. They included the Philistines, the Hittites, the Amorites, and several other groups. The Israelites began to forget God, who had led them out of Egypt into their Promised Land. God allowed them to be conquered by their enemies. Sometimes, when the Israelites had a hard time with their enemies, they called on the Lord for help. God would raise up a judge to lead them and to defeat the enemy. But after the judge died, they would go back to their sinful ways. The book of Judges tells about thirteen such leaders. Judges 2:11–19 provides a summary of the whole book of Judges.

See The Action Bible *pages 209–241 and the book of Judges.*

JUDGMENT

An action taken against a wrongdoing. In the Old Testament judgment often meant God's punishment of a person or a nation for disobeying Him. During the time of the judges, God often judged the Israelites by letting an enemy country conquer them or treat them harshly. Later, prophets like Isaiah, Jeremiah, Ezekiel, Joel, Zephaniah, and many others preached about God's judgment of Israel and other nations.

In the New Testament, judgment also means to criticize or condemn someone. Jesus said Christians are not to judge each other. Judgment also refers to the end of the world as we know it, when God will judge (or punish) sin and reward those who have lived for God. Old Testament prophets like Joel and Obadiah described this

time as the day of judgment or the "day of the Lord."

See The Action Bible *pages 447, 451 and Joel 1:15; 2:31; Obadiah 15; Matthew 7:1; 12:36; 1 Corinthians 11:27–31. See also* Prophecy/Prophesy.

JUSTICE

Exercising fair judgment about a legal matter. Justice is one of God's characteristics. He is described as just, because He is always fair. Judges who decide legal cases were urged to provide justice for those who were hurt in some way by others. The Old Testament prophet Hosea urged the people of Israel to return to God and keep up a standard of justice.

See The Action Bible *page 436 and Deuteronomy 24:17; Psalm 9:16; Hosea 12:6.*

KINGDOM OF GOD

God's rule over people and places. In the Old Testament, God ruled over the people of Israel. In the New Testament, the kingdom people are Christians. When we say that Jesus is our Lord, we are saying that He is the King of our lives. Jesus mentioned God's kingdom in the prayer He taught His disciples. This means we are praying that all people will recognize God as King and obey Him.

The phrases *kingdom of God* and *kingdom of heaven* mean the same thing. The Jewish people said "kingdom of heaven" because they felt God's name was too sacred to speak.

The Bible speaks of an earthly kingdom of God and a heavenly

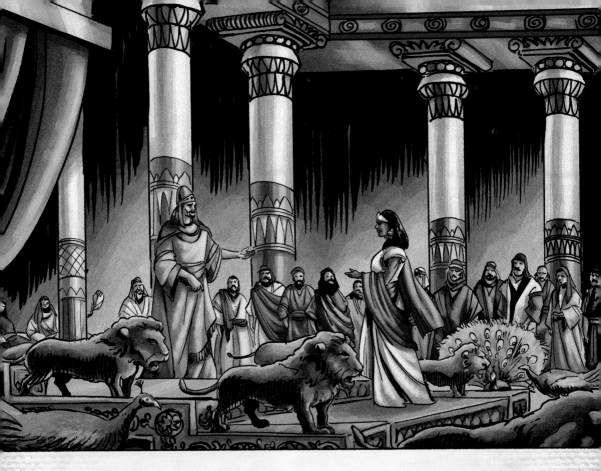

kingdom. God will finally remove evil from all of His creation. Then His kingdom (both earth and heaven) will be free from all sin.

See **The Action Bible** *page 545 and 1 Chronicles 28:5; Matthew 6:10; 13:31–33; Mark 4:26–32; Luke 10:9; 13:18–21; 22:18; 2 Timothy 4:18; 2 Peter 1:11.*

KINGS, 1 AND 2

First and 2 Kings originally were one book but were divided when the Old Testament was translated into Greek. Both are books of history.

First Kings records the stories of Israel's kings, from Solomon (about 970 BC) to Ahab (851 BC). First Kings includes the plan for and the building of Solomon's temple. It includes a long dedication of the temple as well as Solomon's prayer dedicating all the people to the worship of God (8:1–61).

First Kings also tells how the kingdom of Israel was divided into two kingdoms, Israel (northern kingdom) and Judah (southern kingdom), after the death of Solomon. A few of the kings who ruled were good. Many were wicked and worshipped false gods. First Kings tells how God sent prophets such as Elijah to call the people and the kings back to the Lord. Elijah's messages and the miracles God performed for him are recorded in 1 Kings 17–21.

Second Kings continues the history of the two kingdoms, Israel and Judah, from about 850 BC until the destruction of Jerusalem. Israel was defeated and many people were taken captive by Assyria in 722 BC. Judah was conquered by Babylon in 586 BC. Several prophets proclaimed God's judgment because of the wrongdoings of the kings and people of Judah and Israel. These prophets included Elisha, Amos, and Hosea in the northern kingdom and Obadiah, Joel, Isaiah, Micah, Nahum, Habakkuk, Zephaniah, and Jeremiah in the southern kingdom.

See **The Action Bible** pages 348–451 and the books of 1 and 2 Kings. See also Ahab; Athaliah; Jezebel; Josiah; Solomon.

KINSMAN-REDEEMER

A goel—a person, sometimes a relative—who paid the price to buy a slave his freedom. This person also was obligated to avenge the murder of a relative and marry the wife of his dead brother if that brother died before they had a son. After marriage, the firstborn son would be heir of the dead brother. The law of Moses had rules about kinsman-redeemers. Boaz was a kinsman-redeemer who married Ruth.

See **The Action Bible** page 243 and Genesis 38:8; Deuteronomy 25:5–10; Ruth 2:20–4:12.

KIRIATH JEARIM

A fortress-like city about twelve miles west of Jerusalem. About 1050 BC the Philistines captured the ark of the covenant in a battle with the Israelites. Later they returned it to Kiriath Jearim. The ark stayed in a specially built house for twenty years, until King David and many of the people of Israel brought it back to Jerusalem.

See **The Action Bible** page 318 and 1 Samuel 6:21–7:2; 2 Samuel 6:1–15.

KISHON RIVER

A brook in the mountains of what is now northwestern Israel near Lebanon. During the winter, the melting snows from the mountains make it dangerous to cross. On the banks of the Kishon, the army of Deborah and Barak defeated the Canaanites led by Sisera. Many of the Canaanite soldiers were washed away by the raging Kishon when their chariot wheels were bogged down in the mud and water. This was proof to the Israelites that God was with them in the battle.

See **The Action Bible** page 215 and Judges 5:21.

KORAH

A man who, with two of his friends, led a rebellion against Moses during the exodus. God caused the earth to open and swallow Korah, the other leaders of the rebellion, and their followers. This was a dramatic warning to the other Israelites against rebelling.

See The Action Bible *pages 179–180 and Numbers 16; 1 Chronicles 6:22.*

LABAN

The grandnephew of Abraham and brother of Rebekah. Laban's family remained near Haran when Abraham left to go to Canaan. Years later, Abraham wanted a wife for his son Isaac. He sent his most trusted servant back to his relatives near Haran—to the home of Laban's family.

After many years, Jacob, the son of Rebekah and Isaac, ran away to Haran because his brother, Esau, was very angry with him. Jacob fell in love with Laban's daughter Rachel. He agreed to work for Laban seven years in order to earn Rachel as his bride. But Laban tricked Jacob and sent Leah, his older daughter, to be Jacob's wife instead. Jacob asked to work seven more years in order to have Rachel as his wife also. Laban agreed, and Rachel and Jacob were married. After the second seven-year period, Jacob worked for six more years. When he decided to leave, Laban tried to trick him again by cheating Jacob of the wages he had earned. Jacob outsmarted Laban before leaving.

See The Action Bible *pages 66, 79 and Genesis 24:29–50; 29–30. See also Jacob/Israel; Leah; Rachel; Rebekah.*

LAMB

(SEE SHEEP/LAMB)

LAMB OF GOD

A name for Jesus that shows His mission: to sacrifice Himself for all of the wrongs ever committed. That name was especially meaningful to people in Jesus's day when lambs were sacrificed as part of many worship services. When John the Baptist saw Jesus, he used this name. The apostle Peter also called Jesus "the Lamb." In the book of Revelation, a lamb is often a word picture for Jesus.

See The Action Bible *page 743 and John 1:29; 1 Peter 1:18–19; Revelation 5:12–13; 7:14; 13:8; 22:1–3.*

LAMENTATIONS, BOOK OF

An Old Testament book of poems Jeremiah wrote around 580 BC, after Jerusalem was destroyed. Babylon had captured Judah and taken many of the people away. The people left in Jerusalem were suffering. Although they worked very hard, many were hungry. Their friends and families were far away. Jeremiah suffered with them. He put his and their feelings into words in the poems in Lamentations. Even when Jeremiah was very discouraged, he was able to write about God's great faithfulness.

See **The Action Bible** *page 468 and the book of Lamentations.*

LAST SUPPER

The last meal Jesus ate with His disciples before His crucifixion. This Passover meal took place on a Thursday evening in an upper room of a house in Jerusalem.

Almost everything about it was unusual, starting earlier in the day, when Jesus sent Peter and John to find a place for the meal. He told them to enter Jerusalem and then follow a man carrying a water pitcher. When the man arrived at home, the two disciples were to ask to use one of the rooms in the house for the evening. Everything happened as Jesus had described.

After the meal was finished, Jesus shocked His disciples by washing their feet, which was a slave's job. He also announced that one of His disciples would betray Him and that Peter would deny knowing Him. During this meal, Jesus started a tradition now known as Communion. Afterward, they sang a hymn and left for the garden of Gethsemane.

See The Action Bible *page 623 and Matthew 26:17–30; John 13–14. See also* Lord's Supper/Communion.

LAW, THE

(SEE TORAH)

LAZARUS OF BETHANY

A close friend of Jesus. He was the brother of Martha and Mary. Jesus often visited Lazarus's house in Bethany. Jesus didn't rush to help when Lazarus was sick, and Lazarus died. Both Martha and Mary knew of Jesus's power, and each wondered why He didn't come earlier. But Jesus had a special reason: to bring Lazarus back to life. Later, the chief priests wanted to kill Lazarus because so many people heard about the miracle and believed in Jesus.

See The Action Bible *page 604 and John 11:1–46; 12:9–11.*

LEAH

Jacob's first wife and the mother of Reuben, Simeon, Levi, Judah, Issachar, Zebulun, and Dinah. Jacob's second wife was Leah's younger sister, Rachel. Jacob had worked for seven years in order to marry Rachel, but Laban, the women's father, sent Leah to the wedding instead. Jacob was disappointed but worked another seven years for Rachel. Although Leah knew she was not the favorite, she was loyal to Jacob. She went with him to Canaan when he left Laban's house.

See The Action Bible *page 79 and Genesis 29:21–30; 35:23. See also* Jacob/Israel; Rachel; Rebekah.

LEBANON

A mountain range in the southern part of the country also called Lebanon. *Lebanon* means "the white" and probably refers to the snow that covers the tops of the mountains most of the year. The high, rugged peaks are famous for their beauty. Tall trees from these mountains, called the cedars of Lebanon, were used to build the temple of Solomon.

See The Action Bible *page 359 and 1 Kings 5:1–18.*

LEVITES

(SEE PRIESTS)

LEVITICUS, BOOK OF

The third book of the Old Testament has been called "the priests' hand-book" because it sets rules for the worship ceremonies as well as for everyday life. It is named for the tribe of Levi, from which all priests of Israel came. The first seven chapters provide rules for offering sacrifices. Other chapters provide rules about what foods to eat, cleanliness, observing the Sabbath, and other actions. Chapter 16 was especially important. It described the Day of Atonement, the day the high priest entered the Most Holy Place in the tabernacle or temple, and gave an offering for his wrongdoings, his family's, and those of the nation.

See **The Action Bible** *pages 164–165 and the book of Leviticus.*

LIONS

Lions were well-known to the people of Israel, but they are now extinct in the Middle East. They were feared as killers, as in the story of Daniel and the lions' den. David told Saul that he killed lions and bears that tried to take sheep from his flock. Lions were respected for their strength and majestic beauty. Jesus is called the "Lion of the tribe of Judah." This title came from a blessing Jacob gave to his son Judah, who was called "a lion's cub." Jesus was born into the tribe of Judah.

See **The Action Bible** *pages 31, 272 and Genesis 49:8–10; 1 Samuel 17:34–37; Daniel 6; Revelation 5:5.*

LOCUSTS

An insect much like a grasshopper. Swarms of locusts would travel long distances, eating everything green. Locusts were the eighth plague God sent to Egypt before the Israelites were freed. Millions of locusts form multiple swarms. Locusts were also eaten for food. The Old Testament book of Joel was written after crops in Israel had been destroyed by locusts. Locusts were also used as a word picture for a multitude of people. The Midianites who were about to attack Israel were called "locusts."

See **The Action Bible** *page 134 and Exodus 10:1–20; Judges 6:5.*

LORD

(SEE JEHOVAH)

LORD'S DAY/SABBATH

The weekly day of rest and worship and the day set aside to honor Jesus. It was observed on the seventh day of the week (Saturday). Because Jesus rose from the dead on the first day of the week (Sunday), many early Christians used that day to worship and remember Him.

The idea of the Sabbath goes back to creation. The Bible mentions that God "rested" from all His work on the seventh day of creation. This is why keeping the Sabbath is one of the Ten Commandments given to Moses. God meant for the Sabbath to be a day of rest, worship, and remembrance that He brought Israel out of slavery in Egypt.

Later, during the time of Jesus, Pharisees and scribes tried to clarify what could and could not be done on the Sabbath. Jesus regularly worshipped in the synagogue on the Sabbath. He sometimes ignored the long list of the Pharisees' rules if they interfered with helping people. He healed people on the Sabbath, although the Pharisees thought healing was "work" and thus was against the Law.

See The Action Bible *page 149 and Genesis 2:3; Exodus 20:8–11; 34:21; Deuteronomy 5:12–15; Matthew 12:1–14; Mark 2:23–3:6; Luke 4:13–49; John 5:1–18; 20:1–25; Acts 20:7.*

LORD'S SUPPER/ COMMUNION

A special meal to remember Jesus's death and resurrection. As Jesus ate His last meal with His disciples, He took bread, broke it into pieces, and told His disciples to eat it. This was a way of saying that His body would soon be broken on the cross. Then He held up a cup of wine and proclaimed that it was the blood He would soon shed on the cross. Christians through the centuries have continued to take part in the Lord's Supper.

See The Action Bible *page 623 and Matthew 26:26–28; Mark 14:22–24; Luke 22:17–19; 1 Corinthians 11:20–34. See also* Last Supper.

LOT

Abraham's nephew. Lot went with Abraham from Ur to their new home in Canaan. After they reached Canaan, problems arose when their herdsmen quarreled. When Abraham decided

that he and Lot must have separate land, Lot chose the land that looked better for his cattle. But that selfish decision led to trouble for Lot and his family. Lot and his family later moved to nearby Sodom. God later destroyed the wicked cities of Sodom and Gomorrah.

See The Action Bible *pages 48, 53 and Genesis 11:31; 13–14.*

LOT'S WIFE

When God sent two angels to destroy the city of Sodom for the evil actions of its citizens, Lot's family was told to run and not look back. But as Lot's wife looked back to watch fire and brimstone fall on the cities of Sodom and Gomorrah, she was destroyed also. Her body turned into a pillar of salt.

See The Action Bible *page 55 and Genesis 19:15–28.*

LOVE

More than just a feeling of being attracted to someone or of feeling happy with someone—as we do with family, friends, or pets. Love means choosing to be kind and helpful to others even though we may not want to do so. When Jesus was asked to name the greatest commandment, love was the answer He gave: love God; love people.

Love comes from God. God shows His love for us by caring for us all the time. He also showed it by sending His Son, Jesus, to take away our sins.

There are different types of love: the love between friends and the love we are to have for all people.

Unconditional love is the most special kind of love there is. Unconditional love means you continue to love a person regardless of how that person acts. This is the love God shows. God's power helps us love others, even our enemies.

See The Action Bible *pages 555, 617 and Matthew 5:43–48; 22:37–40; John 3:16; 17:26; 1 Corinthians 13; Galatians 5:22; 1 John 2:10–17; 3:14; 4:7–16. See also* Fruit of the Spirit.

LUKE

A well-educated Gentile doctor. He wrote two New Testament books: the gospel of Luke and the book of Acts. He traveled with the apostle Paul, who called him the "beloved physician." His writing style shows his careful attention to details and accuracy— traits he may have learned as a doctor. Scholars believe he may have come from Macedonia (northern Greece). Tradition says he was martyred in Greece.

See The Action Bible *page 708 and Acts 1:1; 20; Colossians 4:14.*

LUKE, GOSPEL OF

Written about AD 60 by the only Gentile gospel writer—Luke, a doctor who traveled with Paul during Paul's missionary journeys. Luke wrote his gospel for Gentiles to record in an orderly way exactly what Jesus said and did. He records the full story of the birth of Jesus and includes a story from the boyhood of Jesus that no other gospel has. Throughout the book, Luke shows Jesus's concern for people. He also points out the many

times Jesus prayed—at His baptism, after cleansing the leper, before calling His disciples, on the Mount of Transfiguration, on the cross, and at His death. Luke also includes many of Jesus's parables, including the Good Samaritan (10:25–37); the lost sheep (15:1–7); the lost coin (15:8–10); and the lost son (15:11–31).

See The Action Bible *pages 523, 526, 593–603 and the gospel of Luke. See also* Luke.

LYDDA

A village, sometimes called Lod, about thirty miles northwest of Jerusalem. Jews returning after the Babylonian exile settled there for a while. Peter helped the people in a church here.

See The Action Bible *pages 672–673 and Ezra 2:33; Nehemiah 7:37; Acts 9:32–38.*

LYDIA

A wealthy businesswoman in Philippi and Paul's first convert in Europe. She heard about Jesus while praying with other women by a river. She believed what Paul told her about Jesus. After her whole family and her servants believed and were baptized, she invited Paul and his traveling companions to stay at her home. The church at Philippi met at her house.

See The Action Bible *page 710 and Acts 16:13–15, 40.*

LYING

Any action or word that is meant to fool someone else. God is truth, and He expects His people to speak the truth. Jesus called Satan "the father of lies." This meant that Satan tries to influence people to lie. All types of lying are considered wrong in the Bible, but especially bad is someone who gives "false testimony"—telling something untrue about another person in order to hurt that person. This is one of the Ten Commandments.

Some lies were fatal. Ananias and his wife, Sapphira, lied to God and died instantly! But people who lied weren't always put to death. When the pharaoh of Egypt ordered the deaths of all newborn boys, two midwives lied to him in order to save the lives of the babies.

See The Action Bible *pages 664–665 and Exodus 1:15–22; 20:16; John 1:17; 8:44; 14:6; Acts 5:1–11. See also* Witness.

LYSTRA

A Roman colony in what is now Turkey. Paul healed a lame man there and returned several times on his missionary journeys. Timothy came from Lystra.

See The Action Bible *page 699 and Acts 14:1–11; 16:1.*

MACCABEES

A priest named Mattathias and his sons were the leaders of a revolt in 168–167 BC to make Syria stop persecuting the Jews in Israel. One of the sons, Judas, was called Maccabeus (meaning "the hammerer") because of his fighting ability. Later all the men in the revolt were called Maccabees. The revolution brought some freedom for the Jews. Judas and his men camped in the mountains and fought against the Syrians and those who sided with the Syrians. The Maccabees tore down

altars to false gods and asked other Jewish people to join them. Syria sent in its army, but the Maccabees defeated the Syrian army.

After driving away the Syrians, Judas Maccabeus worked to restore the worship of God in Palestine. He cleansed the temple and began proper sacrifices to God. An eight-day celebration called the Feast of Dedication (Hanukkah) began during this time. The gospel of John has a record of a time when Jesus attended the Feast of Dedication at the temple.

See The Action Bible *page 518 and John 10:22. See also* Urim and Thummin/Lots.

MACEDONIA

A Roman province in New Testament times located in the northern part of modern Greece. It was the first part of Europe to hear about Jesus. The apostle Paul visited Macedonia many times. Paul first traveled to Macedonia after he had a vision of a man asking

for help. Paul left right away and landed at Philippi, the leading city in Macedonia. There he met Lydia, and when she accepted Christ, the first church in Europe began.

See The Action Bible *page 709 and Acts 16:9–10.*

MAGI/WISE MEN

A name used for the astrologers from the East who came to Bethlehem to honor the child Jesus. Whether there were three or not, the Bible does not mention.

See The Action Bible *page 535 and Matthew 2. See* Frankincense; Myrrh.

MAHANAIM

A city in Gilead to which Ish-bosheth, the son of Saul and David, traveled at different points. David fled from his son Absalom, and Ish-bosheth was brought here to be made king by Abner, the former general of Saul's army.

See The Action Bible *page 343 and 2 Samuel 2:8; 17:24–18:18.*

MAKEUP AND JEWELRY

Makeup has been in existence at least since 2000 BC. Many women, particularly women in Egypt, used kohl sticks to highlight their eyes. Some also used ocher and turquoise malachite to make powders to decorate their eyes. Yet many times in the Bible, women described as "painting their eyes" had bad reputations. Queen Jezebel is an example. She put on makeup and fixed her hair when Jehu, the new king of Israel, came to town.

Oils and perfumes were made from olives, almonds, and the leaves or bark of trees. Some expensive perfumes included aloes, nard, myrrh, and frankincense.

Men and women wore jewelry including necklaces, earrings, nose rings, and rings on toes, ankles, and wrists. The golden calf the people of Israel demanded that Aaron make had been made from melted gold jewelry. A signet ring was worn as a sign of status. It also was pressed on wax and used on documents as a sign that the document was authentic. The pharaoh of Egypt gave Joseph a signet ring and a gold chain as a sign of Joseph's new status in Egypt. Eliezar, the servant of Abraham, gave Rebekah silver and gold jewelry when she agreed to marry Abraham's son Isaac.

See The Action Bible *pages 98, 156, 418–421 and Genesis 24:19–23, 47, 53; 41:42; Exodus 30:22–38; 32:2–4; 2 Kings 9:30; Psalm 133:2; Isaiah 3:18–24.*

MALACHI

The prophet who wrote the last book of the Old Testament. He lived around 450 BC and predicted that those who were not true to God would be judged. In his book, Malachi asked questions to make the people think about their lives. He criticized priests for being careless in conducting worship. He condemned the people who were not giving God their tithes and trying to cheat God. Malachi looked forward to the coming of the Messiah. Although Malachi preached about judgment, he reminded the people that God cared for them.

See The Action Bible *page 516 and the book of Malachi.*

MALTA

An island in the Mediterranean Sea about fifty miles southwest of Sicily. It is now called the Republic of Malta.

See The Action Bible *page 733 and Acts 27:39–28:10.*

MANASSEH

Manasseh and Ephraim were the sons of Joseph by his wife, Asenath, the daughter of an Egyptian priest. They were adopted by their grandfather Jacob. Their descendants formed one tribe of Israel.

When the people of Israel arrived at the Promised Land, the half tribe of Manasseh and the tribes of Reuben and Gad settled east of the Jordan River. Those on the west side were given good land, and they were important among the twelve tribes. Their land stretched from the Jordan River to the Mediterranean Sea through the middle of Canaan. They later became part of the northern kingdom of Israel. Those who stayed on the east side became idol worshippers. All of the people of Manasseh later were taken away as prisoners to Assyria.

See The Action Bible *page 110 and Genesis 41:50–52; 48:8–20; Numbers 32; Joshua 13:8–33; 17:7–10. See also* Ephraim.

MANGER

A feedbox for cattle or horses. It was usually filled with straw, hay, or oats. The most well-known manger was the

one where Jesus was laid when He was born in Bethlehem.

See The Action Bible *pages 533–535 and Luke 2:7–16.*

MANNA

A grain-like food God provided for the Israelites while they wandered in the wilderness. The name *manna* means "What is it?" because that is the question the people asked when they first saw it. In a miraculous way, manna appeared fresh every night on the ground so the people could gather it in the morning. They could use it in many ways. They could grind it up and make cakes, or they could boil it. The Bible says it looked like white seeds or flakes and tasted like wafers made with honey.

See The Action Bible *page 148 and Exodus 16:13–36; Numbers 11:7–9.*

MANOAH

Samson's father. Manoah and his wife had wanted a child for a long time. One day an angel appeared to Manoah's wife and told her that she would have a son and that she should dedicate him to the Lord as a Nazirite. Manoah asked God to send the angel again so they could ask him what to do with their son. When the angel came, he repeated his instructions. The angel's word came true. A son—Samson—was born, and Manoah and his wife raised him according to the strict Nazirite laws.

See The Action Bible *page 222 and Judges 13–14. See also* Oaths and Vows.

MARK/JOHN MARK

The writer of the second gospel and a friend of Peter. John was his Jewish name; Mark or Marcus was his Roman name. In the New Testament, he is called Mark, John Mark, and John. Mark's mother, Mary, lived in Jerusalem in a large house. She was a Christian, and when Mark was a young man, he met many of the early Christian leaders. Peter referred to him as "my son" because of their close friendship. Mark started out with Paul and Barnabas, a relative, on a missionary journey but did not finish it, perhaps because of homesickness or some disagreement with Paul. Mark

went along with Barnabas on his next journey and proved himself. Later Paul highly recommended Mark as a good Christian worker. Mark spent some time with Paul in Rome, and it was probably there he wrote the gospel that has his name.

See The Action Bible *page 694 and Acts 12:12, 25; 13:13; 15:36–41; 2 Timothy 4:11; Philemon 24; 1 Peter 5:13.*

MARK, GOSPEL OF

This gospel was the first of the four to be written—around AD 55–65 by John Mark, a relative of Barnabas. Mark records Jesus's actions more than His words. Mark did not write about Jesus's birth or childhood. He starts with Jesus as a grown man meeting John the Baptist. This gospel tells about Jesus's temptation, His work in His home region of Galilee, and His choosing and training of disciples. It describes many of Jesus's miracles and shows that Jesus was a helper of others as well as Master of the universe.

See The Action Bible *pages 523, 560–561, 696 and the gospel of Mark. See also* Mark/John Mark.

MARRIAGE

A special relationship between a man and a woman that is legally binding. Marriage began in the garden of Eden as a way for human beings to give and receive love and companionship. When God created Eve for Adam, this was the first marriage.

Later, some men had more than one wife. The Bible never says this is good; it simply tells what the people did. In fact, the Old Testament includes many stories about problems that arose when men had more than one wife.

The Bible gives many instructions about marriage. Husbands and wives are to love each other, submit to each other, enjoy each other, and respect each other.

Marriage is sometimes used in the Bible as a word picture of God's relationship with His people. In the Old Testament, God is described as the husband and the people of Israel as His bride. Later, when Jesus came to earth, He described Himself as the Bridegroom and the church as His bride.

See The Action Bible *pages 64, 299, 323 and Genesis 2:24; Matthew 9:15; Ephesians 5:22–33; Revelation 22:17.*

MARS HILL

A little hill in downtown Athens near the temple to the ancient Greek gods. The Greek council met there in New Testament times, and Paul was brought here to explain his message. Paul delivered a famous sermon at this place.

See The Action Bible *page 718 and Acts 17:16–34.*

MARTHA OF BETHANY

A close friend of Jesus. Mary, her brother, Lazarus, and sister, Mary, lived in Bethany, just two miles outside of Jerusalem. Jesus often visited them for meals, and Martha seemed to be the hostess on these occasions.

See The Action Bible *page 597 and Luke 10:38–42; John 11:1–44. See also* Lazarus of Bethany; Mary of Bethany.

MARY MAGDALENE

A follower of Jesus and the first person to whom Jesus appeared after His resurrection. She was called "Magdalene" because she came from the town of Magdala on the Sea of Galilee. Like Jesus, she was a Galilean. The Bible mentions that Jesus cast seven demons out of Mary.

See **The Action Bible** *page 642 and Mark 16:9; Luke 8:2; John 20:11–18.*

MARY, MOTHER OF JESUS

The woman God chose to be the mother of His Son. When the angel Gabriel told her she would give birth to God's Son, she asked, "How can this be?" The angel explained that God would work a miracle through her and that the child to be born would not be Joseph's son, but the Son of God. She responded with a beautiful hymn of praise. Shortly after that she married Joseph, a carpenter to whom she was engaged. Mary remembered all the wonderful events surrounding Jesus's birth and probably shared them later with the apostles and the gospel writers.

When Jesus was twelve years old, Mary and Joseph were amazed that Jesus taught the teachers in the temple. Years later, at a wedding in the village of Cana, she asked Jesus to perform His first miracle. When Jesus was dying on the cross, He asked His disciple John to care for her. Later, Mary seems to have been active in the early church.

See **The Action Bible** *pages 528–544 and Matthew 1–2; Luke 1–2; John 2:1–11; 19:25–27; Acts 1:14.*

MARY OF BETHANY

The sister of Martha and Lazarus. Jesus often visited her family home in Bethany. Mary liked to sit with the disciples and listen to Jesus teach. When Martha scolded her for not helping prepare a meal, Jesus said that Mary had made the better choice. Mary also watched as Jesus brought her dead brother, Lazarus, back to life. Another time Mary was so filled with love for Jesus that she poured expensive perfume on His feet. Jesus appreciated her gift and told those around Him that this was a sign He was being prepared for burial.

See **The Action Bible** *pages 597, 605 and Luke 10:38–42; John 11:2–31; 12:1–8. See also* **Lazarus.**

MASTER

A name for Jesus used in the New Testament, especially in the gospel of Luke. The name showed respect for Jesus as a teacher and guide. The

disciples called Jesus "Master" when they were in the middle of a storm and wanted His help.

See The Action Bible *page 572 and Luke 8:24.*

MATTHEW

A tax collector and one of Jesus's disciples. He was also called Levi. He wrote the first book of the New Testament, the gospel of Matthew. He was well prepared to write a story of Jesus's life, because tax collectors were skilled at writing and keeping records. Also, as a disciple, Matthew was with Jesus during Jesus's ministry. Matthew met Jesus while he was collecting taxes for King Herod Antipas in Galilee. Jesus walked up to him and said, "Follow me." Matthew immediately left his business.

See The Action Bible *page 563 and Matthew 9:9–13; Luke 5:27–32.* *See also* Apostles/Disciples; Tax.

MATTHEW, GOSPEL OF

Matthew, a former tax collector and disciple of Jesus, wrote this gospel in AD 60–65 for Jewish readers. This gospel often shows how Jesus fulfilled the Old Testament prophecies. Jesus was the King the Jewish people had been looking for. Matthew traced Jesus's ancestors back to King David, and then further back to Abraham. Matthew told about the birth of Jesus and the visit of the magi to honor Him. Matthew included several collections of Jesus's teachings. Chapters 26–28 describe the Last Supper, arrest, trial, death, and resurrection of Jesus. Matthew's gospel ends with the Great Commission just before Jesus was taken to heaven.

See The Action Bible *pages 523–525 and the gospel of Matthew. See also* Matthew.

MATTHIAS

(SEE APOSTLES/DISCIPLES)

MEDES

(SEE PERSIA/PERSIANS)

MEDITERRANEAN SEA

An ocean that goes from Gibraltar to the coast of Lebanon (twenty-two hundred miles). Paul and other missionaries sailed on this ocean many times.

See The Action Bible *page 173 and Deuteronomy 11:24; Joshua 16:8; Acts 10:6.*

MELON

The melons eaten by the people of Israel while in Egypt were probably watermelons.

See The Action Bible *page 167 and Numbers 11:5.*

MESSIAH/SAVIOR

The Hebrew word for "anointed one." It applies in a special way to Jesus. The Old Testament nearly always speaks of God as the Savior of His people. He saved His people from Egyptian slavery and delivered them from enemies in many other ways. The Messiah would be a special Savior, one who would bring peace and establish His kingdom. The people of Israel looked forward to the day when this Messiah would come. But many didn't understand what the Messiah would do. They wanted the Savior to defeat their Gentile rulers—the Romans. Instead, the Messiah was a suffering servant who had come to die for wrongs He didn't commit.

When Jesus first began to teach and preach, He went to the synagogue and read a passage about the anointed one from Isaiah 61. He then announced that this passage had now come true.

See **The Action Bible** *pages 23, 541, 600 and Isaiah 61:1–2; Luke 4:16–21; 1 John 4:14. See also* **Christ.**

MICAH, BOOK OF

An Old Testament book written by the prophet Micah just before Israel was conquered in 722 BC. In his book, Micah preached against the sins of the people. Micah predicted that the northern and southern kingdoms of Israel would be defeated by their enemies. But he also told how God would some day bless His people. The Messiah would come to fulfill God's plan. Bethlehem would be the place where the ruler of Israel would be born. Micah reminded everyone that although God sees the sins of His people, He loves and forgives those who repent.

See **The Action Bible** *page 436 and the book of Micah.*

MICAIAH

A prophet sent by God to tell King Ahab of the destruction God had in store for Ahab. While four hundred prophets lied, Micaiah told the truth. God allowed Micaiah to have a vision of God's throne room.

See **The Action Bible** *page 398 and 1 Kings 22.*

MICHAL

(SEE DAVID)

MIDIAN/MIDIANITES

The Midianites were the descendants of Midan, the son of Abraham and his second wife, Keturah. They lived east of the Jordan River in the Sinai Peninsula. Moses married a Midianite (Zipporah). When the Israelites were in the wilderness after they left Egypt, the Midianites seemed friendly to them. Two hundred years after Israel settled in Canaan, the Midianites made life miserable for the Israelites, raiding their villages and trampling their crops. God chose Gideon to drive the Midianites out.

See **The Action Bible** *pages 173, 216 and Exodus 2:15–21; 18:1–11; Judges 6–7.*

MINISTER

A word that means "to serve." It also refers to a person who serves. Today it usually means a pastor. The apostle Paul wrote to Timothy that he had been appointed by God for this kind of service.

See **The Action Bible** *page 391 and 1 Corinthians 9:14; 1 Timothy 1:12; 2 Timothy 1:11.*

MIRACLES/WONDERS

Amazing acts done by the power of God. Miracles may be beyond the known laws of nature, but they are not magic. God performed great wonders and gave many people the power to do great things. In the Old Testament, prophets like Moses, Elijah, and Elisha performed great deeds. In the New Testament, Jesus proved that He was the promised Savior by the

amazing acts He did: healing people of sickness; feeding over five thousand people; turning water into wine; raising dead people to life; and walking on water. The Holy Spirit gave Jesus's disciples the power to do miracles.

See The Action Bible *pages 122–123, 381, 552–553, 577–581 and Exodus 3:1–4:5; 7–15; 1 Kings 17:17–24; 2 Kings 4; Matthew 8:1–2; 14:22–33; John 2:1–11; 6:1–13.*

MIRIAM

An Old Testament prophet and poet. She was the sister of Moses and Aaron. As a young girl, she looked after the baby Moses when he was hidden in a basket on the Nile River to save his life. As an adult, Miriam joined Moses and Aaron on the exodus of the Israelites from Egypt. After escaping from the Egyptians in the miraculous crossing of the Red Sea, Miriam composed a song of praise to the Lord and led the other women in celebrating the victory. But Miriam and Aaron criticized Moses for choosing a wife they didn't think was suitable. For this unwise criticism Miriam was cursed with leprosy. But Moses prayed for her, and God said Miriam would have to stay outside the camp for seven days until she was cured.

See The Action Bible pages 114, 144, 272 and Exodus 2:4, 7–8; 15:20–21; Numbers 12:1–15; 20:1. See also Aaron; Moses; Princess of Egypt.

MIZPAH

A name that means "watchtower." The Bible mentions two places known as Mizpah: the hometown of Jephthah, a judge of Israel, and a town in the territory allotted to Benjamin. The prophet Samuel gathered the people at Mizpah for a special meeting—to get them to give up their idols. But their enemies, the Philistines, decided to attack them. God rescued His people.

See The Action Bible page 255 and Joshua 18:26; Judges 11; 20; 1 Samuel 7.

MOAB

The land east of the Dead Sea. Moses died on Mount Pisgah in Moab. Joshua was chosen on the nearby plains to be Israel's next leader. Some events in the book of Ruth took place in Moab, and Ruth was from this country. This story took place in a time of peace between Israel and Moab. But trouble began again around 850 BC. King Ahab demanded heavy tribute (a kind of tax) from Mesha, the king of Moab. Mesha rebelled, and Jehoram, king of the northern kingdom, and Jehoshaphat, king of Judah, defeated Moab and ruined the land. Moab never again became a strong nation.

See The Action Bible page 247 and 2 Kings 3:4–27.

MOABITES

The nation in the family line of Lot's grandson Moab. They lived east of the southern part of the Dead Sea and were enemies of the Israelites. When the Israelites left Egypt for Canaan, the Moabites refused to let them pass through their land. Almost a hundred years later, the Moabites joined the Ammonites and the Amalekites and ruled over Israel for eighteen years. Finally Ehud, a man from the tribe of Benjamin, killed the Moabite king.

See The Action Bible page 242 and Judges 3:12–25; 11:17–18; Numbers 22:1–25:9. See also Ehud; Moab.

MORDECAI

A relative and adviser to Queen Esther. Mordecai and Esther lived in Susa, the Persian capital, about 486–465 BC. After Esther became the king's wife, Mordecai saved the king's life by warning him of a plot against him. But when an angry Haman tried to have Mordecai and all the Jews killed, Mordecai told Esther she should reveal to the king that she was Jewish and try to get the king to protect her people. Esther succeeded. After Haman's death, Mordecai replaced Haman as chief minister to the king.

See The Action Bible pages 491–505 and Esther 2–10. See also Xerxes/Ahasuerus; Esther; Feasts; Haman.

MOSES

Old Testament prophet and chosen leader of the Hebrew people (the Israelites) as they left slavery in Egypt. Moses wrote the first five books of the Bible. Because he received the Ten Commandments and the Old Testament Law from God, he is known as the "Lawgiver."

Moses's life shows that God's plans cannot be defeated. When Moses was a baby, the pharaoh ordered that all male Hebrew babies were to be killed. Moses's mother placed him in a basket, and Moses's sister, Miriam, watched over it. The basket and baby were found by an Egyptian princess, who adopted Moses. She hired Moses's mother to take care of him until Moses was a little older. In this way, Moses grew up understanding the beliefs and customs of both the Hebrews and the Egyptians.

Moses was not perfect. At times, his temper got the better of him. He killed an Egyptian while trying to defend an Israelite slave and ran away to Midian. There, he lived as a shepherd and the husband of Zipporah, the daughter of a priest. But forty years later, God called Moses to be a shepherd of people instead of sheep!

During their forty years in the wilderness, the people constantly grumbled against Moses and Aaron. Many times Moses was discouraged. Sometimes he disobeyed God. But he was still a great leader. He had to organize a mass of people, settle their arguments, answer their complaints, and try to teach them how to worship God.

Moses and all the other adults (except Joshua and Caleb) who left Egypt were not permitted to enter the Promised Land because of their earlier sins of doubting and disobeying God.

Moses died at age 120 and was buried in the land of Moab.

See The Action Bible *pages 112–189 and the books of Exodus–Deuteronomy.* *See also* Jethro; Zipporah.

MOUNT HERMON

The tallest mountain in northern Israel. It is the source of the streams that become the Jordan River. It is snowcapped most of the year and is one of the most beautiful sights in the area. Some Bible scholars believe that Jesus's transfiguration took place here or on Mount Tabor.

See The Action Bible *pages 584–585 and Deuteronomy 3:8–9; Joshua 11:17; Psalm 133:3.*

MOUNT HOR

The name of two mountains: (1) the mountain where Aaron was buried. This mountain is probably a sandstone mountain in what is now the Sinai Peninsula about one hundred miles south of Jerusalem. It has twin peaks. (2) The mountain that marked the northern boundary of Israel's land. It is probably one of the peaks in what we know as the Lebanon mountain range.

See The Action Bible *page 182 and Numbers 20:22–23; 21:4; 34:7–8; Deuteronomy 32:50.*

MOUNT MORIAH

The place where God told Abraham to offer Isaac as a sacrifice. Isaac was spared, however, when God provided an animal for the sacrifice. The exact location is not known, but many people believe this is the same Mount Moriah on which Solomon built his temple—a rocklike hill in the center of Jerusalem today.

See The Action Bible *pages 60–63 and Genesis 22:2; 2 Chronicles 3:1.*

MOUNT OF OLIVES

Sometimes called Olivet. It is not really a mountain but rather a rounded ridge east of Jerusalem that stands higher than other parts of the city. The Valley of Kidron lies between the city walls and this mountainous ridge. The ridge is about a mile long with four small peaks on it.

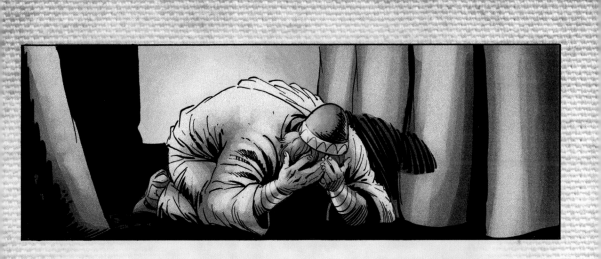

In this wooded area, people came to get away from the heat and crowds of the city. Jesus often taught His disciples there. The garden of Gethsemane, where Jesus prayed before His crucifixion, is somewhere on the hill. Jesus began His triumphal entry into Jerusalem from this place on the Sunday before His crucifixion. He also returned to heaven from this place.

The ridge was important in the defense of Jerusalem. When the Romans destroyed the city in AD 70, the soldiers camped on this hill, where they could get a good view of the city. Today, the Mount of Olives is heavily populated with hotels, homes, businesses, and Hebrew University.

See The Action Bible *page 625 and Matthew 21:1–3; 24:3–25:46; 26:30–46. See also Gethsemane/Garden of Gethsemane.*

MOUNT SINAI

Also known as Mount Horeb, this is the place where Moses went to receive the Ten Commandments from God. It is also the place to which Elijah fled to escape the anger of Jezebel. We are not sure of the exact location of this mountain, but most scholars believe it is one of the mountains in the southern part of the Sinai Peninsula.

See The Action Bible *page 121 and Exodus 19; 1 Kings 19:1–8.*

MOUNT TABOR

A mountain east of Nazareth. Barak mustered his troops here before the battle with the Canaanites. This might also be the place where Jesus was transfigured.

See The Action Bible *page 213 and Judges 4; Matthew 17:1–13.*
See also *Transfiguration, the.*

MOURNING

Showing sadness or sorrow, usually at a person's death, but sometimes because of a wrongdoing. When people in Bible times learned of a death or other tragedy, they often tore their clothes. Sometimes mourners sprinkled dust or ashes on their heads. People often wore clothing made of coarse material (such as goat hair) as a sign of mourning. Another mourning custom was to cover one's head with a heavy veil. Musicians might play mournful music (especially on the flute) to show the family's sadness. Some of these customs are seen in the story of the death of Jairus's daughter.

See The Action Bible *pages 111, 307, 327, 407, 444, 605 and Joshua 7:6; 2 Samuel 1:2; Isaiah 22:12; Jeremiah*

14:3; Mark 5:21–24, 35–43. See *also* Music/Musical Instruments.

MUSIC/MUSICAL INSTRUMENTS

Music was very important in Bible times. Music was used to call people to worship, to battle, or to sound a victory after a battle. Choirs with men and women were an important part of temple worship. The musicians played their part as well. Here are some of the most common instruments musicians played:

Harp and Lyre. A harp was made of wood and had twelve strings. The harp was one of the most important instruments in the temple orchestra. A lyre was a square or triangle-shaped instrument. Like the harp, it was made of wood, but it usually had ten strings instead of twelve and was plucked with a small pick instead of the fingers. The lyre was smaller in size and higher in pitch than the harp. It made a sweet, soft sound. It was one of the temple orchestra instruments. David, a skilled musician, played a lyre to soothe Saul.

Trumpet. A trumpet was a straight tube about eighteen inches long ending in a bell shape, made from either copper or silver. There were always at least two trumpets played at each temple service—and sometimes as many as 120. A trumpet will be blown when Jesus returns to earth from heaven and believers are resurrected.

Shofar. A shofar, a curved ram's horn, is still used in Jewish worship today. Shofars were part of the temple orchestra. A shofar was blown by the priests as a signal in worship

MYRRH

A resin that comes from the commiphora myrrha shrub. When dissolved, its oil is used as medicine or expensive perfume. The wise men who visited Jesus when He was a child gave Jesus myrrh.

See **The Action Bible** *page 537 and Matthew 2:11.*

MYTHICAL CREATURES

If you read Job 39:9–12 in the King James Version of the Bible, you might be surprised to find the unicorn mentioned. But the unicorn was probably a wild ox or an antelope, rather than the single-horned unicorn you read about in fantasy books. Another creature, the leviathan, is mentioned in the book of Job and other places in the Bible. It is one of the "magnificent creatures" God talks about on page 43 of *The Action Bible*. Some scholars think the term refers to a crocodile; others think it is a make-believe creature.

See **The Action Bible** *page 43 and Job 39:9–12; 41:1–10.*

NAAMAN

A commander of Syria's army. Naaman had a huge problem: leprosy. At least his form of leprosy was not contagious. His wife's young Israelite slave told him that a prophet in Israel could cure him. Instead of meeting Naaman, Elisha sent instructions: dip seven times in the muddy Jordan River to be healed. How could a muddy river make a person clean? It couldn't, but God could. When proud Naaman finally obeyed, he was healed of leprosy.

ceremonies. It is still used to announce events such as the Jewish New Year and the beginning of each Sabbath. The Israelites blew shofar horns as the walls of Jericho fell down.

See **The Action Bible** *pages 154, 200–201, 274, 284, 318 and Joshua 6; 1 Samuel 16:23; 2 Samuel 6:45; 1 Chronicles 25; 2 Chronicles 35:25; Nehemiah 7:67; 1 Corinthians 15:52. See also* **Psalms, book of.**

MUSTARD

The mustard seed is small and grows rapidly into a large plant. Jesus used the mustard seed as an example of how the kingdom of God grows.

See **The Action Bible** *page 586 and Matthew 13:31, 32; 17:20; Mark 4:30–32; Luke 13:18–19; 17:6.*

See The Action Bible *page 406*
and 2 Kings 5:1–27.

NABAL

(SEE ABIGAIL)

NABOTH

An Israelite who had a good vineyard next to King Ahab's palace in Jezreel. When King Ahab wanted to buy Naboth's vineyard, Naboth refused. He wanted the land to stay in his family so others could inherit it. Ahab's wife, Jezebel, had Naboth stoned to death. God sent the prophet Elijah to tell Ahab that God would judge him and his wife for the death of Naboth.

See The Action Bible *page 394 and 1 Kings 21.*

NAHUM

An Old Testament prophet who wrote a short book of prophecy. Nothing else is known about the man except that he came from the town of Elkosh—the location of which is not known either. His book is full of poetic, powerful word pictures about God's strength and goodness. Nahum prophesied the defeat of Nineveh, the capital of Assyria. At this time in history (sometime between 663 and 612 BC) the Assyrians were threatening the kingdom of Judah. The idea that Nineveh could ever be defeated seemed impossible. But Nahum's prophecy came true in 612 BC, when Nineveh was conquered by Babylon.

See The Action Bible *page 445 and the book of Nahum.*

NAOMI

(SEE RUTH, BOOK OF)

NARD/SPIKENARD

A fragrant oil made from the roots and stems of the spikenard plant. It was a favorite perfume of ancient people. It was very expensive because it had to be imported from India. This was the ointment Mary placed on the feet of Jesus, as told in John 12:3. Mark 14:3 describes another time when nard was poured on the head of Jesus.

See The Action Bible *page 610 and Mark 14:3; John 12:3.*

NATHAN

A prophet who was a counselor to King David. Nathan often delivered God's messages to David. When David wanted to build a house of worship for God, he talked with Nathan. God told Nathan to tell David that David's son would build the temple, not David. Several years later, Nathan told him that God would judge him for his sin with Bathsheba. When David was old and dying, Nathan learned that Adonijah, one of David's sons, plotted to become king instead of Solomon. Nathan told David and then followed David's orders to make Solomon king. Nathan also wrote a history of the reigns of David and Solomon, but no copies of his work have been saved.

See The Action Bible *pages 319, 349 and 2 Samuel 7; 12:1–25; 1 Kings 1:8–53.* See also **Bathsheba; David.**

NAZARETH

The town in Galilee (between the Sea of Galilee and the Mediterranean Sea) where Jesus grew up. Nazareth had a bad reputation. This is why Nathanael, who became one of Jesus's disciples, questioned how anything good could come from there. Early in His ministry, Jesus preached in the synagogue in Nazareth, but the people became so angry with Him that they wanted to kill Him. Today Nazareth is a large city, and most of the people who live there are Arabs.

See The Action Bible *page 532 and Luke 2:39, 51; 4:16–30; John 1:46.*

NEBUCHADNEZZAR

King of Babylon during its time of greatest glory. He ruled from 605 to 562 BC. Nebuchadnezzar made the city of Babylon beautiful; his hanging gardens were one of the seven wonders of the ancient world. His armies invaded Judah three times—in 605, 597, and 586 BC. In 597, the armies came into the city of Jerusalem and took most of the furnishings of the temple back to Babylon. Thousands of Israelites were forced to leave their country and go to Babylon to live. These included the leaders of Judah.

Nebuchadnezzar was a proud, power-hungry king. He once set up a huge golden image and ordered everyone to worship it. In 586 BC, Nebuchadnezzar's army destroyed Jerusalem and the famous temple Solomon had built. More Israelites were forced to leave Judah and go to

Babylon to live. He died in 562 BC after reigning forty-three years.

See **The Action Bible** *pages 450, 466, 473 and 2 Kings 24–25; Daniel 1–4.*

NEHEMIAH

The governor who led the rebuilding of the walls of Jerusalem and much of the city. He also restored the worship of God among the people. Nehemiah's work began in 445 BC—more than one hundred years after Jerusalem had been destroyed by Nebuchadnezzar, king of Babylon. Nehemiah was a descendant of people who had been taken as exiles from Jerusalem.

Nehemiah was cupbearer to King Artaxerxes of Persia. Nehemiah asked the king to let him return to Jerusalem to rebuild the walls of the city. The king not only gave him permission but later appointed him governor of the area.

See **The Action Bible** *page 513 and the book of Nehemiah.*

NEHEMIAH, BOOK OF

The book of Nehemiah tells the last events of Jewish history recorded in the Old Testament.

See **The Action Bible** *pages 513–515 and the book of Nehemiah.*

NERO

The emperor (Caesar) of Rome who probably had Paul and Peter killed. He began as a good ruler in AD 54. Nero's later rule of terror and cruelty began about AD 63. He had his own mother put to death, as well as some of his most trusted advisers. In AD 64, a large part of the city of Rome burned. Many thought that Nero had ordered the burning of the city. To draw suspicion away from himself, Nero accused the Christians of starting the fire. This became an excuse to begin a terrible persecution of Christians. Some were burned as torches in Nero's own gardens; others were crucified or thrown to wild beasts. The Roman Senate finally decided that Nero should die. But before the death order could be carried out, Nero ordered many senators to be killed and then killed himself in AD 68.

See The Action Bible *pages 736–739 and Acts 25:10–11.*

NICODEMUS

A Pharisee who belonged to the ruling Jewish council. Nicodemus wanted to know what Jesus taught. Because the Pharisees were enemies of Jesus, Nicodemus took his questions to Jesus secretly at night. When the Sanhedrin wanted to condemn Jesus without a fair trial, Nicodemus objected. But he was afraid to be an open follower of Jesus until after Jesus died. Then Nicodemus boldly showed that he was a disciple by helping to bury Jesus's body.

See The Action Bible *page 554 and John 3:1–21; 7:45–52; 19:38–42.*

NILE RIVER

The longest river in the world. It runs nearly 4,132 miles through the middle of Africa to Egypt and the Mediterranean Sea. A very wide plain along the coast of Egypt is flooded each July by the Nile River. This flooding makes the land good for farming. Without the Nile River, the country of Egypt could not have survived. The seven years of famine in Joseph's time were probably caused when the Nile did not flood as usual.

See The Action Bible *page 129 and Exodus 2:1–10; 7–8.*

NINEVEH

One of the oldest cities of the world. It was founded by Nimrod the famous hunter. Archaeological digging has shown that people lived there as early as 4500 BC. When it was the capital of the empire of Assyria, it had beautiful palaces for its kings, temples for its gods, and a canal thirty miles long that ran from a dam to the north.

In the Bible Nineveh is best known as the city to which Jonah went to preach. The people expressed their sorrow over their wrongdoings when Jonah warned them that God would destroy the city. God spared the city then, but it was finally destroyed in 612 BC by the Babylonians, Medes, and Scythians.

See The Action Bible *page 431 and Genesis 10:11; 2 Kings 19:36–37; Jonah 1:2; 3:2–3; 4:11.*

NOAH

A good man who continued to do right when everyone around him was doing wrong. When God sent the flood that destroyed most of the known population, Noah was about six hundred years old. Noah and his three sons (Shem, Ham, and Japheth) and their wives took a male and female of every known animal and bird. Because of the flood, Noah and his family and the animals stayed in the ark almost a year. They had to wait until the land was dry enough so they could walk on the ground, build houses, and grow food again.

One of Noah's first acts when he got out of the ark was to build an altar to worship God. God made an agreement with Noah, promising that He would never again send a flood to destroy all living things. As a proof of His promise, God sent a rainbow across the sky. Noah lived for 350 years after the flood.

See **The Action Bible** *pages 29–37 and Genesis 6:9–9:17; Hebrews 11:7.*
See also **Ark, Noah's; Flood, the.**

NUMBERS, BOOK OF

In the Hebrew version, this fourth book of the Bible is called "In the Wilderness" because of the first phrase of the book. It describes Israel's wanderings in the wilderness. The name *Numbers* comes from the Greek translation of the Old Testament. The ancient translators called it *Numbers* because the beginning of the book and the end of the book tell the number of males over twenty years of age—those who could fight in battles. The book of Numbers also records the sad stories of Israel's rebellion against God, Moses, and Aaron when the twelve spies returned from Canaan. Because of their lack of faith, God decided they would live in the wilderness for forty years—long enough for most of that generation to die. Numbers also includes the strange story of the prophet Balaam and how God would not allow him to curse the Israelites.

See **The Action Bible** *pages 164–189 and the book of Numbers.*

OAK

There were many varieties of oak trees in Palestine. Absalom's long hair was caught in the branches of an oak tree.

See **The Action Bible** *page 345 and Genesis 35:8; 2 Samuel 18:9; Isaiah 2:13.*

OATHS AND VOWS

An oath was a solemn promise a person made that what he or she says is true. In Bible times, there were several methods of taking oaths. Sometimes a person said something like "as the Lord lives." They meant that their words were as dependable as the fact that God is alive. Other times a person made a signal, such as raising his hand toward heaven. In our country, we use oaths in court cases, where a person places his hand on the Bible and says, "I swear to tell the truth, the whole truth, and nothing but the truth, so help me God."

A vow was a voluntary promise to God, made in exchange for something. Jacob vowed to give a tenth of all he had to God, if God would be with him, provide for him, and bring him back home safely. Once a vow was made, it had to be kept or else it was sin. A vow had to be spoken out loud to be binding.

Nazirite Vow. A vow a person took to commit himself or herself to God in a special way for a certain length of time. The time could be anywhere from thirty days to a lifetime. The person who took the vow could not eat anything made with grapes, cut his hair, or touch a dead body. Samson, Samuel, and John the Baptist took this vow for life. Paul took a Nazirite vow for a short time.

In the New Testament, Jesus said everything His followers said should be just as binding as a vow. A simple yes or no should be enough. But if people did make vows, they must keep them faithfully.

See **The Action Bible** *pages 222, 267 and Genesis 28:20–22; Numbers 6:1–21; 30; Deuteronomy 23:21–23; Judges 13:7; 16; 17; 1 Samuel 1:11; Matthew 5:33–37; 23:16–22; Mark 1:6; Luke 1:15; Acts 18:18.*

OBADIAH, BOOK OF

The shortest book in the Old Testament. Not much is known about the prophet Obadiah or when the book was written. The twenty-one verses in Obadiah are about the nation of Edom—descendants of Esau, Jacob's brother. Their country was south of the Dead Sea. Even though the people of Edom and the people of Israel were distant relatives, they were usually enemies. The Edomites sometimes fought with the Philistines against the Israelites. Obadiah predicted that the people of Edom would be punished by God for being proud and for joining other nations in trying to destroy God's people.

See **The Action Bible** *pages 466, 468 and the book of Obadiah.*

OBEDIENCE

Doing what we're told to do. Obedience has been a part of life since the time of Adam and Eve when God gave them one rule to obey. We are commanded to be obedient to God in every way. Jesus encouraged His disciples to remain close to Him by obeying His commands. Obedience is a part of faith. Children are told to obey their parents and to honor them.

See **The Action Bible** *pages 20–21, 28, 181 and Genesis 2:15–17; John 15:10; Romans 1:5; Ephesians 6:1–2; 1 John 5:2.*

OFFERING/SACRIFICE

Gifts to God. They show that a person trusts God and wants to do what He commands. The Old Testament Law gave a long list of instructions about how offerings were to be made, when they should be given, and for what purpose. Offerings were usually animals, wine, oil, or grain and were a symbol of sins confessed and then taken away by God. Christians believe that Jesus Christ was the final, once-for-all sacrifice to bring forgiveness of sins to all who believe in Him.

Some of the offerings mentioned in the Old Testament include the following:

Burnt Offerings. Calves, lambs, rams, or goats burned upon the altar in the temple or tabernacle. The animal had to be in perfect condition. Blood was sprinkled around the altar, and the entire animal (except the skin) was burned up in the fire. Burnt offerings were always for sin.

Drink Offerings. A pouring out of liquids—usually wine and oil (separately or mixed together)—as an offering. They were always given with other sacrifices—never alone.

Evening Sacrifice. One of the daily sacrifices made to God in the tabernacle or temple. Every morning and every evening an animal was burned as a sacrifice to God. With it was offered a grain offering and a drink offering.

Grain Offerings. Vegetable offerings were mixed with fine flour, oil, and flavorings and made into bread or cakes. Sometimes these offerings were burned at the altar. Other times, part was burned and the rest was given to the priest.

Peace Offerings. Given to make peace with God. Any animals normally used for sacrifices were given (except birds). In peace offerings, the breast and shoulder of the animal were given to the priest. The blood was sprinkled on the altar and the fat burned. The person who made the offerings and his friends ate the rest of the meat in the tabernacle or temple. Eating it there showed that God was a guest at the meal.

Sin Offering. A calf, a male or female goat, a female lamb, a dove, or a pigeon. The sin offering was for the sins of an individual that affect his or her life.

Trespass or Guilt Offering. A ram or a male lamb given to God when a person hurt someone else by his sin—as in stealing. In such cases, the person not only had to make a trespass offering to God but also had to pay back what he had stolen or make up the wrong he had done.

Wave Offerings. Motions made by the priest when a peace offering was given. A wave offering meant that the breast of the animal was placed in the high priest's hands and "waved" before the Lord to show that it had been given to God's representative—the priest. In the similar heave offering, the right thigh of the animal (the choicest part) was treated in a similar way as the wave offering and then eaten by the priests.

Other Offerings. Sometimes offerings of gold, silver, or other items were collected for building purposes, for worship, or to help people. David took offerings for the building of the temple. A poor widow gave an offering in the temple that Jesus admired. Paul praised an offering the Philippian church sent to him.

See The Action Bible *pages 25, 61–62, 165 and Genesis 4:3–5; 8:20; Leviticus 1–7; Numbers 28:3–8; 1 Chronicles 29; Mark 12:41–43; Philippians 4:10.*

OG, KING OF BASHAN

(SEE SIHON)

OLIVE

Olives were eaten for food, and olive oil was used in cooking, lamps, medicines, and ointments. Olive wood was used in carpentry. Olive trees grow well in the rocky soil, require very little water, and produce fruit for hundreds of years. When Noah sent a dove to find dry land, the dove brought back a branch from an olive tree.

See The Action Bible *page 35 and Genesis 8:11; Zechariah 4:3.*

OXEN

Oxen are bulls with their sex glands removed. Because they were strong, they were usually used to pull wagons, plows, and other farm implements. Almost every Israelite farmer had an ox. Oxen were also frequently used as offerings to God. Job had thousands of oxen. When the ark of the covenant was returned to Israel, it was placed on a cart pulled by oxen. Elisha sacrificed a pair of oxen when he followed Elijah.

See The Action Bible *pages 40, 318 and 2 Samuel 6:6; 1 Kings 19:19–21; Luke 14:19.*

PALESTINE

(SEE ISRAEL)

PALM

Date palms have grown in Israel for at least five thousand years. When Jesus rode into Jerusalem on the Sunday before His crucifixion, the crowds took branches of palm trees and went out to meet Him. The Christian church calls the Sunday before Easter Palm Sunday.

See The Action Bible *pages 213, 612 and Matthew 21:1–11; John 12:13.*

PAPHOS

A town on the island of Cyprus to which Paul, John Mark, and Barnabas paid a visit. Here, they met a sorcerer named Elymas who tried to stop them from preaching the gospel to Sergius Paulus.

See The Action Bible *page 696 and Acts 13:6–12. See Cyprus; Elymas.*

PARABLE

A story that teaches a lesson. Each parable in the Bible usually points out one spiritual truth and teaches a lesson by comparing one situation with another. Jesus often taught with parables. Usually Jesus's parables were easily understood by His listeners, but sometimes He had to explain what they meant. Some of Jesus's parables include the Good Samaritan, the lost son, the lost coin, and the sower.

See The Action Bible *pages 568–570, 600–604 and Luke 10:29–37; 15.*

PASSOVER

(SEE FEASTS)

PATMOS

The small island where John was exiled about AD 95. The Roman emperor Domitian sent him there because of his Christian faith. While John was there, God sent him remarkable visions. John wrote about these visions in the book of Revelation. The island of Patmos is only about sixteen square miles and is located about thirty-five miles off the coast of Asia Minor (now Turkey). The island is now known as Patino.

See The Action Bible *page 741 and Revelation 1:9.*

PAUL/SAUL OF TARSUS

A missionary and preacher of the gospel and the writer of thirteen New Testament books. Paul's name was Saul, but after he became a believer in Christ, he was known as Paul. Paul grew up in a strict Jewish home in Tarsus, a Roman city in what is now southeastern Turkey. In Tarsus, he also learned a trade—tent making.

At first, Paul was against Christianity, which was known as "the Way." When he was about thirty years old, he watched with approval as Stephen, the first Christian martyr, was stoned to death for blasphemy. While headed for Damascus to persecute Christians, Paul saw Jesus in a blinding vision. After being blind for three days, Paul received his sight through Ananias. He began preaching in synagogues and met with threats upon his life. Eventually Barnabas, a Christian leader from Jerusalem, asked him to come to Antioch, where a new church was growing.

About AD 48, the church at Antioch sent Saul, Barnabas, and John Mark on a trip to Cyprus and parts of Asia Minor (Turkey). They preached in Jewish synagogues but were often mistreated by others. When Paul and Barnabas were ready to make their second missionary journey, they had an argument and went their separate ways. Paul visited some of the churches he had started on his first journey.

After a short time, he began his third journey, returning to many of the same cities again. He lived at Ephesus for three years before returning to Jerusalem. When he arrived, he was arrested on false charges. A Jewish mob would have killed him if he had not been rescued by a Roman officer. When Paul saw that he could not receive a fair trial, he appealed to Caesar. This meant his case would be determined by Emperor Nero himself. Paul could do this because he was a Roman citizen.

Paul was sent to Rome as a prisoner about AD 60. As a prisoner, he wrote Colossians, Philemon, Ephesians, and Philippians. The letters of Paul to Timothy and Titus show that Paul was released by Nero probably in the spring of AD 63. But by AD 64, Paul was again in prison in Rome. He was executed in AD 66 or 67 as part of Nero's persecution of Christians.

See The Action Bible *pages 686–739 and Acts 9; 11–28; and the letters written by Paul. See also* Ananias of Damascus; Asia Minor; Damascus; Mark/John Mark.

PENTATEUCH

(SEE TORAH)

PERGA

A large city in Asia Minor (Turkey). Paul and Barnabas went through the city twice on their first missionary journey. At that time, Perga had a huge temple to the Greek goddess Artemis. Today the city is known as Murtana.

See The Action Bible *page 696 and Acts 13:13; 14:25.*

PERSECUTE/ PERSECUTION

To harm or destroy, sometimes by injury or torture. Usually people are persecuted because of their beliefs. Prophets were sometimes persecuted in the Old Testament. Daniel, for example, refused to stop praying to God and was therefore thrown into a den of lions. In New Testament times,

many who believed in Jesus were persecuted. The disciples were thrown into prison, beaten, and killed because of their beliefs. Many first-century Christians were often persecuted because they would not say, "Caesar is Lord." The New Testament teaches that Christians should be prepared for persecution.

See The Action Bible *pages 300, 685 and Daniel 6; Luke 21:12; John 16:33; 2 Timothy 3:12.*

PERSIA/PERSIANS

A country and an empire that were very strong during one period of Old Testament history. The country was the part of the Middle East roughly similar to the present country of Iran. The Persian ruler Cyrus began building the Persian Empire in 559 BC. Persia defeated Nebuchadnezzar and the Babylonians and became the ruling empire from about 539 to 331 BC. During this period, Persia controlled not only Israel but also Egypt and eastern Greece. In 539 BC, Cyrus permitted many of the Jews who had been captured earlier to return to Israel and rebuild the temple and the city of Jerusalem. Persia was finally defeated by Alexander the Great of Greece.

The Medes were the people of the land of Media (the northwest part of Iran today). A fierce, warlike people, they often joined with the Persians to fight the Assyrians and the Egyptians. Darius the Mede was the first ruler of this empire after it defeated Babylon.

See The Action Bible *page 483 and 2 Chronicles 36:20–23; Ezra 1:1–8; 4:5–24; 6:1–12; Esther 1:1–3; Isaiah 13:17; Daniel 5:31–12:13. See also* Xerxes/Ahasuerus; Esther.

PETER/SIMON

The leader of the twelve disciples and a leader in the first-century church. His original name was Simon. Jesus gave him the name Cephas or Peter, which means "rock." He was originally a fisherman who lived in Capernaum in Galilee. He was married, but we know nothing about his wife or whether they had children. But the Bible tells us that Peter had a mother-in-law, who was later healed of a fever by Jesus. Peter first met Jesus along the shore of the Sea of Galilee. He and his brother, Andrew, both left their work to follow Christ.

Peter was the first of the disciples to recognize and say that Jesus was the Messiah. Many stories in the Gospels show Peter to be full of energy, a man who often seemed to act before he thought. He sometimes bragged, as when he told Jesus that all others might turn away from Him, but he never would. Within a few hours, Peter denied that he even knew Jesus. He deeply regretted what he did.

Peter tried to defend Jesus when the soldiers came to arrest Him. He cut off the ear of one of the men, but Jesus healed it. Peter was one of two disciples who ran to the tomb on Easter morning and found that Jesus's body was gone. The risen Jesus also served breakfast to Peter and some of the disciples. Jesus forgave Peter for denying Him.

When the Holy Spirit came at Pentecost, Peter preached a sermon. Afterward three thousand people became Christians. The Holy Spirit helped Peter and the other apostles to do amazing things. A lame man was healed at the temple gate. Peter brought a woman back to life. God also gave Peter a special vision to show him that the gospel was for the Gentiles as well as Jews. As a result, he went and preached to Cornelius and his family. Later, when Peter was imprisoned, God sent an angel to free Peter.

Peter wrote letters—1 and 2 Peter—to Christians in Asia Minor (now Turkey). Most scholars believe that Peter eventually went to Rome, where he was executed by the emperor Nero.

See The Action Bible *pages 549, 581, 583, 624, 649, 656 and Matthew 16:13–20; 26:31–35, 69–75; Luke 5:1–11; John 18:10–11; 20:1–10; 21; Acts 2–5; 10:1–11:18; 12:1–19; and 1 and 2 Peter. See also* Cornelius; Tabitha.

PETER, 1 AND 2

Written by the apostle Peter between AD 62 and 69 to Christians in northern Asia Minor (now Turkey). Peter may have visited some of these Christian groups earlier, but the apostle Paul had not. Peter wrote the first letter to encourage the Christians to have joy and trust God even though they would be facing persecution. Many scholars think Peter was in Rome when he wrote this letter and could see that Emperor Nero's persecution of the church would probably spread to other areas. Peter wrote his second letter to warn about false teachers. Knowing that he would not live much longer, Peter wanted the readers to beware of those who taught wrong things.

See The Action Bible *page 740 and the books of 1 and 2 Peter. See also* Peter/Simon.

PHARAOHS OF EGYPT

The title of the rulers in ancient Egypt, just as president is the name of the top official in the United States. Joseph, son of Jacob, served as second in command under a pharaoh who realized how wise and talented Joseph was. Moses was raised in the home of a pharaoh. But after that pharaoh died, God sent terrible plagues upon Egypt because the current pharaoh— perhaps Thutmose III—would not let the Israelites leave his country, where they were slaves. This pharaoh later drowned with his army in the Red Sea when they tried to pursue the people of Israel after they left Egypt.

Throughout Israel's history, pharaohs of Egypt made alliances with kings of Israel and Judah or went to war against them. When the Persian Empire grew, the Egyptians were conquered around 525 BC and served the Persians. The Egyptians gained their independence around 404 BC, but Alexander the Great later conquered Egypt.

See The Action Bible *pages 46, 97–98, 112–144 and Genesis 41; Exodus 1–15.*

PHARISEES

The strictest and most influential group of Jews in the time of Jesus. They studied the Old Testament and were determined to keep every rule in it. Many traditions and interpretations of the Old Testament had grown through the centuries, and the Pharisees tried to follow these too. They did not like when Jesus made friends with the people they considered "sinners"—like tax collectors. They objected when Jesus healed people on the Sabbath. Jesus often criticized their unloving attitudes. Some of the leaders of the New Testament church had once been Pharisees—men such as the apostle Paul, Nicodemus, and probably Joseph of Arimathea.

See The Action Bible *page 561 and Matthew 9:10–13; 12:1–14; 23; Mark 15:1, 42–46; Luke 5:21; 23:50–54; John 3:1–15; Philippians 3:4–6.*

PHILEMON, BOOK OF

In AD 61, Paul wrote this short letter to Philemon, a believer living in Colossae (now southwestern Turkey). Philemon had a slave named Onesimus, who ran away and probably went to Rome, where he met Paul and became a Christian. Paul sent Onesimus back to Philemon with this letter, urging Philemon to receive Onesimus not as a slave but as a fellow believer.

See The Action Bible *page 734 and the book of Philemon.*

PHILIP

A deacon and evangelist. Philip was a Greek-speaking Jewish man and one of seven deacons chosen to provide food for poor widows in Jerusalem. After Stephen was stoned to death, Philip went to the city of Samaria to preach. Many people believed in Jesus, and God did some miracles of healing through Philip. Philip met an Ethiopian palace official who was reading the book of Isaiah in a chariot. Philip explained that Jesus was the Messiah about whom the prophet Isaiah had written. The Ethiopian believed in Jesus, and Philip baptized him. Then the Holy Spirit led Philip away to preach in other towns. Philip later lived in Caesarea. Paul the apostle often stayed with him when he traveled to Caesarea. Philip had four unmarried daughters who were prophets.

See **The Action Bible** *pages 550, 671 and Acts 6:1–6; 8:4–8, 26–40; 21:7–10. See also* **Ethiopian Officer.**

PHILIPPI

A major city in northeastern Macedonia, an area that is now part of Greece. Philippi was a Roman colony. Many retired Roman soldiers lived there, and the people had all the legal rights of Roman citizens. This city was the first place in Europe to hear the gospel. Paul went to Philippi on his second missionary journey after God sent him a vision of a Macedonian man asking for help.

See **The Action Bible** *page 710 and Acts 16:1–40; the book of Philippians.*

PHILIPPIANS, BOOK OF

Written by the apostle Paul to the church at Philippi (now part of Greece) while he was imprisoned in Rome in AD 61 or 62. This letter has the nickname "the joy letter," because of its joyful message, despite Paul's difficult circumstances. Paul had a closer relationship with this church than with any other. His love for the Philippians shows clearly in this letter. He wrote of his joy in remembering them and of their joy in the Lord. The idea of joy or rejoicing appears sixteen times in this short letter.

See **The Action Bible** *page 735 and the book of Philippians.*

PHILISTIA/ PHILISTINES

A nation along the coast of the Mediterranean Sea in southern Canaan. The Philistines were wealthier and more advanced in using tools and crafts (particularly metals) than the Israelites. They were enemies of the Israelites and fought many battles against them during the time of the book of Judges and during the reigns of Saul and David—about 1400 to 1050 BC. A Philistine woman, Delilah, tricked Samson into telling the secret of his great strength. The giant whom David killed with a sling and a stone was a Philistine. The Israelites never fully conquered the Philistines.

See **The Action Bible** *pages 222, 276 and Judges 14–16 and the books of 1 and 2 Samuel.*

PIGS

Pigs and hogs were declared "unclean," and therefore could not be eaten by the people of Israel. The Gentiles in Israel and surrounding areas raised pigs. Jesus told a parable of a son who left home and became a pig keeper—a shameful job for a man of Israel. Jesus also drove a legion of demons out of a man and allowed them to go into a herd of pigs.

See **The Action Bible** *pages 491, 602 and Leviticus 11:7–8; Mark 5:1–17; Luke 15:15–16.*

PILATE/PONTIUS PILATE

The Roman governor of Judea during the time of Jesus's death. He was responsible for keeping peace among the Jews. Pilate never got along well with the Jews. He did not understand them or their beliefs about God. The Jewish historian Josephus wrote that Pilate outraged the Jews by using temple money to build an aqueduct. He also brought shields decorated with figures of Roman emperors into Jerusalem.

When Jesus was on trial before him, Pilate realized that Jesus was innocent of the charges against Him. However, Pilate did not want to get into more trouble with the Jews, so he allowed Jesus to be executed. He was removed from his position about six years later. History does not record what happened to him after that, although Christian tradition says he later killed himself.

See **The Action Bible** *page 629 and Matthew 27:1–26; John 18:28–19:16.*

PILLAR OF FIRE AND CLOUD

The sign God used to lead the Israelites through the wilderness. God showed this miraculous sign to the Israelites as they were fleeing from the army of the pharaoh. It continued to guide them all during the forty years before they entered Canaan. The cloud was seen during the day and the fire at night.

See **The Action Bible** *page 139 and Exodus 13:21–22; 14:19–24; 33:8–11; Deuteronomy 31:14–23.*

PISIDIAN ANTIOCH

(SEE ANTIOCH)

PLAGUES ON EGYPT

Ten disasters God allowed to convince the pharaoh to let the Israelites leave Egypt. Although some of these plagues could be considered natural disasters, their timing was arranged by God to fulfill His purpose for the Hebrews. The plagues:

1. Water became blood.
2. Frogs swarmed throughout all of the land.
3. Swarms of gnats (lice, sand flies, or fleas) came.
4. Swarms of flies came in great numbers.
5. Cattle became diseased. While the cattle of the Egyptians died, the cattle of the people of Israel survived.
6. Boils or sores infected people and animals.
7. Hail destroyed animals and crops.
8. Locusts ate the crops that were just coming out of the ground and had not been destroyed by the hail.
9. Darkness covered the land for three days.
10. The oldest child in each family and the firstborn cattle

all died. The Israelites were protected by God from this terrible plague by sprinkling the blood of the Passover lamb on their doorposts.

See **The Action Bible** *pages 129–137 and Exodus 7–12.*

POTIPHAR AND HIS WIFE

Potiphar was a captain of the pharaoh's guard. Potiphar bought Joseph as a slave. Potiphar soon recognized Joseph's keen mind and organizing ability and placed him in charge of running his household. Potiphar's wife liked Joseph, but Joseph rejected her when she flirted with him. When Potiphar's wife made a false accusation against Joseph, Potiphar had Joseph imprisoned.

See **The Action Bible** *page 94 and Genesis 39. See also* Joseph, son of Jacob.

PRAY/PRAYER

A conversation with God. But prayer is much more than asking God for things we want. Prayer includes praising God, giving thanks for His blessings, admitting when we've done wrong, asking Him for help, and asking God

to help other people. Isaac prayed for his wife to give birth. Hannah prayed for a son. Solomon prayed a prayer of dedication when the temple was completed. Jesus prayed often: when He was baptized, when He chose His disciples, whenever He healed people, and especially when He faced hard times. When the disciples asked Jesus to teach them to pray, Jesus taught them a prayer we call the Lord's Prayer.

The Bible teaches that when we pray we must have faith that God hears and will answer our prayers. The Holy Spirit will lead us in praying if we ask Him. We also must have a forgiving heart if we want God to forgive us.

See The Action Bible *pages 68, 599 and 1 Samuel 1:27; 1 Kings 8:22–61; Matthew 6:9–13; Mark 11:24–26; 14:32–42; Luke 3:21; 6:12–13; John 14:13–14; 17.*

PRIDE

A refusal to depend on God and a belief that one person is better than others. Miriam admitted to pride when she criticized Moses. King Nebuchadnezzar was proud, but God humbled him. The Pharisees showed their pride with their refusal to believe that Jesus was the Savior sent from God.

See The Action Bible *pages 172, 422, 486 and Numbers 12; Proverbs 8:13; 13:10; Isaiah 25:11; Daniel 4; 1 Corinthians 13:4; James 4:6.*

PRIESTS

Priests led the worship of God and offered sacrifices in the temple and tabernacle. From the time of Moses to the New Testament, all priests of Israel were from the tribe of Levi.

While other nations also had priests, the Bible describes three kinds of priests of Israel:

The High Priest. Aaron was the first high priest. The high priests were to come from Aaron's family line. The high priest, like other priests, offered sacrifices in the tabernacle and later in the temple. His most important work, however, came once a year on the Day of Atonement. On that day he put aside his beautiful clothes and put on a plain linen ephod. Then he entered the Most Holy Place to sprinkle blood on the mercy seat of the ark of the covenant to offer a sacrifice for his sins and for the sins of the people. Although the high priest was meant to be the spiritual leader of Israel, the high priests Annas and Caiaphas opposed Jesus and worked to bring His death.

Priests. The sons of Aaron—Nadab, Abihu, Elezar, and Ithamar—were the first priests. Later priests were divided into twenty-four groups. They took

turns working in the tabernacle and later in the temple. Only the priests could offer the sacrifices that the people brought to God. Part of these offerings went to the priests and their families. Because the priests did not own land, the Israelites were required to give one-tenth of their earnings or harvest to the tribe of Levi, and one-tenth of that was given to the priests.

Whenever someone was healed of an illness, he was to show himself to a priest. In this way, he could be allowed to worship at the tabernacle or temple.

Levites. They were assigned to help the priests take care of the tabernacle, and later the temple. Some Levites were singers and musicians; others were gatekeepers and assistants to the priests who offered sacrifices. Levites were assigned forty-eight cities where they could live and have pastureland. The Levites, in turn, were to give one-tenth of whatever they received to the priests. Levites began their service when they were twenty-five years old and worked until age fifty.

See The Action Bible *pages 164–165, 289, 319 and Exodus 28; Leviticus 16; Numbers 1–4; 1 Samuel 1–4; John 11:47–57; 18:12–32. See also* Clothing.

PRINCESS OF EGYPT

The daughter of the pharaoh of Egypt who became the adoptive mother of Moses. Having found the baby in a basket on the Nile, the princess hired Moses's mother, Jochebed, to nurse him until he could be returned to the princess. This princess may have been the one who became Queen Hatshepsut of the eighteenth dynasty of Egypt.

See The Action Bible *pages 115–116 and Exodus 2:1–10. See also* Pharaohs of Egypt.

PRISCILLA

(SEE AQUILA AND PRISCILLA)

PRISON

A place where a person accused or convicted of a crime was held. In ancient times, people were sometimes put in prison simply because they could not pay their debts. Joseph, son of Jacob, was thrown in prison for a crime he didn't commit. Often the prisoners in Bible times were beaten and then placed in chains or stocks. Often their food was only bread and water. Sometimes a prisoner who had not been proved guilty but was awaiting trial would be permitted to stay in his own house with guards to watch him. This was true of Paul in Rome.

See **The Action Bible** *page 95 and Genesis 39; 2 Chronicles 18:26; Matthew 25:34–36; Acts 16:22–34; 28:16.*

PROMISED LAND

(SEE CANAAN/ CANAANITES; ISRAEL)

PROPHECY/PROPHESY

A prophecy is a special message from God spoken through a prophet usually about a future event. To prophesy means to speak that message. Sometimes God used dreams or visions to speak to a prophet. God also spoke to His prophets directly, as He did with Moses. Prophets were often unpopular, because they told of God's judgment. Jeremiah was imprisoned several times because he courageously spoke God's message to the people of his day. Prophets like Nathan, Elijah, Isaiah, and Ezekiel spoke to the kings of their time, often bringing messages of God's judgment for wrongdoing.

The prophets sent by God often warned about false prophets—those who weren't sent by God but claimed to speak for Him. Micaiah challenged the false prophets who spoke to King Ahab and King Jehoshaphat. Paul wrote about prophecy as a spiritual gift.

See **The Action Bible** *pages 188, 396, 445–448, 657 and Numbers 12:6; 2 Samuel 12:1–14; 1 Kings 21:17–29; 22:1–28; 2 Kings 20:1–11; Isaiah 6; 1 Corinthians 12:10; 14:1–6. See also Dreams and Visions; Judgment.*

PROVERB

A wise saying. Solomon, the wisest king in history, wrote over three thousand proverbs.

See **The Action Bible** *page 357 and 1 Kings 4:32; the book of Proverbs.*

PROVERBS, BOOK OF

An Old Testament book of wise sayings. Many were written by King Solomon, the son of David. Some sections were apparently written by Agur (Proverbs 30) and Lemuel (Proverbs 31:1–9). The purpose of the book is to help people gain wisdom. Most of the proverbs tell what a wise person does and contrasts his acts with those of a foolish person.

See **The Action Bible** *page 357 and the book of Proverbs.*

PSALMS, BOOK OF

An Old Testament book of 150 songs containing prayers and praise to God. David wrote many of the psalms. The

psalms had their greatest use as a hymnbook when the Jewish people returned from exile in Babylon and rebuilt the temple.

The psalms were divided into five sections: Book 1 (Psalms 1–41); Book 2 (Psalms 42–72); Book 3 (Psalms 73–89); Book 4 (Psalms 90–106); and Book 5 (Psalms 107–150). Some of the psalms are called Messianic psalms because they describe the coming of the Messiah, Jesus Christ. The Messianic psalms are Psalms 2, 22, 72, and 110. When Jesus was dying on the cross, He quoted Psalm 22:1.

The hymn Jesus sang with the disciples at the end of the Last Supper was probably from Psalms 113–118. Paul and Silas sang hymns when they were in jail. Christians are told to sing hymns to encourage each other as well as to praise God.

See **The Action Bible** *pages 318–319 and the book of Psalms; Matthew 26:30; Acts 16:25; Ephesians 5:19; Colossians 3:16.*

QUARRY

A place from which stones are taken for building purposes. It also refers to the process of cutting or removing stones. Archaeologists have found quarries dating back to Bible times. In one quarry, the limestone was relatively soft until it was exposed to air for a long time; then it became hard and durable. The workers made slits in the soft stone and then inserted wedges of wood. Then they poured water over the wedges. When the wood swelled, the rock split into pieces that could be moved. Scholars think this may have been the way that huge stones were prepared for Solomon's temple.

See **The Action Bible** *page 360 and 1 Kings 6:7. See also* **Temples.**

QUEEN OF SHEBA

The ruler of the Sabean kingdom in Arabia during the time of Solomon. This kingdom was about fifteen hundred miles from Israel. She came to see King Solomon, probably on a trading mission as well as to ask questions to test his wisdom. Solomon and the queen exchanged gifts before she returned to her own country.

See **The Action Bible** *pages 364–365 and 1 Kings 10:1–13.*

RACHEL

The beautiful, favorite wife of Jacob, and the mother of Joseph and Benjamin. She was also Jacob's cousin and the daughter of Laban. She met Jacob after he fled from his brother Esau's anger. Although Jacob fell in love with her and agreed to work for Laban for seven years in order to marry her, Laban tricked Jacob into marrying Leah. In exchange for another seven years of work, Jacob was allowed to marry Rachel.

For a long time, Rachel could not have children and was jealous of Leah. When she finally had a son, Joseph, the child was Jacob's favorite. Rachel later had another son, Benjamin, but Rachel died in childbirth.

See **The Action Bible** *page 79 and Genesis 29–31; 35:16–19. See also* **Jacob/Israel; Joseph, son of Jacob; Laban; Leah.**

RAHAB

One of the women mentioned in the family line of Jesus. Although she lived in Jericho, she let two Israelite spies stay in her home. Messengers from the king of the city told Rahab to turn the men over to them, but she hid them under stalks of flax on her roof. In return for their safety, Rahab asked the spies to protect her and her family during the Israelite invasion. They agreed, and she helped them escape by letting them down over the walls of the city using a scarlet rope. The spies told her to hang the rope from her window so the Israelite soldiers would know which house was hers. She followed their orders, and Joshua had Rahab and her family brought out of Jericho before the city was burned.

See **The Action Bible** *pages 193–195 and Joshua 2; 6; Matthew 1:5; Hebrews 11:31; James 2:25.*

RAINBOW

The arch of the seven colors of the prism often seen in the sky after or during rain. God gave the rainbow as the sign of His agreement to protect the earth from another flood. God gave this sign to Noah after the floodwaters decreased. The prophet Ezekiel and the apostle John saw the rainbow as a sign of God's glory.

See **The Action Bible** *page 37 and Genesis 9:8–17; Ezekiel 1:28; Revelation 4:3. See* **Flood, the.**

RAMS

Rams are mature male sheep, often used for sacrifices, but also used for meat. Their skins were used as coverings in the tabernacle, and their horns were commonly used for trumpets. God provided a ram for Abraham to sacrifice, rather than his son Isaac.

See **The Action Bible** *page 62 and Genesis 22:12–14; Exodus 25:5.*

REBEKAH

The wife of Isaac and the scheming mother of Jacob and Esau. Rebekah was the sister of Laban. When Abraham wanted a bride for his son Isaac, he sent his servant Eliezar back to his relatives at Haran to find a suitable woman. There Eliezar met Rebekah at a well and asked her for some water. She not only gave him water, but also watered all his camels. This was a big job, because camels that have been traveling drink many gallons of water.

Once Rebekah agreed to go with Eliezar, she became the wife of Isaac. But they had no children for twenty years. Finally God answered their prayers, and twins were born—Esau and Jacob. Esau was the firstborn, but Rebekah loved Jacob more and wanted him to get the birthright that belonged to the firstborn. Esau was so angry that Rebekah had to send Jacob

back to Haran to stay with her family to be safe.

See The Action Bible *pages 64, 71–77 and Genesis 24:1–28:9; 49:31.*

REBEL/REBELLION

Opposition to someone in authority. Korah led a rebellion against Moses and Aaron. God punished Korah, his followers, and the people of Israel who sided with them. During the time of the judges, the people of Israel regularly rebelled against the Lord and were conquered by their enemies as a result. When Moses and Aaron sent spies to look over the land of Canaan, the people of Israel rebelled against the Lord by believing the bad report of ten of the spies.

See The Action Bible *page 345 and Judges 2–6; Numbers 14; 16. See also* Sin/Disobedience.

RED SEA

A large body of water thirteen hundred miles long, stretching from the Indian Ocean up to the Suez Canal. Although the Red Sea is salty, its waters are green and clear, and many fish and other forms of life thrive there. A marshy area that may have once been a northern finger of the Red Sea between the Mediterranean and the Gulf of Suez was important in the Old Testament. This area, more properly called the "Sea of Reeds," probably was the water that God miraculously separated to let the people of Israel cross as they fled from the Egyptians.

See The Action Bible *page 140 and Exodus 13:17–14:30.*

REDEEM/REDEMPTION

Paying the price for land or someone enslaved so that the land can be returned to its original owner, or the slave can be set free. In the Old Testament, Boaz bought (or redeemed) a piece of land from Naomi. In the New Testament, redemption is a word picture to show how Jesus, by His death and resurrection, redeemed—freed—us from our slavery to sin. On the cross, Jesus gave His life to set people free. He made possible a new life and new freedom to live as God's children.

See The Action Bible *page 23 and Ruth 4:1–7; Job 19:25; Psalm 19:14; Romans 3:24; 1 Corinthians 6:20; Galatians 3:13; Titus 2:14; Hebrews 9:12. See also* Kinsman-Redeemer; Salvation.

REHOBOAM

The foolish son of King Solomon. He was king when the Israelites divided into two separate kingdoms—Judah and Israel. When Rehoboam began to reign after the death of his father, Solomon, around 932 BC, he wanted to raise the taxes. But the people felt their taxes had been too high when Solomon was king. When Rehoboam consulted with his advisers, the older ones told him to reduce taxes. But the younger advisers—his friends—told him to threaten to make life harder for the people so that they would know who was in charge.

Rehoboam took the advice of his friends and raised the taxes. The people of the northern part of the kingdom rebelled. Jeroboam, a young official who had worked for Solomon, became the leader of the northern ten tribes. Only the tribes of Judah and Benjamin stayed with Rehoboam. Rehoboam was not able to reunite the kingdom. When he went to war against the north, God stopped him.

See **The Action Bible** *page 370 and 1 Kings 11:43–12:33; 14:21–31.*

REPENTANCE

Sorrow for sin, and turning away from that sin to serve God and do right. Repentance involves admitting before God that what we did or said was wrong, feeling sorrow for that wrongdoing and the hurt it caused God or others, and most importantly, turning from wrong acts to right acts. As we turn away from sin, we turn back to God. To accept Jesus's gift of new life, we must admit that we've done wrong. The Holy Spirit leads us to ask for forgiveness.

See **The Action Bible** *page 546 and Matthew 3:2, 8, 11; 4:17; Acts 5:31; 11:18; 20:21; 26:20; 2 Peter 3:9.*

RESURRECT/ RESURRECTION, THE

Resurrect. The return to life again after being dead. Two kinds of resurrection are mentioned in the Bible. One is the kind Jesus gave to Lazarus when Jesus brought him back from the grave after being dead four days. Jesus also raised the daughter of Jairus and the son of the widow of Nain from death. All of these people came back to the usual kind of physical life. And they all died again at the end of their earthly lives. Old Testament prophets like Elijah and Elisha also raised people from the dead.

The Bible promises that all Christians will be resurrected from the dead at some point in the future. Our new bodies will not be like our old bodies. They will be cool, amazing bodies that will never wear out. This is the kind of body Jesus had at His resurrection. In this final resurrection, God's people will live forever with Him, while those who rejected Him will be forever separated from God.

See **The Action Bible** *page 606 and 1 Kings 17:17–24; 2 Kings 4:18–37; Daniel 12:2; Mark 5:35–43; Luke 7:11–17; John 11:1–44; Acts 24:15; Romans 6:5; 8:11; 1 Corinthians 15:12–57.*

Resurrection, the: Jesus's return to life after His death on the cross. Many people saw Jesus die, and a Roman soldier even used a sword to pierce His side to be sure He was dead. He was buried in a tomb with guards posted outside to be sure no one could steal the body. Because Jesus died near sundown on the day that would begin the Sabbath, the burial customs could not be completed that day or the next day. So on the third day some of the women who were His friends returned to put burial spices on Jesus's body. But there was no body! Instead, they found angels, who told them that Jesus was alive once more. Soon after, the risen Jesus appeared several times to His disciples. They touched Him and ate with Him and assured themselves that He was truly alive.

See **The Action Bible** *page 643 and Matthew 28; Mark 16; Luke 24; John 20.*

REVELATION, BOOK OF

The last book of the New Testament. John wrote it on the island of Patmos, where he had been exiled because of his faith in Christ. Revelation tells how God gave John visions of the future church and the future earth. It is filled with strange word pictures using beasts, dragons, angels, thrones, scrolls, trumpets, and bowls. It is somewhat like the Old Testament prophecies of Daniel and Ezekiel, because it tells what will occur at the end of time. John wrote to seven churches that were facing hard times around the close of the first century. He wrote to encourage them to stay true to their faith in Jesus Christ. He then tells of God's judgment upon the world to come, where the forces of Satan and evil are overcome in battle

by Jesus Christ. Then a new heaven and a new earth are prepared, where God and His people enjoy each other forever.

See **The Action Bible** *pages 742–744 and the book of Revelation.*

REVENGE/VENGEANCE

Getting back at someone who wronged you. God established laws so that the people of Israel would not take revenge against each other. God said that taking revenge was His responsibility. Only He could judge fairly. David wanted revenge when Nabal treated David and his men unfairly. But Abigail stopped David from unlawfully taking revenge.

See **The Action Bible** *pages 296–297, 343 and Leviticus 19:18; 1 Samuel 25; Nahum 1:2; Romans 12:19.*

RHODA

A young servant in a house in Jerusalem where a group of Christians had gathered to pray for the release of the apostle Peter from prison. When she heard a knock at the gate of the house, she went to see who was there. When she heard Peter's voice, she was so surprised she forgot to open the gate! Instead, she ran inside to tell the others Peter had come. They did not believe her until they finally went to the gate, where Peter was still knocking.

See **The Action Bible** *page 682 and Acts 12:12–17.*

RIGHTEOUS/ RIGHTEOUSNESS

Right and lined up with God's will. Job and Noah were considered righteous men, but they weren't perfect.

In the Old Testament, God gave commands like the Ten Commandments that He expected people to follow. But no person except Jesus has ever perfectly obeyed every one of God's laws. We all choose to sin at times, but God has made it possible for us to share in His righteousness. Jesus, the only perfect man who ever lived, died for our sins. When we accept His death in our behalf, God enables us to live according to His will.

See **The Action Bible** *page 40 and Genesis 6:9; Job 1:1; Isaiah 64:6; Romans 3:19–26; 2 Corinthians 5:21. See also* **Commandment.**

ROMANS, BOOK OF

Written by Paul around AD 58 to Christians he had never met in the city of Rome. In this letter, Paul talks about the "righteousness of God"— righteousness given to believers thanks to the death and resurrection of Jesus. Paul was very careful to point out that although salvation is a free gift of God, it does not mean that Christians may go on sinning because God forgives them. We are to use the power of God's Spirit to defeat sin.

See **The Action Bible** *page 721 and the book of Romans.*

ROMANS/ROMAN EMPIRE

The ruling government all around the Mediterranean from about 27 BC to AD 450. It began as a small city-state in Italy and grew into an empire that controlled most of the world of that day. It reached from Britain, France, and Germany in the north to Morocco in Africa and east to what is now Turkey and Lebanon. As Rome conquered and

controlled these areas, it brought some degree of peace that lasted about five centuries. This peace also permitted trade to grow. Roman money became the common currency throughout the world.

In the time before Jesus, the city-state had a form of democracy with a senate representing the citizens. Later the emperor became more and more powerful. By about AD 100, the emperor of Rome was even worshipped as a god in some places. The Romans insisted that everyone must say, "Caesar is Lord." Because Christians refused to say that, they were persecuted throughout the Roman Empire. Despite persecution, the peace and the ease of travel that Rome established helped the church

to grow and spread throughout the world of that day.

See **The Action Bible** *page 519 and throughout the New Testament. See also* **Augustus Caesar; Nero; Pilate/Pontius Pilate.**

ROME

The capital of the Roman Empire. The city began about six centuries before Jesus's birth. Built on seven hills, Rome lies about ten miles up the Tiber River off the west coast of Italy. At the time of Jesus, more than a million people lived there. By the third and fourth centuries AD, the city had lost its glory and had less than half a million people. Most Roman emperors lived in the city of Rome, and some of them were considered gods by the citizens.

Early Christians were severely persecuted in Rome. Many were killed. Christians sometimes hid and worshipped in tunnels called catacombs beneath the city. Most scholars believe that the wicked city John wrote about in the book of Revelation was the city of Rome. Rome later became an important Christian center.

See **The Action Bible** *page 731 and Revelation 17–18.*

ROOF

(SEE HOUSE)

RUTH, BOOK OF

An Old Testament book that tells the story of a romance between a foreign widow and the relative of her mother-in-law, Naomi, in the time of the judges. The story took place sometime between 1300 and 1010 BC.

Naomi and her husband, Elimelech, and their two sons, Mahlon

and Kilion, went to live in Moab during a famine in Israel. After the famine was over, Naomi's husband died, and she wanted to return home. Ruth, a Moabite woman, was married to Mahlon, who also died. Ruth pledged her loyalty to Naomi and returned to Bethlehem with Naomi. To get food, Ruth gleaned grain in the fields of Boaz, a relative of Naomi. Boaz saw the young widow working hard in the field and began asking questions about her. Eventually Boaz and Ruth were married and had a son, Obed. Ruth was the great-grandmother of King David and is one of the ancestors of Jesus.

See **The Action Bible** *pages 242–247 and the book of Ruth; Matthew 1:5. See also* **Gleaning.**

SACRIFICE

(SEE OFFERING/SACRIFICE)

SALVATION

Saved through the death of Jesus from the penalty and power of sin. Often in the Old Testament, salvation referred to a person or a group being saved from physical danger. When the Israelites were crossing the Red Sea in their escape from Egypt and the pharaoh's army was close behind them, Moses told them that they would see the "salvation" of God. This meant their rescue when the Egyptian army was destroyed in the Red Sea.

The New Testament records only one time when Jesus used the word *salvation.* He told Zacchaeus the tax collector that salvation had come to

his house. Jesus meant a spiritual salvation, for Zacchaeus was not in any physical danger.

The apostle Paul makes it clear that spiritual salvation means being freed from sin—both its power over our lives and the judgment it brings from God. This kind of salvation comes through faith in Jesus, who gave His life so we could enter into the new life He made possible.

See The Action Bible *page 144 and Exodus 14:13; Luke 19:9–10; Romans 1:16. See also* Gospel, the; Redeem/Redemption.

SAMARIA/SAMARITANS

The name of a city and an area in Israel. It is not always clear in the Old Testament whether a verse refers to the area or to the city. During most of the 210-year history of the northern kingdom (Israel), the city of Samaria was its capital. For this reason, the name *Samaria* often refers to the whole northern kingdom. King Omri made Samaria the capital city of Israel about 880 BC. Later his son, King Ahab, built an elaborate palace there,

decorated with so much ivory that it was called "the ivory house." Ahab and his wife, Jezebel, made it a place of luxury and idol worship. The city was finally destroyed by the Assyrians in 722 BC after a three-year siege. Most of it was burned, but it was later rebuilt.

In the New Testament, Samaria refers to an area about forty miles wide and thirty-five miles long right in the middle of Israel. Judea was south of it and Galilee was north. The people who lived in Samaria did not follow the same rules of Judaism as the people in Judea and Galilee. Terrible hatred existed between Samaritans and the Jews of Israel during the time of Jesus. For this reason, most Jews would not travel through Samaria; they would take a much longer route so they wouldn't have to go through this province. Jesus, however, traveled through Samaria, and on one such trip He had an important conversation with a woman at a well.

See The Action Bible *page 403 and 1 Kings 16:24, 28; 22:38–39; John 4:3–6. See also* Assyria; Israel.

SAMSON

An Old Testament judge who had unusual, God-given strength, but was not very wise. An angel announced Samson's upcoming birth to his parents and told Samson's mission: to help free Israel from its Philistine rulers. But Samson never fully lived up to this potential. He continually made poor choices. He even married a Philistine woman!

At the weeklong wedding feast, Samson gave a riddle to thirty men who were guests. When the men could not guess the riddle after several days, they told Samson's wife she would have to get the answer or they would burn down her father's house. She tricked Samson to get the answer. When his wife was given to another man to be his wife, Samson later took revenge by tying the tails of three hundred foxes to flaming torches and let the foxes loose in the Philistine grain fields. The grain harvest was destroyed. The Philistines took revenge against Samson, but Samson killed one thousand of them with the jawbone of a donkey.

Samson met his match with Delilah, another Philistine woman. He was later captured by the Philistines and blinded. Standing between the two pillars, Samson prayed to God for the strength to push them down. As the walls and ceiling fell, thousands of Philistines were killed—and so was Samson.

See The Action Bible *pages 223–241 and Judges 13–16. See also* Delilah; Oaths and Vows.

SAMUEL

A prophet, priest, and the last judge of Israel. He was born in answer to the prayers of his mother, Hannah. Later, as a prophet, priest, and judge, Samuel told the Israelites they must stop worshipping false gods. He called all the people to a meeting at the city of Mizpah, where he offered a sacrifice to God and asked Him to forgive the people.

For most of his life, Samuel acted as a judge of the Israelites. When he was an old man, the Israelites told Samuel they wanted a king to rule them. Like Eli, Samuel had sons who did wrong things. God told Samuel they could have a king, but they should know that a king would cause them a lot of trouble. Samuel anointed Saul as the first king of Israel.

When King Saul did not follow God's commands, Samuel warned him that God would make someone else king. God told Samuel to anoint David as the new king. Later, when Saul tried to kill David, David stayed at Samuel's home. All of Israel was sad when Samuel died.

See The Action Bible *page 249 and 1 Samuel 1–25. See also* Hannah.

SAMUEL, 1 AND 2

The two parts were one book until about 200 BC, when the Bible was translated into Greek. The translators then divided it into two parts, and it is now known as 1 Samuel and 2 Samuel. Although the books are named after Samuel, who was a judge, prophet, and priest, no one knows who wrote them. First Samuel tells the history of the Israelites from the birth of Samuel to the death of King Saul. Second Samuel records the events during David's rise to the throne of Israel (chapters 1–10) and the problems that occurred after David's sin with Bathsheba (chapters 11–24).

See The Action Bible *pages 248–352 and the books of 1 and 2 Samuel.*

SANHEDRIN

The Jewish council of leaders in Israel in New Testament times. They were under the authority of the Roman rulers, but they had the final say in religious matters. The current high priest served as president. The seventy members included former high priests, heads of important families in Jerusalem, scribes, and Pharisees. Historical records do not show exactly how members were chosen or how long they served. The Sanhedrin usually met in one of the temple buildings or courts every day except on the Sabbath or feast days. Because the Roman Empire ruled the area, the Sanhedrin could not execute a prisoner without the permission of the Roman ruler. That is why Jesus had to be brought before Pilate as well as the Sanhedrin. After they healed a lame beggar, Peter and John were dragged before the Sanhedrin and told not to preach in Jesus's name. The power of the Sanhedrin ended after Jerusalem was destroyed in AD 70.

See The Action Bible *page 662 and Mark 14:53–65; 15:1–11; Luke 23:1–12; Acts 4; 23:1–10.*

SAPPHIRA

(SEE ANANIAS OF JERUSALEM)

SARAI/SARAH

The wife of Abraham. At first her name was Sarai. God promised Abram that he and Sarai would be the parents of a nation of people. After many years, God kept His promise, and Sarah, at age ninety, gave birth to a boy. He was named Isaac, which means "laughter." Sarah died when she was 127, and Abraham buried her in a cave in a field he bought.

See The Action Bible *pages 44–52, 56 and Genesis 11:29–12:20; 16:1–17:19; 18:1–15; 21:1–14; 23. See also* Abram/Abraham.

SAUL, KING OF ISRAEL

The son of Kish, and Israel's first king. When the prophet Samuel anointed him king, Saul was a tall, handsome young man who knew how to work hard. He was humble and did not consider himself worthy to be king. God used him to win some battles against the Philistines, one of Israel's toughest enemies.

Although Saul was brave, he was not a good king. After David killed Goliath, Saul became jealous of David's popularity and tried repeatedly to kill him, even though David was close friends with Saul's son Jonathan. But David always escaped.

Saul also was impatient and did not always obey God's commands. Once he made a sacrifice to God instead of waiting for the priest Samuel to make the sacrifice. Another time he disobeyed God and kept some sheep and cattle he found in the camp of the Amalekites after they were defeated. Later, Saul went to a woman who claimed to speak to the dead. He wanted to know what would happen in a battle with the Philistines. Saul learned that he would die in battle. Saul and his three sons were killed in the same battle.

See The Action Bible *pages 258–305 and 1 Samuel 9–32. See also* Witch of Endor.

SCAPEGOAT

On the Day of Atonement, two goats were chosen. One goat was sacrificed. The other goat was released into the wilderness as a symbol for the removing of the sins of the high priest and the people. The high priest would place his hands on the goat before sending the goat away, thus giving the sins to the goat.

See The Action Bible *page 165 and Leviticus 16.*

SCEPTER

A rod or baton that symbolized the authority of a ruler. Some scepters were long and thin like a curtain rod; others were short and flat. King Ahasuerus held out his scepter to Queen Esther to show that she had his permission to speak.

See The Action Bible *page 500 and Esther 4:9–5:8.*

SCORPION

Ancient scorpions were about two to four inches long and the deadliest of insects. Scorpions were often mentioned as symbols of pain and betrayal. Rehoboam, the son of Solomon, told the people of Israel that he would whip them with scorpions—an expression that meant he would treat them harshly. His words also implied the use of a whip called a "scorpion," which stung like the tail of a scorpion. The apostle John later saw a vision of a terrible creature in the end times that will cause pain to people like the sting of a scorpion.

See The Action Bible *page 370 and 1 Kings 12:11; Revelation 9:5–6.*

SCROLL

(SEE WRITING)

SEA OF GALILEE

Sometimes called the Lake of Gennesaret, the Sea of Tiberias, and the Sea of Chinnereth. It is a freshwater lake about thirteen miles long and eight miles wide in northern Israel near where Jesus grew up. There were nine large, thriving cities around the lake. Only Tiberias still exists, plus one tiny village, Magdala.

The Sea of Galilee had a rich fishing industry. Four of Jesus's disciples fished for a living in the Sea of Galilee. Many of Jesus's sermons and miracles took place along the shore. The sea was known for its sudden and violent storms. Jesus rescued His disciples in two such storms. Jesus sometimes taught large crowds from a boat anchored near the shore.

See The Action Bible *page 173 and Matthew 14:22–34; Mark 4:1, 35–41; Luke 5:1–11; John 6:16–21.*

SECOND COMING OF CHRIST

The night before Jesus was crucified, He told His disciples He would return. When He ascended to heaven, two angels told the disciples that Jesus would come again in the same manner as they had seen Him go. He will return for His people to take them to be with Him forever. Although Christians sometimes argue about when and how the second coming will occur, most agree that Jesus will return in a way that will be clearly visible.

See The Action Bible *page 651 and John 14:3; Acts 1:11; 1 Thessalonians 4:13–18; 2 Thessalonians 1:6–12; Revelation 19:11–27.*

SENNACHERIB

(SEE ASSYRIA; HEZEKIAH)

SERMON ON THE MOUNT

A sermon Jesus preached on a mountainside in His first year of ministry. It began with the Beatitudes and ended with the parable of the wise and foolish builders. Many of the sayings in this section are repeated in other parts of the Gospels. Since Jesus taught in many places, He no doubt repeated His teachings over and over.

See The Action Bible *page 566 and Matthew 5–7.*

SERPENT/SNAKES

Many different types of snakes were mentioned in the Bible. Adders or asps were poisonous snakes, probably similar to cobras. On the island of Malta, Paul was bitten by a viper, but survived. *Serpent* in the Bible seems to refer to a poisonous snake. In the story of the temptation of Adam and Eve in the garden of Eden, a serpent tempted Eve. Because of that incident, a snake, viper, or serpent is often used as a word picture for sin or for something evil. John the Baptist called the Pharisees a "brood of vipers." But Jesus told His disciples to be "shrewd as snakes and as innocent as doves."

See The Action Bible *pages 22, 123, 733 and Genesis 3:1–14; Psalm 58:4; Matthew 10:16; Luke 3:7; John 1:29; Acts 28:3–6; Romans 3:13; 2 Corinthians 11:3; Revelation 20:2.*

SHADRACH, MESHACH, ABEDNEGO

Daniel's three friends, along with Daniel, were taken from Judah to Babylon when King Nebuchadnezzar invaded Israel in 605 BC. Like Daniel, they were trained for three years in the king's court. Their names were also changed from the Hebrew names of Hananiah, Mishael, and Azariah to the Babylonian names Shadrach, Meshach, and Abednego.

King Nebuchadnezzar made an idol ninety feet high, which all his officers were to worship. Shadrach, Meshach, and Abednego refused because they worshipped God, so

the king had them thrown into a fiery furnace. The furnace was so hot, the men who threw Shadrach, Meshach, and Abednego in were killed instantly. Then an amazing thing happened. As the king looked into the furnace, he saw four men walking around instead of three. God sent an angel to be with the three men. They left the furnace unharmed.

See **The Action Bible** *pages 470, 476 and Daniel 1–3.*

SHEEP/LAMB

Sheep are mentioned more often in the Bible than any other animal. The earliest mention is in Genesis 4:2, where Abel, the son of Adam and Eve, "was a keeper of sheep" (KJV). Sheep were kept more for their milk and wool than for their meat. The needs of the sheep kept many people living as nomads. The sheep needed pasture and water, so the shepherd and his household moved with the sheep from place to place. Sheep needed constant care. This is why God's people were called "sheep." David describes God as a Shepherd in Psalm 23. This description was based on the well-known habits of shepherds in caring for their sheep. Jesus later called Himself the Good Shepherd.

Lambs were the animals most frequently used as a Jewish sacrifice. They were used at the Passover feast, in the morning and evening burnt offerings in the tabernacle, and for many other sacrifices. For the Israelites, the lamb was a symbol of innocence and gentleness. John the Baptist called Jesus the "Lamb of God."

See **The Action Bible** *pages 24, 325, 594, 649 and Genesis 4:2; Psalm 23:1; 100:3; John 1:29; 10:11. See also* **Lamb of God.**

SHIELD

Shields (sometimes called bucklers) were large or small objects that soldiers carried to protect themselves from the spears and swords of enemies. Shields were usually wickerwork (thin, flexible twigs woven together) or leather stretched over a wooden frame. The leather was oiled before battle to preserve it or to make it glisten.

See **The Action Bible** *page 149 and Isaiah 21:5.*

SHIP/BOAT

The Israelites were farmers rather than sailors because they had no harbors. Most of the Mediterranean coast was usually controlled by their enemies, the Philistines and the Phoenicians, who were the main shipbuilders and sailors of the Mediterranean world.

The New Testament mentions Galilean fishing boats and merchant ships. The Galilean boats had small sails and oars, and could carry about twelve men and a load of fish. Jesus sometimes preached from these boats. Many of His disciples were fishermen and were used to sailing on the Sea of Galilee. Once they were terrified during a squall and feared that their boat would sink. Jesus, however, calmed the storm and kept the boat afloat.

Ships were important to Paul's journeys across the Aegean and Mediterranean Seas. There were no special ships for passengers, so Paul traveled on merchant ships that carried grain and other cargo.

See The Action Bible *pages 704, 708, 731–733 and Matthew 8:23–27; 14:22; Mark 4:1; Luke 5:3; Acts 27; 2 Corinthians 11:25. See also* Paul/Saul of Tarsus; Shipwreck.

SHIPWRECK

The destruction of a ship. Travel in Bible times was pretty risky, especially in the Adriatic Sea with its high winds. Paul was shipwrecked more than once. When the disciples sailed with Jesus on the Sea of Galilee, they were terrified during a storm. For experienced fishermen to be frightened, the storm was a big deal. But Jesus calmed the storm and prevented their ship from sinking.

See The Action Bible *pages 731–733 and Matthew 8:23–27; Acts 27:27–28:6; 2 Corinthians 11:25. See also* Ship/Boat.

SHOWBREAD/ HOLY BREAD

Twelve loaves of bread, representing the twelve tribes of Israel. The loaves were placed on a special gold-covered table in the tabernacle (later the temple) each Sabbath by the priests. This bread was also called the "bread of the Presence," referring to the presence of God. The twelve loaves were arranged in two rows on a table in the Holy Place of the tabernacle or temple. When fresh loaves were brought each Sabbath, the old loaves were removed and could be eaten only by the priests. David and his hungry men, however, ate these special loaves while on the run from Saul.

See The Action Bible *page 289 and Exodus 25:30; Leviticus 24:5–9; 1 Samuel 21:1–7; 1 Chronicles 9:32. See also* Tabernacle/Tent of Meeting.

SIHON

An Amorite king living in Heshbon, a city in Moab, during the time of the Israelites' exodus from Egypt. Sihon refused to allow the people of Israel to pass through his land and decided to go to war with them. His ally was Og, another Amorite king of a region called Bashan. Both kings were defeated.

See The Action Bible *page 185 and Numbers 21:21–35; Deuteronomy 2:24–37; Joshua 12:2–5. See also* Amorites.

SILAS

One of Paul's companions on his second missionary journey. He is sometimes called Silvanus. Like Paul, he was a Jew and a Roman citizen. The church in Jerusalem sent Silas with Paul and Barnabas to the Christians in Antioch to explain the decisions that had been made about Gentile Christians keeping the Jewish Law.

Silas later returned to his home in Jerusalem while Paul and Barnabas stayed in Antioch. However, when Paul and Barnabas separated, Paul chose Silas to go with him on the second missionary journey. Silas was beaten and imprisoned with Paul in Philippi. They then went on to Thessalonica. After a three-week stay that ended in a riot, they continued on to Berea. Silas and Timothy stayed in Berea for a short time while Paul went on to Athens.

Silas and Timothy joined Paul in Corinth and stayed there for some time. From Corinth, Paul wrote two letters back to the church at Thessalonica. Silas is mentioned in both of them (he

is called Silvanus). Scholars believe Silas may have helped Paul in writing these letters. Silas also served as a scribe for the apostle Peter.

See **The Action Bible** *page 707 and Acts 15:22–17:15; 2 Corinthians 1:19; 1 Thessalonians 1:1; 2 Thessalonians 1:1; 1 Peter 5:12. See also* **Paul/Saul of Tarsus.**

SILVER

Silver was used as money and also to make things: cups and crowns for kings and nobles, jewelry, idols, and the trumpets, bowls, and other furnishings in the tabernacle and temple. Silver was refined in furnaces. Judas agreed to betray Jesus for thirty pieces of silver. Many silversmiths in Ephesus made silver statues of the Greek goddess Artemis.

See **The Action Bible** *pages 619, 723 and Exodus 25:3; Leviticus 27:16; Matthew 26:14–16; Acts 19:24. See also* **Coins/Money.**

SIMON OF BETHANY

A Pharisee who had leprosy. After inviting Jesus to have dinner in his home, Simon found fault with Jesus for permitting a woman with a bad reputation to anoint Him with expensive ointment.

See **The Action Bible** *page 610 and Matthew 26:6–13; Luke 7:36–50.*

SIMON OF CYRENE

Cyrene is a city in North Africa. A man named Simon from this city was in Jerusalem when Jesus was crucified. The soldiers made him carry Jesus's cross.

See **The Action Bible** *page 635 and Luke 23:26; Acts 2:10; 11:20.*

SIN/DISOBEDIENCE

Any act or thought that goes against God and His will. When we sin, we sin against God, who is perfect. Sin separates us from God. Every person beginning with Adam has sinned. The penalty for sin is eternal separation from God. God knew that it's impossible for us to get rid of our sin or our guilt alone. But because He wants us to be free to love Him and

be friends with Him, He sent His Son, Jesus, to die for our sins so the penalty of our sin can be removed. There is one sin God won't forgive. Jesus said, "Whoever blasphemes against the Holy Spirit will never be forgiven; they are guilty of an eternal sin" (Mark 3:29 NIV). This means a person rejects God by claiming that God's power is evil. When a person rejects God and the forgiveness He offers, his sin can't be forgiven.

See The Action Bible pages 172, 447 and Psalm 51:9; Isaiah 53:6; Matthew 1:21; 12:32; Mark 3:29; Luke 12:10; John 3:16, 18; Romans 3:23; 1 Corinthians 15:3; 2 Corinthians 5:21; Hebrews 10:26–29; 1 Peter 2:24; 1 John 1:7–9; John 5:16. See also Blasphemy.

SISERA

Commander of the army of Canaanites whose king was Jabin. The Canaanites were difficult to fight, for they had nine hundred chariots of iron, and the Israelites had none. Deborah and Barak gathered men from other tribes to fight Sisera's forces and defeated his army. Sisera fled on foot, hiding in the tent of a woman named Jael who later killed him.

See The Action Bible page 213 and Judges 4. See also Deborah.

SLAVERY

A system in which a person can be owned by another person. Slavery was an accepted part of life in Bible times. Many times in war, people were captured and forced into slavery. The people of Israel lived as slaves for over four hundred years in Egypt until Moses and Aaron were sent to free them. Joseph was sold into slavery by his brothers.

There were rules in the Old Testament about slaves. A person could sell himself or herself into slavery. He or she could be free from slavery after six years. The apostles Paul and Peter gave advice to slaves and those who owned them. Both urged that slaves be obedient. The masters of the slaves were to treat their slaves kindly.

Because of these rules, some people have fooled themselves into believing that God approves of slavery. But the slave trade practiced in the seventeenth through the nineteenth centuries and in some parts of the world today was harsh and cruel and not at all acceptable to God.

See **The Action Bible** *pages 93, 95, 117–118 and Genesis 37:26–28; 39; Exodus 1–3; 21:1–11, 20–21; Leviticus 25:39–55; Ephesians 6:5–9; 1 Timothy 6:1–2; 1 Peter 2:18–21. See also* **Philemon, book of.**

SLING

A common weapon for hunting animals and for war. It was not like our slingshots. The sling was made of two narrow strips of leather joined in the middle by a wider piece where the stone was held. The person using it tied one end to his wrist and twirled

the other end above his head before releasing the stone. Seven hundred left-handed men from the tribe of Benjamin were so skilled that they could "sling stones at an hair breadth, and not miss" (Judg. 20:16 KJV). David killed the giant Goliath with such a sling. Men with slings were a regular part of the armies of Israel.

See **The Action Bible** *pages 272, 280 and Judges 20:16; 1 Samuel 17:40–50.*

SODOM

A city God destroyed during the time of Abraham. Scholars do not know where the city was located, for no traces of it have been found. Lot and his family went to live in Sodom after he separated from Abraham. Later, God told Abraham He was going to destroy Sodom and another city, Gomorrah, because of the evil behavior of the people. Abraham pleaded with God, and for the sake of Abraham, God warned Lot to take his family and run away.

See **The Action Bible** *page 52 and Genesis 18:16–19:29. See* **Lot;** **Lot's wife.**

SOLOMON

The third and last king of the united kingdom of Israel, reigning from 970 to 930 BC. He was the son of David and Bathsheba and was well-known for his great wisdom. While he was king, Israel experienced a golden age. He developed a strong army and maintained peace with the countries around him.

He is most remembered for the beautiful temple to God that he commissioned, based on plans of his father, King David. It took seven years to build. It replaced the tabernacle, where the people had worshipped for about four hundred years.

Solomon started his reign with great promise. He asked God for wisdom, and God gave him his request. He wrote some of the psalms, many of the proverbs, and was believed to have written the books of Ecclesiastes and Song of Solomon. However, as Solomon grew older, he married many foreign wives and began to worship their gods. So, God promised to take away part of the kingdom from Solomon's family line after Solomon's death.

See The Action Bible *pages 328, 353–359 and 1 Kings 1–11; Psalms 72; 127; the books of Proverbs, Ecclesiastes, Song of Solomon. See also* Temples.

SON OF GOD

A title used in the New Testament to show that Jesus was the unique Son of God—born of the Holy Spirit. Although Jesus did not describe Himself as the Son of God, He agreed when others called Him that. At Jesus's baptism, and also on the Mount of Transfiguration, a voice from heaven said, "You are my beloved Son; with you I am well pleased" (Mark 1:11 ESV).

Jesus taught the disciples that His relationship to God was different from their relationship to God. He often spoke of "My Father" rather than "our Father." Only when He taught the disciples to pray did He say, "Our Father." The gospel of John and the letters of John often speak of Jesus as God's Son. Paul spoke of Jesus as the Son of God in his preaching and his letters.

See The Action Bible *page 593 and Mark 1:11; 9:7; John 3:16; Acts 9:20; Romans 1:4.*

SON OF MAN

Jesus's favorite name for Himself. It is used over seventy times in the Gospels. With this term, Jesus identified Himself as a true man as well as being the Son of God. He often spoke of Himself this way when talking about the need to suffer and to give His life for the sins of all people. The Old Testament prophet Ezekiel also was called "son of man."

See The Action Bible *page 670 and Ezekiel 4:1; Mark 9:31; 14:41, 62; Luke 18:31–33; 21:27–28; John 13:31.*

SONG OF SOLOMON, BOOK OF

(SEE SOLOMON)

SOUL

The part of a person that is not physical. The soul is a way to describe the feelings, will, and desires of a human being. Moses told the people of Israel to "love the LORD your God with all your heart and with all your soul and with all your strength" (Deut. 6:5 NIV). This means loving God with everything that makes you who you are.

See The Action Bible *page 529 and Deuteronomy 6:5; Psalm 23:3; Matthew 10:28.*

SPIES/SCOUTS

In Bible times spies were sent to enemy territories to find out about military strength or to spread rumors that would hurt the enemy. Moses sent twelve spies into Canaan. Later, Joshua sent two spies to Canaan. In the New Testament times, the chief priests sent spies to find some charges against Jesus.

See The Action Bible *pages 173–176, 193 and Numbers 13–14; Joshua 2:1–24; Luke 20:19–20.*

SPIRITUAL GIFTS

Special abilities that God gives to His people. The Holy Spirit works through people as they use their gifts. These gifts are to be used to help people learn about Jesus and to help other Christians grow in their faith. Some of the gifts Paul mentions in his letters are the following: prophecy, teaching, helping, encouragement, speaking in tongues, hospitality, working miracles, healing, and being a pastor, evangelist, administrator, or apostle.

When the Holy Spirit came at Pentecost, He gave Jesus's disciples the ability to speak in languages other than their own. When Peter and John healed the man begging at the Beautiful Gate, this was another gift of the Spirit. Barnabas, a missionary who traveled with Paul, was called the "Son of Encouragement," because of his spiritual gift.

See The Action Bible *pages 654, 659 and Acts 4:36; Romans 12:6–8; 1 Corinthians 12; 14; Ephesians 4:7–13. See also Feasts; Barnabas; Paul/Saul of Tarsus.*

STAFF/ROD

A shaft of wood used for support in walking or climbing. Although in many sections of the Bible, *staff* and *rod* had the same meaning, sometimes a rod was a stick used to punish someone. The staffs or rods of Moses and Aaron were used by God to work miracles. A staff was often a sign of authority. A shepherd used his rod or staff to beat off attacking animals or to rescue lost sheep. He used his staff to count the sheep every day or to grab a sheep that had fallen in a crevice.

Aaron's staff was probably a straight piece of wood made from an almond tree. Aaron's staff turned into a serpent when he threw it down before the pharaoh. When God told Moses to stretch out the staff, the waters of the Nile turned into blood. The staff was used in other plagues. Later, when Korah and others tried to get the people to rebel against Aaron's authority as high priest, his staff became part of a test to show that Aaron was God's choice. Twelve staffs (one for each tribe of Israel) were placed in the tabernacle. The next morning, only Aaron's staff had buds, blossoms, and ripe almonds. Aaron's staff later was placed inside the ark of the covenant.

See **The Action Bible** *pages 123–124, 129, 143, 181 and Exodus 7:8–20; 8:16–19; Numbers 17:1–11; Psalm 23:4; Hebrews 9:4. See also* **Ark of the Covenant.**

STAIRWAY OF JACOB

While traveling to the home of his uncle Laban in Haran, Jacob had a dream of a great stairway. Some Bible translations mention a ladder, others a stairway. On it, angels traveled to and from the earth. This was a sign of God's commitment to take care of Jacob and be his God. Jesus later referred to Jacob's dream but mentioned that angels would come down from heaven, just as they did in Jacob's dream, only they would come down to the earth and return to heaven on the Son of Man. By this Jesus meant that He was the only way to God.

See **The Action Bible** *page 78 and Genesis 28:10–22; John 1:51.*

STAR OF THE EAST

The light that guided the wise men to Bethlehem. Many astronomers have tried to figure out what caused this star to shine at that time in such a distinct way, since the movement of most stars is so exact that their positions can be determined for centuries ahead or centuries past. One idea is that it was the result of a conjunction of the planets Jupiter and Saturn that is known to have occurred about 7 BC. It could also have been a supernova—a faint star that suddenly becomes brighter and then fades slowly for no known reason. Whatever the star was, God planned whatever was necessary to make it shine at the right time.

See **The Action Bible** *pages 535–537 and Matthew 2:1–12.*

STEPHEN

The first Christian known to die for his faith. He was one of seven deacons in the church in Jerusalem who were

chosen to be in charge of giving food and money to poor widows. Through the power of the Holy Spirit, Stephen performed miracles and preached before the Jewish council when he was accused of blasphemy. Those who listened became so angry they took him outside the city and stoned him to death.

See The Action Bible *page 669 and Acts 6–7.*

STONES OF REMEMBRANCE

When Joshua led the people of Israel to cross the Jordan River into Canaan, God caused the waters of the Jordan River to stop flowing. Joshua and the men of Israel gathered stones from the middle of the Jordan to remember the occasion. Twelve stones were taken— one for each tribe.

See The Action Bible *page 197 and Joshua 3–4.*

STRAW

(SEE BRICKS)

SUSA

The capital city of the Persian Empire. Xerxes ruled from this city. Esther was made queen here.

See The Action Bible *page 489 and the book of Esther.*

SWORD/DAGGER

Swords are the weapons most frequently mentioned in the Bible. Normally they were long, broad knives with a handle. Some swords had two sharp edges, some only one. They were usually carried by the soldier in a sheath on his left side. A dagger is a smaller sword. A sword is often used in the Bible as a word picture for the judgment of God or for violence of any kind. Jesus said, "All who take the sword will perish by the sword" (ESV). A sword is also used as a word picture of the power of the Word of God.

See The Action Bible *pages 23, 150, 187, 210, 429 and Genesis 3:24; Judges 3:15–17; Matthew 26:52; Ephesians 6:17; Hebrews 4:12. See also* Ehud.

SYCAMORE FIG

The sycamore tree Zacchaeus climbed in order to see Jesus was a sycamore fig tree. The fig tree is a slow-growing tree that needs special care. Jesus cursed a fig tree that didn't produce fruit.

See The Action Bible *page 609 and Mark 11:20–22; Luke 19:4. See also* Zacchaeus.

SYNAGOGUE

A place where Jewish people meet together to read the Old Testament and worship God. *Synagogue* can refer to the building in which they meet and to the people who meet there. Many historians believe that synagogues began after the Jewish people were taken into exile in Babylonia in 597 BC. Since they had no temple, they began to gather together on the Sabbath to read and worship.

By New Testament times, synagogues were common throughout the Mediterranean area, wherever there were ten or more Jewish families in a city. Most synagogues were simple buildings, unlike the temple in Jerusalem. Each synagogue had a wooden chest in which the Old Testament scrolls were kept wrapped in a linen cloth. Those who read from the scrolls stood on some kind of platform. Jesus and Paul regularly attended synagogue.

The people usually sat on benches along the walls. Sometimes there was a gallery or balcony where the women sat. Some scholars think that in some synagogues women were seated on one side and men on the other, or women were seated in a separate room. In some areas, women may not have been permitted in the synagogue.

See The Action Bible *page 716 and Luke 4:16; Acts 17:2.*

SYRIA

(SEE DAMASCUS)

TABERNACLE/TENT OF MEETING

The Israelites' sacred tent for worship. The tabernacle was a symbol to the people of God's presence with them. They used it during their wanderings in the wilderness on their exodus from Egypt. It was used for worship and sacrifice until it was replaced by King Solomon's temple.

The tabernacle was about forty-five feet long and fifteen feet wide. It was made from cloth drapes and animal skins held up by acacia wood supports. Only the priests entered the tabernacle. A heavy curtain embroidered with red, purple, and blue cherubim divided the tabernacle into two smaller rooms.

The room nearest the entrance was called the Holy Place. It had an altar for incense. It also had golden candlesticks with seven branches and a table for special bread.

The room beyond the Holy Place was called the Holy of Holies or the Most Holy Place. It was the most sacred place in the tabernacle and temple. Only the high priest could enter this area, and only on the Day of Atonement. The ark of the covenant was kept in this section.

When the tabernacle was taken apart for moving, the ark and the two altars were carried by Levites.

See **The Action Bible** *page 162 and Exodus 25–27; 35–40. See also* **Ark of the Covenant; Bronze/ Copper; Showbread/Holy Bread.**

TABITHA

A Christian who lived at Joppa. She showed her love for Jesus by making clothing for those in need and helping in other ways. When she became ill and died, other Christians learned that Peter was in a nearby town and sent for him. When Peter arrived, he prayed beside Tabitha's body. By the power of the Holy Spirit, he raised her from the dead.

See **The Action Bible** *page 675 and Acts 9:36–42. See also* **Joppa.**

TABLE OF SHOWBREAD

(SEE SHOWBREAD/HOLY BREAD)

TABLETS OF THE LAW

Stone slabs or tablets on which Moses received the Ten Commandments from God. When Moses brought them down from his meeting with God on Mount Sinai, he found the Israelites worshipping a gold calf they had made in the forty days while he had been gone. In anger, Moses threw down the tablets, breaking them. God called Moses to cut two new slabs of stone and take them up the mountain to receive the Law again. This time Moses put the tablets of the Law into the ark of the covenant, which was placed in the tabernacle and later in King Solomon's temple. The tablets were lost forever when the temple was destroyed by the Babylonians in 586 BC.

See The Action Bible *page 158 and* Exodus 24:12–18; 32:15–20; 34:1–35.

TARSUS

A city ten miles from the northeast coast of the Mediterranean Sea. Tarsus was the birthplace and early home of the apostle Paul. Although it was located in what is now Turkey, it was then the capital of the Roman province of Cilicia. During Paul's time the city had a famous university. Tarsus was also famous for its goats' hair cloth.

See The Action Bible *pages* 431, 686 and Acts 21:39.

TAX

Money paid by citizens to support their rulers. Taxes were collected by the government and by the religious leaders in Bible times. Early Old Testament taxes included a half shekel yearly for the support of the tabernacle. This was equal to about 160 grains of barley or 8 grams of silver. This might be worth about five dollars today. Both rich and poor paid the same tax. After the Israelites demanded a king, the people had to pay heavy taxes, just as Samuel had warned. King Solomon put such heavy taxes on the people that after he died the northern tribes revolted, and the kingdom was divided.

During New Testament times the Roman rulers of Israel used local Jewish people to collect taxes for them. These men agreed to collect a certain amount for the government. Anything extra became their salary. Many tax collectors became rich that way and were hated by others because they worked for the Roman government and were not always honest.

A census for taxation brought Mary and Joseph to Bethlehem at the time of Jesus's birth. Later, when Jesus was an adult, Jesus told Peter that he would find a coin in a fish's mouth to pay the temple tax. Amazing! The Pharisees tried to trick Jesus once by asking Him if taxes should be paid to Caesar. Jesus had a good answer for them!

See The Action Bible *pages 562, 615–617 and Exodus 30:13–15; 1 Samuel 8:11–18; Matthew 17:24–27; Luke 2:1–7; 20:20–26.* See also Matthew; Zacchaeus.

TEL-ABIB

The place in Babylon where Ezekiel and other people from Israel lived after being exiled there by King Nebuchadnezzar of Babylon.

See The Action Bible *page 456 and Ezekiel 3:15.*

TEMPLES

The permanent place of Jewish worship through much of the Old Testament and New Testament periods. Between 950 BC and AD 70, three different temples were built on the same hill in Jerusalem—Mount Moriah, the place where Abraham was going to sacrifice Isaac.

Solomon's Temple. King Solomon ordered the building of the first temple in 950 BC to replace the tabernacle. Its basic floor plan resembled that of the tabernacle. It took seven years to build the temple itself and thirteen more to finish the other buildings that were part of the complex. Many of the furnishings were made of gold or bronze. The temple was considered one of the most beautiful buildings in the world. The nation of Israel was very proud of it. Between 950 and 586 BC, however, some of the kings allowed the worship of idols inside this temple that had been dedicated to God. Other kings took treasures from the temple to pay off foreign attackers. King Josiah removed the pagan altars, cleaned up and repaired the temple, and restored it to its proper use. The Babylonians destroyed this temple in 586 BC when they burned Jerusalem.

Zerubbabel's Temple. The building of this temple was supervised by Zerubbabel, the governor of the Jews returning from Babylon, and Jeshua, the high priest. It was completed in 515 BC. No description of this temple exists, but it probably followed the same pattern as Solomon's temple. Although it was beautiful, it was much simpler and less expensive than Solomon's. Some Jews wept because it was so modest compared to Solomon's temple. The returning Jews had little money for the building.

Herod's Temple. Herod's temple was begun about 20 BC. It took more than forty-six years to build. This was the temple in which Jesus was presented as a baby and later traveled to regularly for the required feasts. Herod's temple was burned and destroyed along with the rest of Jerusalem in AD 70 by the Romans. But the foundation of one wall remains today—the Western Wall, or Wailing Wall. Many people go there to worship and pray.

See The Action Bible *pages 353, 359, 511, 526 and 2 Samuel 7; 1 Kings 6–8; 2 Kings 21–23; 2 Chronicles 2–7; Ezra 1–8; Luke 2:21–38; John 2:12–25. See also* Veil of the temple.

TEMPT/TEMPTATION

The lure or pressure to do something wrong. Satan tempts us to do evil, sometimes working through our own desires. Satan first appeared in the form of a serpent to Eve, who gave in to the temptation Satan offered. Satan used these same ideas to tempt Jesus in the wilderness after Jesus fasted forty days. But Jesus resisted the temptation by using verses from the Bible. His resistance showed that He was the Son of God and that resistance is possible. Although we often fail, God offers help when we are tempted.

See **The Action Bible** *pages 21–23, 548 and Genesis 3; 22; Matthew 4:1–11; Mark 1:12–13; Luke 4:1–13; 1 Corinthians 10:13; Hebrews 2:18; 4:15.*

TEN COMMANDMENTS

(SEE COMMANDMENT)

TENT

A movable shelter made of cloth or skins supported by poles—the regular living place of many Old Testament people and of shepherds and soldiers in the New Testament. Most tents in Bible times were made of goats' hair cloth. Often the covering appeared striped because of the addition of patches over worn or torn places. People slept inside on coarse straw mats and cooked on stoves that were only a group of stones at the tent entrance, or a hole in the ground. When Rebekah arrived with Eliezar to marry Isaac, Isaac brought Rebekah to his mother's tent. The tabernacle used by Israel in the wilderness was a tent.

See **The Action Bible** *pages 63, 163 and Genesis 18:10; 24:67; Exodus 26.*

TESTAMENTS, OLD AND NEW

Testament means "agreement." The Old Testament laid the foundation for the time when Jesus would come and teach more about God. The Old Testament tells about God's concern for the Hebrew nation and His instructions on how it was to live and worship. The New Testament is the new agreement God made with people through the life, death, and resurrection of Jesus.

The Old Testament. The first part of the Bible has thirty-nine books that record what happened from the time God created the world until the time of Malachi, the last prophet—about 400 BC. The first five books—Genesis, Exodus, Leviticus, Numbers, and Deuteronomy—are called the Law and were written by Moses. The next group of books, the books of history, record what happened to the people of Israel from the time they entered Canaan until about 400 BC. These books are Joshua, Judges, Ruth, 1 and 2 Samuel, 1 and 2 Kings, 1 and 2 Chronicles, Ezra, Nehemiah, and Esther. Five books of poetry appear next in the Old Testament: Job, Psalms, Proverbs, Ecclesiastes,

and the Song of Solomon. After the poetry books come the books of the major prophets: Isaiah, Jeremiah, Lamentations, Ezekiel, and Daniel. After these come twelve short books known as the minor prophets: Hosea, Joel, Amos, Obadiah, Jonah, Micah, Nahum, Habakkuk, Zephaniah, Haggai, Zechariah, and Malachi.

The New Testament. A collection of twenty-seven books written about the life of Jesus, the early church, and the Christian faith. They were written between the years AD 50 and 90. There are four kinds of books in the New Testament: the Gospels (Matthew, Mark, Luke, and John); Acts; the epistles (Romans; 1 and 2 Corinthians; Galatians; Ephesians; Philippians; Colossians; 1 and 2 Thessalonians; 1 and 2 Timothy; Titus; Philemon; Hebrews; James; 1 and 2 Peter; 1, 2, and 3 John; and Jude); and the book of Revelation.

See The Action Bible *pages 17–515, 521–744 and the books of the Old and New Testaments. See also* Torah.

THANKSGIVING

(SEE WORSHIP/PRAISE)

THESSALONIANS, 1 AND 2

Paul wrote both letters around AD 51 to the church he started in Thessalonica during a stay of only three weeks. His coworkers Silas and Timothy had been with him. Paul had been forced to leave Thessalonica because of opposition from Jewish leaders. He went on to Berea, then Athens, and finally Corinth, but sent Timothy back to Thessalonica from Athens. After Timothy returned to Corinth with a good report of the new church in Thessalonica, Paul wrote the first letter to the Thessalonians. The people of Thessalonica were so excited about the promise of the second coming of Jesus that some had given up their jobs. Paul wrote to tell them that no one knows for sure when Christ will come again. Each person must live in a way that pleases God. The second letter was written a few months after the first letter to encourage these new Christians to remain faithful to Christ, even through persecution.

See The Action Bible *pages 710, 716–719 and 1 and 2 Thessalonians.*

THESSALONICA

The chief seaport of Macedonia. Sometimes called Salonika, it is now the second-largest city in modern Greece. In New Testament times it was an important trade city. Paul visited here on a missionary journey, but had to leave after three weeks because of persecution. However, the church he started there grew vigorously. He later sent Timothy to Thessalonica to help the new Christians.

See The Action Bible *page 716 and Acts 17:1–10.*

THOMAS

One of Jesus's twelve disciples. He was also called Didymus, which probably meant he was a twin. Although he is most remembered for his doubting, the Gospels show how much he loved Jesus. When Jesus went to Bethany to heal Lazarus, most of the disciples hesitated because they were afraid. They knew that Jewish leaders wanted to get rid of Jesus. Yet Thomas was willing to go with Jesus.

Later, Thomas showed his honesty and sincerity when he asked where Jesus was going after Jesus foretold His coming crucifixion. Thomas was not with the other disciples when Jesus appeared after His resurrection. When Thomas heard about it, he said he would not believe unless he could see and feel Jesus's body. Yet as soon as Jesus appeared, Thomas was convinced.

See The Action Bible *pages 566, 646 and John 11:16; 14:5; 20:24–29.*

THORNS

Thorns are plants with sharp points. They are common in Israel and are mentioned several times in the Bible. The crown of thorns placed on Jesus before His crucifixion was probably made from a thornbush now known as the Christ thorn.

See The Action Bible *page 570 and John 19:1–3.*

THRONE

Special chairs for kings or other heads of state on official occasions.

Because rulers sit on thrones, a throne is often used as a word picture for authority and power. Thrones were often beautifully decorated. Solomon's throne was made of ivory and gold and had twelve lion figures on its six steps. In visions, Isaiah, Ezekiel, Daniel, and John the apostle saw God on a throne. The New Testament also speaks of Jesus sitting on a throne to judge and rule the world, and Christians reigning with Him with justice and fairness.

See The Action Bible *page 419 and 1 Kings 10:18–20; Isaiah 6:1–3; Ezekiel 1:4–28; Daniel 7:9–10; Revelation 3:21; 4; 20:4–6.*

TIMOTHY

A close friend and helper to the apostle Paul. Timothy was the son of a Gentile father and a Jewish mother (Eunice), who was a Christian. His grandmother Lois also was a Christian. Timothy became like a son to Paul. When Paul was in prison or faced other hardships, Timothy was the person he wanted most to see.

Timothy joined Paul in Lystra on Paul's second missionary journey. After they were driven out of Thessalonica by Jewish persecution, Paul sent Timothy back to help the Christians there. Several times Paul sent Timothy to churches as his representative.

Timothy was with Paul during much of his third missionary journey. During the last years of Paul's life, Timothy served as a leader over the churches in Ephesus. Two books of the New Testament—1 and 2 Timothy—are letters that Paul wrote to Timothy at Ephesus. The second letter of Paul to Timothy was probably written while Paul was in prison in Rome, shortly before his death.

See The Action Bible *page 707 and Acts 16:1–5; Philippians 2:19–24; 1 Thessalonians 1:1; 2 Thessalonians 1:1; and throughout 1 and 2 Timothy.*

TIMOTHY, 1 AND 2

First Timothy was probably written about AD 63, while Paul was in Philippi between his first and second imprisonments in Rome. Timothy was serving as the leader over the churches in Ephesus. Paul treated Timothy like a son. Paul and Timothy had a deep friendship, and these letters are full of advice from Paul. Second Timothy is the last known letter of Paul before he was executed in Rome around AD 64. Knowing that he was near the end of his life, Paul wrote about Jesus as the conqueror of death, and the joy he was going to have in being with Christ. Paul warned Timothy that he probably would suffer persecution as Paul had.

See The Action Bible *page 738 and the 1 and 2 Timothy.*

TITUS

A friend and helper of the apostle Paul. He was a son of Gentile parents and may have become a Christian after listening to Paul preach. Later, he went with Paul to Jerusalem to meet with Jewish Christians there. These Jewish Christians did not realize that a Gentile could become a Christian without becoming a Jew first. In time, Titus became so well accepted that he was given many responsibilities among the early churches. Later, Titus became a pastor of the church on the island of Crete. Paul wrote a letter to him there.

See The Action Bible *page 726 and 2 Corinthians 2:13; 7:5–16; Galatians 2:1–10; the book of Titus.*

TITUS, BOOK OF

A letter from the apostle Paul to his friend Titus. Titus was a Christian leader on the island of Crete, where the church had many problems. Paul reminded Titus that pastors and leaders in a church must be holy people. They must be able to live happily with their own families if they are going to work well with the larger church family. They must be honest in all they do and not be lazy.

See The Action Bible *page 738 and the book of Titus.*

TOMB

A burial place, usually a natural or artificial cave. Early tombs were often natural caves in the rocky hills. Old Testament people often were buried in vaults or caves with their ancestors. Long after Abraham buried Sarah in a cave at Machpelah, his sons and their sons buried their dead in this area.

In New Testament times, Jews were buried in caves in stone cliffs. Several bodies might be in each tomb. Each body was wrapped in grave clothes and prepared with spices. One

opening was the entrance to all the ledges prepared for the bodies. Jesus, however, was buried in an empty new tomb, one bought by Joseph of Arimathea.

Tombs in Rome were called catacombs. These were large underground networks of caves and corridors. Niches in the walls served as ledges for bodies. Each niche could be sealed with bricks or a marble slab. When persecution was bad, early Christians hid in the catacombs.

See **The Action Bible** *page 641 and Genesis 23:14–20; 47:30; John 19:38–42.*

TONGUES OF FIRE

One of the signs of the Holy Spirit's arrival at Pentecost. All of the disciples, the brothers of Jesus, and some of the women following Jesus had gathered together in Jerusalem. Suddenly a sound like a mighty wind filled the house. Tiny flames seemed to rest on each person in the room as they were all filled with the Holy Spirit. Fire is usually one of the signs of God's presence.

See **The Action Bible** *page 654 and Acts 1:14, 2:1–13. See also* **Feasts.**

TORAH

Torah is the Hebrew word for the Law of God and refers to the first five books of the Old Testament, which were probably written by Moses around 1445–1406 BC.

See **The Action Bible** *pages 17–189 and the books of Genesis, Exodus, Leviticus, Numbers, and Deuteronomy.*

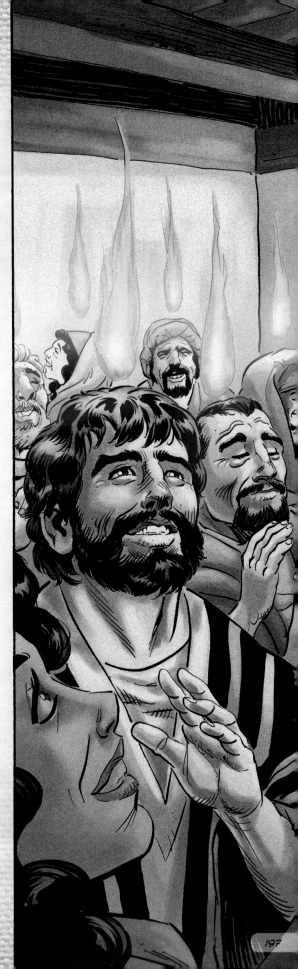

TOWER OF BABEL

A place where people began speaking different languages after God was displeased with them. At the time of the building of the tower, everyone spoke one language. The people tried to build a tower to the heavens. Their idea was to make a ziggurat—a tower with a series of levels, one on top of the other, each smaller than the one below it. At the top of such ziggurats was usually a shrine to a god. But God caused them to speak different languages so they could no longer understand one another. The people had no choice but to stop working on the tower. Many scholars believe the tower of Babel was in Babylon, located in what is now Iraq.

See **The Action Bible** *page 38* and **Genesis 11:1–9.**

TRANSFIGURATION, THE

A change in form or appearance. The word is used to describe the time when a dramatic change took place in Jesus's physical appearance as the disciples Peter, James, and John watched. This event took place on Mount Tabor or Mount Hermon shortly before His last trip to Jerusalem. As Jesus was praying, His face began to shine like the sun. His clothes became dazzling white. Moses and Elijah appeared and talked with Jesus about His coming death. Jesus's disciples were amazed and terrified.

See The Action Bible *pages 584–585 and* Matthew 17:1–8; Mark 9:2–8; Luke 9:28–36. *See also* Mount Hermon; Mount Tabor.

TREASON

An attempt to overthrow the government or to switch one's loyalties to another country. *Conspiracy* is another word used for treason. Queen Athaliah, who murdered most of her grandsons to take the throne of Judah, screamed, "Conspiracy!" when Jehoiada, the priest, anointed Josiah king of Judah. Jesus was accused of blasphemy and treason against Rome when He was crucified.

See The Action Bible *pages 427, 635 and* 2 Kings 11:12–14; Luke 23:13–25.

TREASURY

A place where valuable things are kept or placed. When King Hezekiah showed a group of Babylonian ambassadors his treasury, the prophet Isaiah predicted that Hezekiah's treasures would one day be taken away. In the temple where Jesus worshipped, tithes and taxes were paid at the treasury, or collection box. Jesus once sat near the treasury as He watched a poor widow bring her offering.

See The Action Bible *page 201 and Deuteronomy 28:12; 2 Kings 20:12–21; Mark 12:41.*

TREE OF THE KNOWLEDGE OF GOOD AND EVIL

A special tree that grew in the middle of the garden of Eden. God used this tree to test the obedience of Adam and Eve. God commanded Adam and Eve not to eat its fruit. There was probably not much special about the fruit—the sin was in disobeying God's command.

See The Action Bible *page 21 and Genesis 2:8–3:7. See also* Adam and Eve; Fall, the.

TRIAL

A legal matter decided before a judge. According to the Law given to Moses, two or three witnesses were required to convict a person of a crime.

The most well-known trial in the Bible is the trial of Jesus. It had three parts. After Jesus was arrested in the garden of Gethsemane, He was immediately brought to Jerusalem, to the Jewish council. Caiaphas, the high priest, was in charge of the trial. Caiaphas and his followers were jealous of Jesus's popularity. They found people to tell lies about Jesus so they could have an excuse to send Him to Pilate to be executed. Only Pilate, the representative of Rome, could have Jesus condemned to death. There they accused Jesus of treason— of saying He was a king.

To the Romans this was a serious crime, for it could mean Jesus was trying to stir up a rebellion. Pilate didn't think Jesus was a threat to the emperor, but he did not want the Jewish leaders to be angry with him. So he thought of a way to avoid the problem. Jesus was from Galilee—an area under the ruler Herod Antipas. Herod happened to be in Jerusalem then, so Pilate sent Jesus to him. But Herod sent Jesus back. Then Pilate had another idea. During the Passover feast, the custom was to release a Jewish prisoner. If the Jews chose Jesus for release, it would solve his problem. But the crowd was stirred up by the Jewish leaders. The people demanded that Barabbas, a murderer, be released. Pilate washed his hands to try to show that the guilt was not his. Then he sent Jesus to be crucified.

See **The Action Bible** *pages 627–633 and Deuteronomy 19:15–21; Matthew 26:57–27:26; Mark 14:53–15:15; Luke 22:54–23:25; John 19:1–16. See also* **Herod; Sanhedrin; Witness.**

TRIUMPHAL ENTRY/ PALM SUNDAY

Jesus's kingly entrance into Jerusalem on the Sunday before His crucifixion. He came riding a colt, a sign that He was on a mission of peace, not war. Conquering generals rode on horses or in chariots. Jesus rode the donkey colt to fulfill a prophecy by the Old Testament prophet Zechariah. As Jesus entered the city from the Mount of Olives, His followers shouted and sang, "Blessed is he who comes in the name of the Lord! ... Hosanna in the highest!" (Mark 11:9–10 ESV) Palm branches were laid in the road for the colt to walk on. Some people even spread their clothes in the road. Their enthusiasm filled the city. Each Palm Sunday we remember that day.

See **The Action Bible** *page 612 and Zechariah 9:9; Mark 11:1–11.*

TROAS

A Roman colony in the northwestern part of Asia Minor. Paul traveled here on two of his missionary journeys.

See **The Action Bible** *page 709 and Acts 16:8, 11; 20:5–6; 2 Corinthians 2:12.*

TRUTH

A fact; something that can be trusted. Truth is an absolute: something that acts as a standard for all other things. God is the source of all truth. He is the "true" God. The idols that many nations worshipped (Baal, Dagon, and so on) were "false" gods—not real. Jesus described Himself as "the truth." This meant that Jesus came from God. Everything He said and did was "the truth"—a true representation of God. When Jesus was put on trial before Pilate, Jesus explained that He was sent by God to testify to the truth. Pilate then asked, "What is truth?" Pilate had no idea what truth was!

Witnesses in trials were ordered to tell the truth. After all, a person's life often was at stake! Truth can also be described as important teachings and messages that come from God. Jesus taught people the truth of God and His kingdom. In many of his letters, Paul urged Christians to be obedient to the truth.

See **The Action Bible** *pages 381, 624 and Zechariah 8:16; John 8:32; 14:6; 18:37–38; Galatians 5:7.*

TYRE

An island city along the coast of what is now Lebanon. It is usually mentioned in connection with Sidon, another city of the Phoenicians. About fifty miles north of Nazareth, Tyre was a center of trade in ancient times and was famous for the purple dyes produced there. Ships from Tyre sailed all around the Mediterranean. During some of the Old Testament period, Tyre was a kingdom by itself and threatened Israel. Later Tyre was conquered by Assyria, then Egypt, Babylonia, and Persia. Three chapters of the book of Ezekiel discuss the fall of Tyre.

Jesus once visited the area of Tyre and healed the daughter of a Greek woman. Paul once stayed there for seven days with Christians. When he left, he and the Christians from Tyre, including children, had a prayer meeting together on the beach.

See **The Action Bible** *page 359 and Ezekiel 26–28; Mark 7:24–31; Acts 21:3–7.*

UPPER ROOM

The place where Jesus had the Last Supper with the disciples. It may have been the same upper room where the disciples met together to pray after Jesus ascended into heaven. It probably was a second-floor room built on the flat roof of the home of a friend of Jesus. Such rooms were commonly used as guest rooms and often had outside stairways.

See **The Action Bible** *page 621 and Mark 14:12–25; Luke 22:7–13; Acts 1:12–14.*

UR

The city where Abraham was born and grew up. It was near the north end of the Persian Gulf in what is now Iraq. Ur was a center of advanced learning in Abraham's day; it had libraries, schools, and many temples to idols. Ur was also a trading center. Ships carried alabaster, copper ore, ivory, gold, and hardwoods to trade at Ur. God called Abraham out of Ur and sent him to the land of Canaan.

See The Action Bible *page 44 and Genesis 11:28, 31; 15:7; Nehemiah 9:7.*

URIAH

The Hittite husband of Bathsheba and a loyal soldier in King David's army. David schemed to have Uriah put to death in order to marry Bathsheba. David told the commander of his army to put Uriah in the front lines, where he would likely be killed. Uriah was killed, and David later married Bathsheba, but he was punished by God for his sin.

See The Action Bible *page 321 and 2 Samuel 11:1–12:15.*

URIM AND THUMMIN/LOTS

Objects used by priests to discover God's choice in a matter. The Bible never describes these objects, only that they were thrown. Some have speculated that they were a way of prayerfully drawing straws in order to make a decision. We know only that they were a fair way for the Israelites to divide the land of Canaan. After Judas died, Matthias was chosen to be the twelfth disciple by casting lots. Lots also played a big part in the Feast of Purim.

See The Action Bible *page 261 and Numbers 26:52–56; 1 Samuel 10:20–24; Luke 1:9; Acts 1:26.*

UZZAH

An Israelite man who died instantly after touching the ark of the covenant. The ark was so holy it was not to be touched. After the Philistines returned the ark they stole from Israel, it was kept in the house of Abinadab, Uzzah's father. When King David and many people in Israel went to retrieve the ark, it was placed on a new cart pulled by oxen. Uzzah and his brother, Ahio, drove the cart. During the journey, the oxen stumbled, and Uzzah reached out to steady the ark and died.

See The Action Bible *page 318 and 2 Samuel 6:1–7; 1 Chronicles 13. See also* Ark of the Covenant.

VEIL

(SEE CLOTHING)

VEIL OF THE TEMPLE

A pair of thick curtains about eighteen inches apart that hung at the entrance of the Holy of Holies (or Most Holy Place in some versions of the Bible) in the temple. The veil hid the ark of the covenant and the mercy seat from the view of the people.

The curtains were woven with blue, purple, and scarlet thread with pictures of cherubim worked into them. In the early days, no one could go behind the veil except the priests.

Later, only the high priest could enter behind the veil, and even he could go only once a year—on the Day of Atonement. At Jesus's death, the veil in the temple was ripped by a miracle from top to bottom. This act showed that because of Jesus's death, all people could now come into God's presence by faith in Jesus.

See The Action Bible *page 639 and Exodus 26:31–33; 36:35; Leviticus 16:2–28; Numbers 18:7; Matthew 27:51; Hebrews 10:20. See also* **Tabernacle/Tent of Meeting; Temples.**

VINEYARD

Grapes were grown in ancient Egypt and Canaan even before Abraham's time. The hilly areas of Judea and Samaria were good for growing grapes. A vineyard was usually surrounded by a wall of stones or thorny hedges to keep out wild animals. Most vineyards had a tower for a watchman, a winepress hollowed out of rock, and a vat, which held the wine. Jesus once told a parable that described the planting of a vineyard. Grapevines needed much

care. Each spring they had to be pruned and the dead branches burned. Jesus used this as a word picture of how God helps each Christian become a better person.

During the harvest, sometimes the whole family guarded the vineyard against thieves. The time of stamping out the juice was one of great happiness. The people sang as they crushed the grapes with their feet. The wine was kept in new goatskin bags.

See The Action Bible *page 394 and Matthew 21:33–41; John 15:1–8.*

WALL

(SEE CITY)

WATERPOTS

Clay pitchers used in ancient times by people who had to haul water from wells or springs to their houses or to troughs for their animals. Each clay pot held several gallons of water. At the wedding in Cana, Jesus performed His first miracle by turning the water in large waterpots (20–30 gallons) into wine.

See The Action Bible *page 552 and Genesis 24:15–20; Luke 22:10; John 2:1–11.*

WEIGHTS AND MEASURES

In ancient times, units of measurement weren't always the same from culture to culture. The people of Israel had their own system, as did the Babylonians, Egyptians, and Canaanites. Some units of measure had to do with money. God warned the people of Israel not to use dishonest scales to measure silver or gold.

Cubit. While many modern translations use the word *feet* instead of *cubits*, a cubit was approximately the measurement from the hand to the elbow. Noah was told to make the ark "300 cubits" long.

Shekel. About four-tenths of an ounce—a standard unit of measurement. Abraham gave four hundred shekels of silver—a huge amount of money—for the cave of Machpelah, where Sarah was buried. Joseph was sold as a slave for twenty shekels of silver.

Talent. A talent was a way of measuring gold and silver. A talent was about seventy-five pounds. After winning a war against the Ammonites, David took a crown from the defeated king that weighed one talent. In Jesus's parable of the talents, talent was a way of saying "a large amount of money."

See The Action Bible *pages 68, 92, 614 and Genesis 6:15; 23:14–20; 37:28; 2 Samuel 12:30; Proverbs 11:1; Micah 6:11; Matthew 25:15–28. See also* Gold; Silver.

WELL

A hole dug in the ground to find water. Since water was very scarce in dry Israel, wells were important for people and animals. When a well was dug, rocks were placed around it and a cover over it to keep animals or people from falling in. Some wells were shallow; others were very deep. Sometimes dry wells or cisterns were used as hiding places. Often people fought over wells. Joseph's brothers threw him into an old, dry well. Among the famous wells in the Bible are the well where Jacob met Rachel, the well of Bethlehem, and the well at Sychar, where Jesus met a Samaritan woman.

See The Action Bible *page 65 and Genesis 29:1–10; 37:23–28; John 4:4–42.*

WHEAT

Wheat was the most common grain in Israel. The King James Version often calls wheat "corn." Jesus told a parable about wheat.

See The Action Bible *pages 99, 570 and Matthew 13:24–30.*

WIDOWS

In ancient times, widows were usually poor because most women did not inherit anything from their husbands. All property was inherited by sons. In Old Testament times, a widow wore special clothes to show she was a widow. The Old Testament Law had a rule that the Israelites were to use some of the Levites' tithes to feed widows. God would punish anyone who cheated or harmed widows.

The prophet Elijah stayed with a poor widow in Zarephath during a three-year famine. God provided food for them. Using the power of God, Elijah brought the dead son of the widow back to life. In the New Testament, the early church in Jerusalem appointed seven men to see that widows had enough food. The apostle Paul wrote to Timothy that the church should help older widows if they had no relatives to care for them.

See The Action Bible *pages 380, 618, 658 and Exodus 22:22–24; Deuteronomy 14:28–29; 1 Kings 17:7–24; Acts 6:1–6; 1 Timothy 5:3–16; James 1:27. See also* Elijah.

WILDERNESS

This is not a sandy wasteland like the Sahara. It usually refers to an area where grass grew but needed more rain to make it good farmland. An Israeli desert (or wilderness) was often a place where sheep grazed. The people of Israel wandered in the wilderness for forty years after leaving Egypt.

See The Action Bible *pages 59, 173 and Exodus 16–Deuteronomy 34.*

WINE

Fermented grape juice. Workers put grapes into the winepress and then walked and stamped on the grapes to press out the juice. The grape juice flowed through a hole near the bottom of the winepress into a smaller vat. Then the juice was made into wine. In Bible times, it was used as a drink, a medicine, and a disinfectant. Wine was also poured out as a special drink offering to God, a symbol of gratitude or willingness to change.

In the Bible, wine is spoken of both as a blessing and as a curse. Isaac blessed his son, wishing him plenty in grain and wine. But the prophet Hosea said wine takes away understanding. Jewish priests were commanded not to drink wine when they were on duty, and Nazirites were never to drink wine. In Old Testament times, wine was not mixed with water, but during the time of Jesus it was. The apostle Paul told Christians not to be drunk with wine but to be filled with the Spirit.

See The Action Bible *page 552 and Genesis 27:28; Leviticus 10:9; 23:12–13; Numbers 6:1–21; 15:5; Proverbs 20:1; 23:29–35; Luke 10:34; Ephesians 5:18.*

WISDOM

Learning, skills, common sense, and good judgment. A skill such as weaving or building was considered wisdom. Some parts of the Old Testament are called Wisdom Literature. They include Proverbs; Ecclesiastes; Job; and Psalms 19, 37, 104, 107, and 147–148. The Old Testament book of Proverbs applies wisdom to daily life situations such as raising children, handling money, telling the truth, and controlling anger. In Proverbs 8, wisdom is described as a woman who invites people to listen to her wisdom and live by it.

God is the source of wisdom. In the beginning of his reign, King Solomon asked God for wisdom, and God gave it to him. Solomon became known as the wisest king on earth. Job told some examples of the wisdom of God. Following God's commands is a sign of wisdom. If you need wisdom, you can ask God for it.

See The Action Bible *pages 353, 357 and Exodus 28:3; Deuteronomy 4:6; 1 Kings 3:4–28; 10:23–24; Job 28:20–28; Psalm 111:10; 1 Corinthians 1:24, 30; Colossians 2:3; James 1:5–8.*

WITCH OF ENDOR

A medium who lived in the town of Endor during the reign of King Saul. Mediums claimed to be able to speak to the dead. God had told the Israelites that they should not go to mediums, whose information came from Satan. But when the Philistines started a war against the Israelites, King Saul went to this woman and asked her to bring Samuel's spirit back from the dead. The women was shocked to see an old man in a robe. Saul learned that he and his sons would die the next day.

See The Action Bible *page 302 and Deuteronomy 18:10–14; 1 Samuel 28:3–25; 1 Chronicles 10:13–14.*

WITNESS

A person who tells the truth about what he has seen and knows no matter what it costs. The word *martyr* comes from the Greek word meaning "witness." A witness was to speak the truth in court. Another type of witness is someone who tells others the truth about Jesus.

The Ten Commandments includes a rule against "bearing false witness." This means lying. Queen Jezebel found men who would be false witnesses in order to steal the vineyard of Naboth. The men who told lies at Jesus's trial also were false witnesses.

God wants His people to be His witnesses about Jesus. The disciples were eyewitnesses to the death and resurrection of Jesus, and they told about it. When Jesus was taken into heaven, He told the disciples that they were to be His witnesses to the end of the earth.

See The Action Bible *page 649 and Exodus 20:16; Deuteronomy 19:15–19; 31:26; 1 Kings 21:7–14; Matthew 26:60; Luke 24:46–49; John 16:7–15; Acts 1:8; 2:32; Romans 8:15–17; Hebrews 10:15–18; 1 John 4:2.*

WOMAN AT THE WELL

This unnamed Samaritan woman talked with Jesus by a well in Samaria. Jesus's conversation with the woman amazed His disciples, because Jewish men didn't normally talk to women in public and because the Jews and the Samaritans didn't get along.

Jesus's knowledge about the woman proved that He was no ordinary man. The woman had a bad reputation in her town, which was proved when she came out to gather water in the middle of the day. Usually, women gathered water at the beginning of the day or during the evening when the weather cooled off. Because of Jesus's kindness, this woman quickly ran to tell everyone about Him.

See The Action Bible *page 556 and John 4:1–42.*

WORLD

Has several meanings in the Bible:

1. *The Earth.* Genesis 1–2 tell about the creation of the world, or earth.
2. *Wherever People Live.* Jesus told His disciples to go into "all the world" and preach the gospel.

3. *The Roman Empire.* At the time of the birth of Jesus, Caesar Augustus wanted "all the world" to be taxed.

4. *Greek Culture.* When Paul preached in Ephesus, a silversmith said that "the whole world" worshipped the goddess Artemis (Diana).

5. *The World to Come.* This involves not only a new physical place, but also a new way of life.

6. *The People Who Live on the Earth.* This is the meaning in John 3:16. Jesus told His disciples that the "world" hated Him because He pointed out its sins.

7. *Those Who Are Not Living the Way God Wants People to Live.* Jesus told the Pharisees that they were "of this world" but He was not. Paul said he had died to this world's ideas of doing whatever pleases oneself. True holiness is to keep oneself unstained from the world's basic idea of "me first."

See The Action Bible *pages 555, 649 and 1 Samuel 2:8; Mark 16:15; Luke 2:1; John 3:16; 7:7; 8:23; Acts 19:27; Galatians 6:14; Ephesians 2:2; Hebrews 6:5; James 1:27; 1 John 2:15–17; Revelation 11:15. See also* Idol/Idolatry.

WORSHIP/PRAISE

To honor and adore someone who is worthy of such high honor. The English word was originally *worthship* to show that the one being honored was worthy of praise. True worship involves not only the things we do but also the thoughts and feelings we have as we do them.

God wants His people to worship only Him. During Jesus's temptation, when Satan promised to give Him all the kingdoms of the world if He worshipped him, Jesus told him, "You shall worship the Lord your God and him only shall you serve" (Matt. 4:10 ESV).

God is worshipped publicly and privately. After the people of Israel left Egypt, they worshipped God publicly at the tabernacle set up in the wilderness. Later, when the temple was built in Jerusalem, the Israelites worshipped together in a more highly organized way. The people sang many psalms as part of their worship in the temple.

First-century Christians met in homes to worship God. Their worship included preaching, reading the Scriptures, praying, singing, celebrating the Lord's Supper, and using other gifts the Holy Spirit gave them. Today, Christians meet in church buildings and other places to worship God.

See The Action Bible *pages 134, 298 and Psalm 135:1–6; Matthew 4:10; Acts 2:42; 1 Corinthians 14:26;*

Ephesians 5:19–20; Revelation 19:10.
See also Tempt/Temptation.

WRATH OF GOD

God's anger with sin. The Old Testament prophets often talked about the wrath of God and what He would allow to happen to the people if they turned away from Him. Because God is holy and loves us, He is angry when we turn away from Him and fail to become all He wants us to be. If God did not care about us, He would not be angry when we mess up or try to mess up the lives of others.

When the people of Israel grumbled or rebelled against God, they felt God's wrath in the form of plagues, fires, and enemy nations that conquered them for a time. Jesus came to die for our sins and to free us from the punishment of God's wrath. When Jesus died on the cross, God poured out His anger on Jesus to make forgiveness with God possible. In the final judgment, all people who refuse Christ's way of salvation must face the wrath of God.

See The Action Bible page 168 and Numbers 11:1; Deuteronomy 1:26–36; Psalm 110:5–6; Romans 1:18; 1 Thessalonians 5:9.

WRESTLING

A popular sport during New Testament times. Paul may have watched wrestling matches in Corinth. He used wrestling as a word picture of the way Christians must struggle against Satan. The most famous wrestling match in the Bible was between Jacob and God's angel.

See The Action Bible page 86 and Genesis 32:24–30; Ephesians 6:12.

WRITING

Probably began in Bible lands about 3500 BC. Early writing involved simple pictures or lines that later developed into other symbols that were more like an alphabet.

Paper didn't exist in Bible times. Many people used chisels on stones for permanent records. When Moses was given the Ten Commandments from God, they were written on stone tablets. Sometimes people covered stones with plaster and then wrote in the plaster while it was still soft.

Many other common items were used for writing. Engraving on gold is mentioned in Exodus 28:36. Wood was sometimes coated with wax or clay and then used as a writing tablet. This is probably the kind of tablet Zechariah used when he was unable to speak. Broken pieces of pottery also were used. People could write on them with ink and then wash the writing off and use the pieces again.

Papyrus, a plant growing in water and swampy places, was used often for important letters or documents. The insides of the papyrus stalks were cut into thin strips, glued on top of each other crisscross, and then left under something heavy to make them stick together. When the sheets were dry, they were polished with stone and glued together to form long strips—scrolls—for writing. The scroll that King Jehoiakim burned was made of papyrus.

Parchment was an expensive writing material made from the skins of sheep or goats. It was made by removing the hair from the skins, soaking them in lime, and then stretching them on frames. The skins were finally rubbed smooth with chalk or pumice stone. Parchment lasted much longer than papyrus. For this reason, scribes often used parchment in making copies of Old Testament writings.

See The Action Bible *pages 158, 447–448 and Exodus 24:12; Deuteronomy 27:2–8;*

Judges 8:14; Job 19:24; Jeremiah 17:1; 32:14; 36:23; Ezekiel 2:9–10; 37:16–17; Luke 1:63. See also Zechariah, the priest.

XERXES/AHASUERUS

A powerful king of the Medes and the Persians. The name *Ahasuerus* is the Hebrew name for Xerxes. Xerxes reigned from about 486 to 465 BC and was the son of Darius. After becoming angry with his queen, Vashti, he decided to find a new wife. He later chose Esther, the cousin of Mordecai, to be the new queen. At the request of Haman, his chief officer, Xerxes wrote a law that all Jews were to be killed on a certain day. When Esther explained to the king about this evil plan, Xerxes ordered Haman to be executed. The Jews were allowed to protect themselves from harm.

See The Action Bible *pages 489–505 and the book of Esther. See also* Darius; Esther.

YOKE

A wood frame that harnessed two animals together for heavy work. Oxen were often yoked to pull a plow, wagon, or other farm equipment. The yoke was also a symbol of obedience for people. Jeremiah wore a yoke as a sign that the people were to submit to the conquering Babylonians. In the New Testament, yoke is a word picture for demands or burdens. Jesus invited people to take His yoke to join themselves to Him and His work. Loving and serving Him may look hard, but it is really easy when He helps us.

See The Action Bible *page 461 and Jeremiah 27:2–8; Matthew 11:28–30.*

ZACCHAEUS

The chief Jewish tax collector in Jericho during the time of Jesus. Zacchaeus was so short he had to climb a tree to see above the crowds and look at Jesus as He walked past. Jesus surprised Zacchaeus by stopping beneath the tree to announced that He would be staying at Zacchaeus's house. The crowds were surprised that Jesus would go to the house of a tax collector. But Zacchaeus showed his sorrow over his past wrong actions by giving half of his riches to the poor and repaying those he had cheated with four times the original amount.

See The Action Bible *page 609 and* Luke 19:1–10. *See also* Tax.

ZAREPHATH

A town near Sidon on the coast of the Mediterranean. Elijah traveled here during a three-year famine and stayed with a poor widow.

See The Action Bible *page 380 and 1 Kings 17:7–24. See also* Widows.

ZECHARIAH, THE PRIEST

A priest during New Testament times and the father of John the Baptist. He and his wife, Elizabeth, both followed God's commands, but were childless until their old age. One day while Zechariah was burning incense in the temple, the angel Gabriel appeared to announce that Zechariah and

Elizabeth would have a son. Zechariah didn't believe and asked for some sign that the angel's words were true. He was given a sign: he would not be able to speak until his son was born. Zechariah and his wife rejoiced at their son's birth and named him John.

See The Action Bible *page 526 and Luke 1:5–25, 57–80. See also* John, the Baptist.

ZECHARIAH

A prophet from a family of priests. His family returned to Jerusalem from the Babylonian exile to help rebuild the temple. He began prophesying about 520 BC and may have continued on and off for many years. The first part of his ministry was during the same period as the prophet Haggai. He helped encourage the people to rebuild the temple.

The book of Zechariah includes the five prophecies of Zechariah to the group of Jews who had returned to Jerusalem. The first prophecy encouraged the people to show they were sorry for their wrong actions by changing their ways. The second prophecy reminded the people to complete the temple. In the third prophecy, gold and silver were fashioned into a crown for Joshua, the high priest. This was a symbol for the promised Savior, who would be both priest and king to His people. In the fourth prophecy Zechariah urged the people to be fair with each other. In the fifth prophecy, the prophet looked into the future and made many references to the coming Messiah. Zechariah also predicted that the Savior would enter Jerusalem riding on a donkey.

See The Action Bible *page 511 and Ezra 5:1–2; the book of Zechariah. See also* Triumphal Entry/Palm Sunday.

ZEDEKIAH

The last king of Judah. After King Nebuchadnezzar of Babylon captured Jehoiachin, the previous king of Judah, Nebuchadnezzar chose Zedekiah to be king. Zedekiah was twenty-one years old at the time, and ruled for eleven years. He did not obey God's commands, nor would he listen to the advice of the prophet Jeremiah.

Jeremiah told Zedekiah that the Lord wanted Zedekiah to surrender to the Babylonians and spare the city from destruction. The Babylonian army had surrounded the city, and all food supplies were cut off. Instead of following Jeremiah's advice, Zedekiah and his soldiers tried to flee. He was captured and his sons were killed. Zedekiah was blinded and the city was destroyed in 586 BC.

See The Action Bible *page 461 and 2 Kings 24:17–25:7; Jeremiah 34; 37:1–39:7.*

ZEPHANIAH

A prophet and great-grandson of Hezekiah, king of Judah. His prophecies are in the Old Testament book of Zephaniah. He lived in Jerusalem and prophesied in the court of Josiah, king of Judah, between 641 and 609 BC. His prophecies seem to refer to the time before Josiah tried to turn his people back to God. Other prophets during his time included Nahum, Habakkuk, Huldah, and Jeremiah. Zephaniah fearlessly spoke against the evils of his time and told

of God's approaching judgment. His prophecies also spoke of the hope that Israel would be restored as a strong nation.

See **The Action Bible** *page 447 and the book of Zephaniah.*

ZERUBBABEL

The governor of the people of Israel who returned to Jerusalem between 539 and 529 BC after many years of exile in Babylon. Zerubbabel was the grandson of King Jehoiachin and was charged with rebuilding the temple. The prophets Zechariah and Haggai had to keep encouraging Zerubbabel and the high priest Jeshua to get the work done. However, soon after they began, the work was halted by the king of Babylon. Twenty years later, in 520 BC, Zechariah and another prophet, Haggai, encouraged the Israelites to go back to their work on the temple. Four years later, in 516 or 515 BC, the temple was completed.

See **The Action Bible** *page 509 and Ezra 2–8; Haggai 1–2.*

ZION

(SEE JERUSALEM)

ZIPPORAH

The wife of Moses. Her father was Jethro, a priest of Midian. Moses met Zipporah after he fled from Egypt. She and her six sisters were drawing water for their father's flock, but some shepherds drove them away. Moses protected the sisters and helped them. Their grateful father invited Moses to live with them and eventually gave Zipporah to Moses as his wife.

Zipporah and Moses had two sons, Gershom and Eliezer. When Moses returned to Egypt after forty years in Midian, Zipporah and their two sons went with him. Sometime during the conflict with Pharaoh or the beginning of the exodus, Moses sent Zipporah and their two sons back to her father's home. After Moses and the Israelites crossed the Red Sea, Zipporah, her two sons, and her father came to the Israelite camp near Mount Sinai. The Bible states that after a short visit, Jethro returned home. It does not say whether Zipporah and her sons stayed with Moses or went back to Midian.

See **The Action Bible** *page 120 and Exodus 2:15–22; 4:18–30; 18:1–7. See also* Jethro.

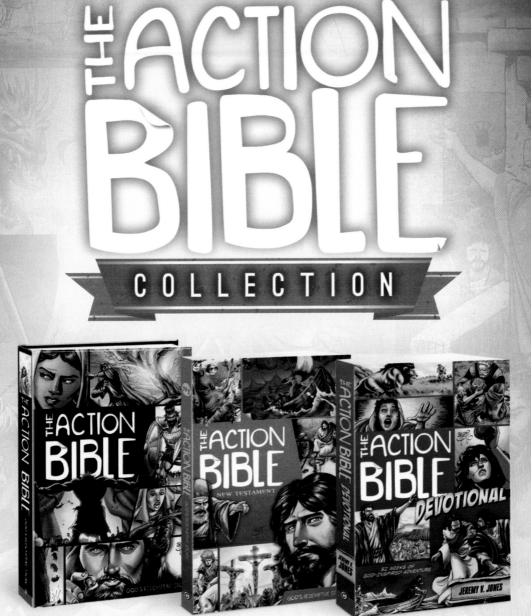